America's Defense Meltdown

America's Defense Meltdown

PENTAGON REFORM FOR PRESIDENT OBAMA AND THE NEW CONGRESS

Edited by Winslow T. Wheeler

*Thirteen non-partisan Pentagon insiders,
retired military officers, and defense specialists speak out*

A Center for Defense Information Book

STANFORD SECURITY STUDIES
an Imprint of Stanford University Press
Stanford, California

Stanford University Press
Stanford, California

*America's Defense Meltdown: Pentagon Reform for President Obama and the
New Congress* was originally published by World Security Institute's
Center for Defense Information, 1779 Massachusetts Avenue, NW,
Washington, D.C. © 2008 Center for Defense Information

The views expressed in CDI publications are those of the authors.

Printed in the United States of America on acid-free, archival-quality
paper.

Library of Congress Cataloging-in-Publication Data
is available.

ISBN: 978-0-8047-6931-0 (pbk.)

The Center for Defense Information

The World Security Institute's Center for Defense Information (CDI) provides expert analysis on various components of U.S. national security, international security and defense policy. CDI promotes wide-ranging discussion and debate on security issues such as nuclear weapons, space security, missile defense, small arms and military transformation.

CDI is an independent monitor of the Pentagon and Armed Forces, conducting research and analyzing military spending, policies and weapon systems. It is comprised of retired senior government officials and former military officers, as well as experienced defense analysts. Funded exclusively by public donations and foundation grants, CDI does not seek or accept Pentagon money or military industry funding. CDI makes its military analyses available to Congress, the media and the public through a variety of services and publications, and also provides assistance to the federal government and armed services upon request.

ABOUT THE AUTHORS

Thomas Christie began his career in the Department of Defense and related positions in 1955. He retired from the Pentagon in February 2005 after four years as director of Operational Test & Evaluation. There he was responsible for advising the secretary of defense on policy and procedures for testing weapon systems and for providing independent evaluations of the test results to both the defense secretary and Congress. He earlier served as director of the Operational Evaluation Division at the Institute for Defense Analyses, where he was also intimately involved in DOD weapons testing. Between 1985 and 1989, he was director of program integration in the Office of the Secretary of Defense, responsible for developing processes for managing the defense acquisition system. Prior to that, he had served in two separate positions under the assistant secretary of defense (Program Analysis and Evaluation): director of Tactical Air Division and deputy assistant secretary of defense for General Purpose Programs. Before coming to the Pentagon in 1973, Christie was the director of the Weapon System Analysis Division at the Air Force Armament Laboratory, Eglin Air Force Base, Fla., where he had begun his career as a weapons analyst.

Col. Robert Dilger (U.S. Air Force, ret.) started in the Air Force as an enlisted man and then entered flight training to become an F-86 pilot. He was the squadron weapons expert and a member of the European fighter wing's F-86 weapons team. He later flew F-84 fighters for the Air National Guard and was recalled to active duty during the Cuban missile crisis. Later, he was in the fighter wing's "tactics shop" at Da Nang Air Force Base in Vietnam, serving under the famous "No Guts, No Glory" Col. "Boots" Blesse. Dilger was shot down over Vietnam by anti-aircraft artillery on his 187th mission in the war and was credited with one "kill" in an F-4. He received three Silver Stars, four Distinguished Flying Crosses and a Purple Heart for his war service. His next job was as an instructor in charge of air-to-air training at the Air Force Weapon's School, Nellis Air Force Base, Nev. – the Air Force's famous "top gun" school. Upon graduation from the Army War College in 1975, he became the armament director of the A-10 in charge of the 30-mm cannon and its ammunition. There, he reduced the cost of the ammunition to one-eighth its earlier expense and improved its effectiveness – doing so with a novel program that re-competed the production contract year after year.

Bruce I. Gudmundsson served in the Marine Corps Reserve for 20 years, joining as a private in 1977 and retiring as a major in 1997. The author of seven books and several hundred articles, he is a historian who specializes in the internal workings of military forces (their structure, training, doctrine and culture) as well as the way that these things influence their ability to adapt to changing circumstances.

William S. Lind served as a legislative aide for armed services for Sen. Robert Taft, Jr., R-Ohio, from 1973 to 1976 and held a similar position with Sen. Gary Hart, D-Colo., from 1977 to 1986. He is one of the founders of the American military reform movement and anticipated the debate over maneuver warfare with an article in *Military Review* in March 1977, "Some Doctrinal Questions for the United States Army." He is author of the "Maneuver Warfare Handbook" (Westview Press, 1985) and co-author, with Gary Hart, of "America Can Win: The Case for Military Reform" (Adler & Adler, 1986). Mr. Lind was heavily involved with the adoption of maneuver warfare doctrine by the U.S. Marine Corps in the early 1990s, assisting with the writing of FMFM-1, "Warfighting" and FMFM 1-1, "Campaigning," and co-authoring FMFM 1-3, "Tactics." Mr. Lind has also written widely for both professional and popular publications.

Col. Douglas Macgregor (U.S. Army, ret.) was awarded the bronze star with "V" device in 1991 for valor for his leadership of the 2nd Squadron, 2nd Armored Cavalry Regiment that destroyed an Iraqi Republican Guard Brigade in the first Gulf war. After that, in November 1997, Macgregor was assigned to Supreme Headquarters Allied Powers Europe (SHAPE) where he became the director of the Joint Operations Center during the Kosovo Air Campaign. In January 2002, Macgregor was directed by the secretary of defense to present the CENTCOM commander with a concept for intervention in Iraq. The plan assumed a no-notice armored attack on two axes and that Iraqi Army and administrative structures would be retained. Though modified in unfortunate ways, major elements of his concept were adopted. He is also author of four books, including "Breaking the Phalanx" (Praeger, 1997) and "Transformation Under Fire" (Praeger, 2003), which have significantly influenced thinking about transformation inside America's ground forces. His newest book, "Warrior's Rage: The Battle of 73 Easting" will appear in 2009.

Col. Chet Richards (U.S. Air Force, ret.) is a consultant and writer based in Atlanta. He is the author of "If We Can Keep It: A National Security Manifesto for the Next Administration" (Center for Defense Information, 2007), "Certain to Win: The Strategy of John Boyd Applied to Business" (Xlibris, 2004) and other publications on Third and Fourth Generation Warfare. He holds a doctorate in mathematics and is adjunct professor of strategy and quantitative analysis at Kennesaw State University.

Lt. Col. John Sayen (U.S. Marine Corps, ret.) served in the Marine Corps' artillery, armor and military intelligence. He retired in 2002. During his last years of service, he worked at the Pentagon analyzing and reporting on trends in international affairs that would affect U.S. interests. Mr. Sayen has published two books on the Army and the Marine Corps and numerous articles for military and historical periodicals. He currently works as the senior contract doctrine writer at the Marine Air Ground Task Force (MAGTF) Staff Training Program at Marine Corps Base Quantico, Va.

Pierre Sprey consulted for Grumman Aircraft's research department from 1958 to 1965, then joined Secretary of Defense Robert McNamara's "Whiz Kids" in the Pentagon. There, in 1967, he met the Air Force's brilliant and original tactician, Col. John Boyd and quickly became a disciple and collaborator of Boyd's. Together with another innovative fighter pilot, Col. Everest Riccioni (U.S. Air Force), they started and carried out the concept design of the F-16 air-to-air fighter, then brought the program to fruition through five years of continuous bureaucratic guerilla warfare. More or less simultaneously, Sprey also headed up the technical side of the Air Force's concept design team for the A-10 close support fighter. Then, against even steeper opposition than the F-16 faced, he helped implement the A-10's innovative live-fire, prototype fly-off competition and subsequent production. Sprey left the Pentagon in 1971 but continued to consult actively on the F-16, the A-10, tanks and anti-tank weapons, and realistic operational/live-fire testing of major weapons. At the same time, he became a principal in two consulting firms; the first doing environmental research and analysis, the second consulting on international defense planning and weapons analysis. During this period, Sprey continued the seminal work of Col. Richard Hallock (U.S. Army/Airborne) in founding the field of combat history/combat data-based cost effectiveness analysis for air and ground weapons. During the late 1970s, Colonel Boyd and Sprey, together with a small, dedicated group of Pentagon and congressional insiders, started the military reform movement. Attracting considerable attention from young officers, journalists and congressmen, the movement led to establishment of the Congressional Military Reform Caucus and to passage of several military reform bills in the early '80s. Sprey continues to work with reform-minded foundations and journalists. Numerous articles, books and theses have described the work of Colonel Boyd and Sprey on the F-16, A-10 and military reform. These include Robert Coram's "Boyd: The Fighter Pilot Who Changed the Art of War" (Little, Brown and Company, 2002) and James Fallows' "National Defense" (Random House, 1981).

James P. Stevenson is the former editor of the Navy Fighter Weapon School's *Topgun Journal*; author of "The Pentagon Paradox" (Naval Institute Press, 1993), a history of the Navy's F-18 Hornet development; and of "The $5 Billion Misunderstanding" (Naval Institute Press, 2001), a history of the Navy's failed A-12 Avenger II stealth bomber program. He also served as the assistant managing editor of *Air Safety Week* and west coast correspondent for *Defense Week*. He has written many articles in professional and popular journals and has lectured on numerous occasions on national security and aviation issues.

Maj. Donald E. Vandergriff (U.S. Army, ret.) served for 24 years of active duty as an enlisted Marine and Army officer. He has had numerous troop, staff and educational assignments in the United States and abroad. Donald Vandergriff was named ROTC instructor of the year 2002-2003 and the 3rd ROTC Brigade instructor of the year for 2003-2004. Vandergriff is a frequently published authority on the U.S. Army personnel system, Army culture, leadership development, soldier training, and the emergence of Fourth Generation Warfare. He has authored many articles and briefings, as well as four books: "Spirit, Blood and Treasure: The American Cost of Battle in the 21st Century" (Presidio Press, 2001), "The Path to Victory: America's Army and the Revolution in Human Affairs" (Presidio Press, 2002), "Raising the Bar: Creating and Nurturing Adaptability to Deal with the Changing Face of War" (Center for Defense Information, 2006) and "Manning the Future Legions of the United States: Finding and Developing Tomorrow's Centurions" (Praeger Security International, 2008). Vandergriff is currently a contractor in support of the Army Capabilities Integration Center Forward at Crystal City, Va.

Col. G.I. Wilson (U.S. Marine Corps, ret.) is a retired veteran. He was a close associate of the late Col. John Boyd.

Winslow T. Wheeler is the director of the Straus Military Reform Project at the Center for Defense Information in Washington, D.C. He has authored two books: "The Wastrels of Defense" (U.S. Naval Institute Press, 2004) about Congress and national security, and "Military Reform" (Praeger Security International, 2007). From 1971 to 2002, Wheeler worked on national security issues for members of the U.S. Senate and for the U.S. Government Accountability Office (GAO). In the Senate, he was the first – and according to Senate records the last – individual to work simultaneously on the personal staffs of a Republican and a Democrat. Wheeler is the editor of this anthology.

DEDICATION AND ACKNOWLEDGEMENTS

Genuine reform often requires swimming against strong currents of conventional wisdom and a refusal to pander to politically driven notions of what is and is not acceptable to think and do at the time. Governments often refuse to acknowledge and act on serious problems that undermine a nation's security – subsequently to be noted by even the most routine of historians to have been blind and foolish. The real test of statesmanship – no matter how unpopular the recognition of needed action may be among the blinkered paragons of contemporary conventional wisdom – is to note and act on the problems before they overwhelm the state.

For the wisdom and the moral courage to see and then act, the authors of this volume wish to recognize the memory of Col. John R. Boyd (U.S. Air Force). For the strength of character and extraordinary generosity of spirit that made this volume possible, the authors wish to thank and recognize Philip A. Straus, Jr., the founder of the Straus Military Reform Project of the Center for Defense Information, along with the additional support of the Stewart R. Mott Charitable Trust and its founder and guiding light, the late Stewart R. Mott, and the many private individuals who also contributed to the support of this work.

The authors also wish to thank the staff of the World Security Institute and the Center for Defense Information for their spirited support, diligent work and skillful professionalism in the completion of this book. Especially to be noted are Bruce Blair, Theresa Hitchens, Drew Portocarrero, Suzanne Ostrofsky, Ron Hinrichs, Deniz Ozdemir, Laura McHugh, Valerie Reed and Ana Marte.

TABLE OF CONTENTS

PREFACE

The mere notion of a "meltdown" within the U.S. military may seem ridiculous to many. America's armed forces are surely the best in the world, perhaps even in history. Democrats and Republicans, liberals, moderates and conservatives in Washington all agree on at least that. On what basis does a bunch of lesser known, if not obscure, analysts make such a preposterous assertion?

The vast majority, perhaps even all, of Congress, the general officer corps of the armed forces, top management of American defense manufacturers, prominent members of Washington's think-tank community and nationally recognized "defense journalists" will hate this book. They will likely also urge that it be ignored by both parties in Congress and especially by the new president and his incoming national security team.

It is not just that following the recommendations of this book will mean the cancellation of numerous failing, unaffordable and ineffective defense programs, as well as the jobs, and more importantly careers, those programs enable. The acceptance of data and analysis presented in this book, and the conclusions and recommendations that flow from them, would require the elite of Washington's national security community to acknowledge the many flaws in their analysis of weapons, Pentagon management and leadership of the nation in a tumultuous world. In too many cases, it would also require those elites to admit their own role in the virtual meltdown of America's defenses.

Our equipment is the most sophisticated and effective in the world. We easily whipped one of the largest armies in the Middle East, not once but twice, and we have now clearly mastered a once difficult and ugly situation in Iraq. Success in Afghanistan will not be far away, once we devote the proper resources there. Those who take comfort in the last three sentences are the people who need to read and consider the contents of this book the most. Reflect on the following:

- America's defense budget is now larger in inflation adjusted dollars than at any point since the end of World War II, and yet our Army has fewer combat brigades than at any point in that period, our Navy has fewer combat ships and the Air Force has fewer combat aircraft. Our major equipment inventories for these major forces are older on average than at any point since 1946; in some cases they are at all-time historical highs in average age.

- The effectiveness of America's "high-tech" weapons does not compensate for these reduced numbers. The Air Force's newest fighter, the F-35, can be regarded as only a technical failure. The Navy's newest destroyer cannot protect itself effectively against aircraft and missiles, and the Army's newest armored vehicle cannot stand up against a simple anti-armor rocket that was first designed in the 1940s.

- Despite decades of acquisition reform from Washington's best minds in Congress, the Pentagon and the think tanks, cost overruns in weapon systems are higher today, in inflation adjusted dollars, than any time ever before. Not a single major weapon system has been delivered on time, on cost and as promised for performance. The Pentagon refuses to tell Congress and the public exactly how it spends the hundreds of billions of dollars appropriated to it each year. The reason for this is simple; it doesn't know how the money is spent. Technically, it doesn't even know *if* the money is spent. Even President George W. Bush's own Office of Management and Budget has labeled the Pentagon as one of the worst managed agencies of the entire federal government.

- At the start of the wars against Afghanistan and Iraq, the Pentagon's senior military leadership failed to warn the nation's civilian leaders of the tremendously difficult mission they were being asked to perform. Indeed, most of the military hierarchy did not even comprehend the difficulties of those missions and misperceived that the key issue was the number of military personnel sent to invade and then occupy an alien land in the Middle East. And then, many of them publicly complained that the civilian leadership had made a mess of things, saying so from the comfort of a retirement pension.

- In Congress and the Office of the Secretary of Defense, there have been acrimonious hearings and meetings, but no real oversight to appreciate just how and where programs and policies ran off the tracks. Except for a very, very small handful, no one has been held accountable. Indeed, it is not even apparent that anyone in Congress knows how to perform oversight. If they do, they apparently lack the spine to perform it in a manner Harry Truman, who carried out superb oversight as a senator during World War II, would call competent.

- Perhaps most damning of all, America has permitted itself, and most leaders from both political parties have aggressively pursued, a national security strategy that has torn us apart domestically, isolated us from our allies, made us an object of disrespect in the eyes of those uncommitted to our cause and caused our enemies to find motivation for greater action on their own part. In fact, it is not even clear whether our national leadership understands what an effective national security strategy is, much less how to put one together and exercise it effectively.

And what of the great victories in the Persian Gulf, the 1991 war to liberate Kuwait and the 2003 invasion that toppled Saddam Hussein's hostile regime? Don't those U.S. operations prove our armed forces' historic superiority? America did quickly beat Iraq's armed forces in 1991, and in the early phases of the 2003 invasion, but those victories were both incomplete and against forces best characterized as grossly incompetent – perhaps even the "most incompetent in the world."[1] Against the best of Saddam Hussein's forces, the so-called Republican Guard, America's military commanders in Operation Desert Storm in 1991 failed to capture or destroy the Guard as the single prop to Saddam's regime that enabled him to survive the war. In 2003, the Army's most senior commanders again made fundamental tactical, operational and strategic errors, and in one situation virtually panicked when faced with an enemy that was virtually immobilized by its own incompetence.[2]

The architects of the current war in Iraq slickly proclaim victory in sight thanks to the success of the "surge" there. Politically motivated to their very core, they studiously ignore the internal dynamics in Iraq and the region that have been inestimably more powerful in lowering the violence there. Blind as the proverbial bat, they and even opponents to the Iraq misadventure now proclaim that more of the same in Afghanistan will rescue the collapsing situation there. As Pentagon wags used to remark inside the building, "it's data-free analysis and analysis-free decisions" that are driving U.S. policy.

Many American soldiers, sailors, marines and aviators are rightly honored by the American public for their courage and sacrifice in Iraq and Afghanistan, but quality at the combat-unit level cannot compensate for inadequate leadership at the highest levels.

The authors of this volume seek to inform the new president and the new Congress of the pervasive nature of serious, decades-long problems that are corroding not just our military power, but our national strength. Each chapter addresses the nature of problems as we see them in a discrete sector of our national security apparatus and, just as importantly, proposes solutions based on the nature of the problem – rather than on the limited willingness of political actors to ape reform. These chapters progress from:

- an analysis of America's military heritage relevant to our international situation today in chapter 1,

- to a discussion of the components of a competent national strategy and how to construct and implement one in chapter 2,

- to a wholesale, perhaps even radical, change in how America trains its military leaders to think and operate (a change already beginning to occur in some important corners in the U.S. Army) in chapter 3,

- to two alternative, but not necessarily mutually exclusive, visions of America's ground forces in the Army and Marine Corps in chapters 4 and 5,

- to a prescription to make the U.S. Navy relevant to the 21st century, rather than to the middle of the last century, in chapter 6,

- to a compelling vision of the dogma that ails our Air Force and how to build combat air forces that are both astonishingly inexpensive and devastatingly effective in all forms of warfare in chapter 7,

- to a new plan for the vitally important airlift and support portions of our Air Force in chapter 8,

- to a new paradigm for our reserves and National Guard in chapter 9,

- to what has gone amiss for the last several decades in our weapons acquisition and Pentagon management apparatus in chapter 10,

- to a depiction of the hyper-cost of our shrinking, aging and less effective military forces in chapter 11.

Each author writes for himself and, we believe, the nation. We all can probably find something in each other's chapter with which we disagree, sometimes strenuously. However, all contributors share a common view that our problems are severe and longstanding, that they do not relate to just one political party or ideological faction, and that at the core of our problems and their solution resides a fundamental question of ethics.

We invite a national debate to probe our national security troubles and how best to summon the character and persistence that their solution will require.

ENDNOTES

1. Thomas Withington, "What If We Battled a Real Army?" *Long Island Newsday*, August 27, 2003.

2. For further discussion, see Winslow T. Wheeler and Lawrence J. Korb, *Military Reform: A Reference Handbook* (Westport, CT: Praeger Security International, 2006), Chapter 6.

EXECUTIVE SUMMARY
Chapter Summaries and Recommendations

Chapter 1
Introduction and Historic Overview:
The Overburden of America's Outdated Defenses
Lt. Col. John Sayen (U.S. Marine Corps, ret.)

Our military forces have become high-cost dinosaurs that are insufficiently lethal against most of the enemies we are likely to face. Our forces have also broken free of their constitutional controls to the point where they have essentially become a presidential military. Congress exerts meaningful control neither in peacetime nor in wartime – and has lost all control over going to war. The large peacetime standing army established just before World War II (and maintained ever since) has become a vehicle for misuse by presidents, and multiple other parties both internal and external to the Pentagon.

The large standing forces were supposed to facilitate professional preparation for war, but the essential officer corps never truly professionalized itself. Thus, we were almost invariably unprepared, in mind set and in doctrine, for the conflicts we faced. In both World Wars, Korea, and Vietnam, America hurriedly threw together unprofessionally led armies to fight – too often ineffectively. The result, especially today, has been notably mediocre senior military leadership – with only the rarest exceptions. At the same time, our armed forces have become ruinously expensive, as they simultaneously shrink, age, and become remarkably less capable. In Iraq and Afghanistan, for example, the Army and Marine Corps have been stretched to the limits of their strength to fight enemies not even a tenth as numerous as those they faced in Vietnam. We have become a pampered, sluggish, weak-muscled elephant that cannot even deal effectively with mice.

Chapter 2
Shattering Illusions: A National Security Strategy for 2009-2017
Col. Chet Richards (U.S. Air Force, ret.)

Decisions by the last two Democratic and Republican administrations have left the country deeply in debt, depleted our military strength, lowered our national standard of living, and strengthened those around the world whose goals conflict with ours. Much of this can be traced to the initially politically-popular use of military force to attempt to solve problems that are inherently social, economic or political and therefore do not admit of military solutions. Chief among the examples are Iraq and Afghanistan, where the initial successes against third-rate military opponents have dragged on into separate occupations of a bewildering array of religious, political and ethnic groups, few of which wish to be dominated by Americans. The solution requires the next administration to explicitly restrict the use of our military forces to those problems that only military forces can solve and that the nation can rally to, and to eschew the use of our forces to serve hubris, propaganda or dogma.

The advent of nuclear weapons has limited the utility of military force against other major powers: there will be no replays of World War II. For smaller conflicts, history has shown that military occupations of developing countries or alien cultures will be expensive and very unlikely to succeed. Furthermore, the continuing epidemics of crime and political instability in areas where force was initially successful, as in the former Yugoslavia and the Middle East, show that the West still has no solution to the problem of rebuilding destroyed states.

Recommendations

- The new president needs to formally assess the policy objectives for which military force still has utility in today's world, and propose a program of revamping our force sizes and missions, shaped by the essential requirement to act in concert with America's national ethic and our allies on each of those missions.

- In parallel with this presidential revamping, Congress and the president need to fundamentally change the preparation and presentation of intelligence so that misuse of force based on false pretext becomes far more difficult.

- Congress and the president need to dramatically strengthen regulation of private contractors in the public sector, particularly in the military and intelligence services.

Chapter 3
Leading the Human Dimension Out of a Legacy of Failure
Col. G.I. Wilson (U.S. Marine Corps, ret.)
and Maj. Donald Vandergriff (U.S. Army, ret.)

Institutional failures pervade the current management of military men and women, by far our most important defense resource. The end of the Cold War necessitated fundamental change, yet we remain hobbled by an archaic and dysfunctional personnel system in each of the active military services and their all-important reserves. That archaic system fails to recognize and benefit from the new realities of leading human resources in the 21st century. Without fundamental changes in how we nurture and lead our people, there can be no real military reform.

The military's legacy system is built on flawed constructs: a centralized "beer-can" personnel system, lack of imagination in nurturing leaders, and faulty assumptions about human beings and warfare itself. This concoction is worsened by ingrained behaviors: adversity to risk, preference for the status quo and "group think," preoccupation with bureaucratic "turf battles," and valuing contracts above winning wars.

Recommendations

- The fundamental reform requirement is to learn to lead people first and manage things second. Instead, today we administer people as a subset of managing things.

- The primary route to valuing people is to learn to nurture highly innovative, unshakably ethical thinkers. Sadly, in today's armed forces such people, those who lead by virtue of their courage, creativity, boldness, vision, honesty and sometimes irreverence, are known as mavericks. The military services must learn it is admirable to disagree with, change, and improve the institution the individual serves and remains loyal to. Such change-seeking individuals are the ones who best adapt and prevail in humankind's most stressful circumstance: war. They are the war-winning leaders.

Specific recommendations for bringing such people and such values to the fore are articulated in the chapter.

Chapter 4
Maneuver Forces: The Army and Marine Corps after Iraq
Col. Douglas Macgregor (U.S. Army, ret.)
and Col. G.I. Wilson (U.S. Marine Corps, ret.)

Today's Army and Marine warfighting structures have reached block obsolescence. The strategic conditions that created them no longer exist. The problematic structures are characterized by antiquated, inappropriate World War II-style organizations for combat, inventories of aging and broken equipment thanks to unaffordable and mismanaged modernization programs, heavy operational dependence on large, fixed foreign bases, disjointed unit rotational and readiness policies, and a very troubling exodus of young talent out of the ground combat formations.

Compensating for these deficiencies by binding ground forces more tightly within "networked" systems, such as the Army's misguided Future Combat Systems, does not work and is prohibitively expensive.

Reform lies in changes that promise both huge dollar savings and powerful synergies with proven – not hypothetical – technologies and concepts fielded by the air and naval services. This means a laser-like focus on *people*, *ideas* and *things* in that order.

Recommendations

- Because defined, continuous fronts on the hypothetical World War II model do not exist today and because ubiquitous strike capabilities and proliferating weapons of mass destruction make the concentration of ground forces very dangerous, mobile dispersed warfare is the dominant form of combat we must be prepared to conduct.

- Needed organizational change means new, integrated, more fundamentally "joint" command and control structures for the nation's ground maneuver forces. This approach expands the nation's range of strategic options in modern warfare operations against a spectrum of opponents with both conventional and unconventional capabilities.

- Because Marines are now much more likely to conduct Army-like operations far from the sea than they are to re-enact Inchon-style amphibious landings, it is time to harmonize Army and Marine deployments within a predictable joint rotational readiness schedule.

- The authors focus on ways to reorient thinking, organization, and modernization in the ground maneuver force to:

  1. reshape today's force for new strategic conditions (mobile dispersed warfare);

  2. exploit new technology, new operational concepts, new organizations, and new approaches to readiness, training and leadership; and

  3. extract huge dollar savings through fundamental reorganization and reform.

The authors do not pretend that the changes outlined in the chapter will gain easy acceptance. New strategies, tactics and technologies promising more victories and fewer casualties are typically viewed as threatening by general officers and senior civilians who are comfortable with the status quo.

Chapter 5
A Traveler's Perspective on Third and Fourth Generation War
William S. Lind

While the United States Marine Corps espouses a doctrine of Third Generation (maneuver) War, it is organized and trained only for Second Generation (attrition) Warfare. The chapter proposes an alternative structure that reflects Third Generation doctrine.

Recommendations
- Most Marines should again become "trigger pullers."

- The size of the officer corps above company grades should be drastically reduced.

- A "regimental" system – based on the battalion – would provide mentally and morally cohesive units through unprecedented personnel stability.

- Reserve units should become as capable as active-duty battalions.

- Marines need to convert from line infantry to highly mentally and physically agile, true light ("Jaeger") infantry.

- Marine aviation should be restructured and re-equipped to reflect the "Jaeger Air" close air support concept with less costly and more effective task-designed, single purpose aircraft.

The chapter concludes with a brief look at Fourth Generation War concepts, for which the proposed Marine Corps force structure would also be suitable.

Chapter 6
The Navy
William S. Lind

America's geography dictates that it must remain a maritime power, but today's U.S. Navy remains structured to fight the aircraft carrier navy of Imperial Japan. Reform can only proceed from a fundamental understanding that people are most important, ideas come second, and hardware, including ships, is only third.

Recommendations
- The main personnel deficiency of the Navy is an officer corps dominated by technicians. That reinforces the Navy's Second Generation institutional culture. Reform requires adopting a Third Generation culture and putting the engineers back in the engine room.

- Fourth Generation War demands the Navy shift its focus from Mahanian battles for sea control to controlling coastal and inland waters in places where the state is disintegrating.

- Submarines are today's capital ships, and the U.S. Navy must remain a dominant submarine force while exploring alternative submarine designs.

- Aircraft carriers remain useful "big boxes." However, they should be decoupled from standardized air wings and thought of as general purpose carriers, transporting whatever is useful in a specific crisis or conflict.

- The Navy should acquire an aircraft similar to the Air Force's A-10 so it can begin to effectively support troops on the ground.

- Cruisers, destroyers and frigates are obsolescent as warship types and should be retired; their functions assumed by small carriers or converted merchant ships.

- The Navy should build a new flotilla of small warships suited to green and brown waters and deployable as self-sustaining "packages" in Fourth Generation conflicts. (The Navy's current "Littoral Combat Ship" is an apparently failed attempt at this design.)

Chapter 7
Reversing the Decay of American Air Power
Col. Robert Dilger (U.S. Air Force, ret.) and Pierre M. Sprey

The Air Force's resource allocations and tactical/strategic decisions from the 1930s until today have been dominated by airpower theoretician Giulio Douhet's 1921 assertion that strategic bombardment of an enemy's heartland can win wars independently of ground forces.

The authors' analysis of combat results and spending since 1936 shows the unchanging dominance of that strategic bombardment paradigm has caused the Air Force to:

1. leave close air support capabilities, which have proven far more effective than strategic bombing in determining the outcome of conflicts, essentially unfunded over the last 70 years;

2. habitually underfund effective air-to-air capabilities; and

3. engender serious U.S. military setbacks and unnecessary loss of American lives in each modern conflict America has fought.

The actual combat results of strategic bombardment campaigns in each conflict since 1936 show a consistent pattern of failure to accomplish the assigned military objectives – and often, no noticeable military results at all. Supporting these bombardment campaigns always entailed very high budget costs, far higher than the costs of close support or air-to-air. There were also consistently high losses of aircrew lives in pursuing strategic bombardment – far higher than the losses in close support or air-to-air. In every theater with sustained air opposition, neither strategic bombardment nor close support proved possible without large forces of air-to-air fighters.

Wherever we mounted significant close support efforts (invariably opposed by bombardment-minded senior Air Force leaders) in mobile battle situations – no matter whether we were retreating or advancing – the military gains proved to be remarkable, out of all proportion to the resources expended.

The implications of the last 70 years of combat results for future Air Force aircraft procurement are not hard to grasp.

Recommendations

- First and foremost, we must abandon a business-as-usual procurement process hopelessly centered on aircraft specifically designed for – or compromised for – strategic bombardment.

- For the first time in U.S. history, we need to provide in peacetime for real, single-purpose close air support forces of substantial size. The only aircraft to succeed in real world close support have been ones that are highly maneuverable at slow speeds and highly resistant to anti-aircraft artillery impacts. High speed jets have consistently failed in close support.

- We must provide adequate air-to-air fighter forces to make close support (and perhaps some small amount of deeper "interdiction" bombing) viable in the face of air-to-air opposition.

To actually implement such forces,
- we must abandon wish-list planning that comes up with outrageously expensive, impracticable procurement plans.

- Instead, we must fit our aircraft development and procurement plans within fixed, real world budgets – and make sure we develop and buy aircraft so austerely designed for single missions (and therefore much more effective than multi-mission "gold-platers") that we can procure large, adequate forces.

- The authors present a radically new procurement plan, based on new close support, air-to-air, forward air control, and "dirt-strip" airlift aircraft designs of greatly superior effectiveness and vastly lower unit cost. These will make possible buying over 9,000 new, highly effective airframes over the next 20 years – all *within* current U.S. Air Force budget levels.

Air forces based on these concepts will have unprecedented effectiveness in either conventional or counterinsurgency warfare.

Chapter 8
Air Mobility Alternatives for a New Administration
James P. Stevenson

The Pentagon's current plans for air mobility should not continue; they are not plausible. The United States has the best air mobility capability in the world. Nevertheless, it comes at excessive cost. Even with record-level defense spending, current plans for air mobility are impossible to achieve without huge budget increases – increases which are unnecessary and even counter-productive.

Recommendations

- To reduce the cost of the tanker fleet, the U.S. Air Force should start work on a smaller, cheaper, more tactically effective tanker (KC-Y) as quickly as possible. The Air Force should also stop the currently contemplated buy of large, too expensive KC-X tankers at about 100 aircraft. There exist other innovative ideas to provide more capability at lower cost.

- For strategic air- and sea-lift, the Pentagon should reduce the number of strategic airlifters to approximately 260, which implies retiring C-5As and stopping the buy of C-17s at about 205 aircraft. The Civil Reserve Air Fleet (CRAF) should be increased by at least ten percent. The capacity for fast strategic sealift should be doubled since it dominates the actual fast deployment capabilities of U.S. forces.

- Tactical airlift capability should be about 400 aircraft. The mix of aircraft should include faster retirement of older C-130s, stopping the egregiously high cost C-130J buy at about 100 aircraft, buying more of the smaller, cheaper, more useful-to-the-Army C-27Js, and pursuing a new commercial-derivative airlifter that is more cost-effective than anything in current Air Force plans. The Army's Joint Heavy Lift program should be cancelled.

- For Special Operations air capabilities, the CV-22 should be stopped immediately, replacing it with one or more new, cost-effective helicopters. New variants of the C-130Js and C-27J should replace MC-130s and AC-130s. A new irregular warfare wing of small, manned aircraft should be started instead of less effective unmanned aerial vehicles (UAVs).

The chapter advocates a strategic focus on aerial refueling and Special Operations air warfare, with less emphasis on strategic and tactical airlift. In all cases, innovative solutions that run counter to conventional wisdom allow us to lower costs without loss of overall capability.

Chapter 9
The Army National Guard, the Army Reserve, and the Marine Corps Reserve
Bruce I. Gudmundsson

The chapter lays out the broad outlines of a new approach to the recruitment, organization, and training of reserve forces. Essentially, it would mean a reserve component much more closely tied in outlook and mission to the citizenry it defends.

Recommendations

- A somewhat smaller National Guard should focus on homeland security missions.

- Most units of the Army Reserve and Marine Corps Reserve should be organized as "lifecycle units," organizations in which members remain together for the entire course of their initial terms of service. As such, these units should receive much more training than they currently receive.

- Training schedules and benefits packages should be custom tailored to the civilian occupations of their individual members. For example, units composed of college students – of which there would be many based on the recreated incentives packages – will have longer periods of initial training as well two-month periods of training each summer. Similarly, units composed of people with seasonal occupations would train in their "off-season."

Chapter 10
Long in Coming, the Acquisition Train Wreck is Here
Thomas Christie

After more than four decades of supposedly well-structured defense planning and programming, as well as numerous studies aimed at reforming its multi-billion dollar acquisition system, the Pentagon's decision process governing our defense establishment is clearly broken. We need far-reaching, even radical, remedial initiatives. The evidence supporting the need for drastic action abounds.

Despite the largest defense budgets in real terms in more than 60 years, we have a smaller military force structure than at any time during that period, one that is equipped to a great extent with worn-out, aging equipment.

Granted, the employment of our forces in Iraq and Afghanistan has contributed to the wear and tear on our combat and support equipment, particularly for our ground forces. The bill for repairing and replacing that equipment (reported to be in the hundreds of billions) is mostly yet to be faced. And, more to the point, this only exacerbates the already severe modernization problems faced by all three services. Those problems have been on the horizon for decades and would have plagued our forces even if the war on terror had not evolved as ruinously as it has since 2001.

A fundamental source of DOD's problems is the historically long pattern of unrealistically high defense budget projections combined with equally unrealistic low estimates of the costs of new programs. The net effect is for DOD's leaders to claim that they can afford the weapons they want to buy. Thus, there is no urgency to face up to the needed hard choices on new weapon systems. In addition, there are other looming demands on the budget, such as health care for both active and retired personnel and planned increases in ground forces manpower. Any confidence that DOD's in-house goals can be achieved in the future (even with increased spending) is sorely mistaken.

Recommendations
See below for Chapter 11.

Chapter 11
Understand, Then Contain America's Out-of-Control Defense Budget
Winslow T. Wheeler

As Thomas Christie and Franklin C. "Chuck" Spinney have argued, major U.S. defense components are now smaller, older, and less operationally ready than at any time in recent history. This collapse has occurred in the face of the highest levels of defense spending since the end of World War II. This is not compensated by the (false) illusion that our smaller military forces are more effective due to their "high tech," sophisticated nature. In fact, what many proclaim to be "high tech" is merely high complexity – at extraordinarily high budgetary and operational cost. The armed forces, Congress, and many others seek to solve the problems with still more money, which will only accelerate the shrinking, the aging, and the diminishing of combat effectiveness. In fact, if existing ways of thinking and current processes are employed, more money will guarantee failure. Decades of data make this counterintuitive conclusion unavoidable.

Recommendations
- There can be no recovery without being able to track how DOD spends its money, which is not now done. The first order of priority is to force DOD to comply with federal laws and regulations that require financial accountability – without permitting the exercise of the many loopholes Congress and DOD managers have created and exploited.

- Analytical integrity based on real world combat history must be applied to the rigorous evaluation of DOD programs and policies, now riddled with bias and advocacy. In the absence of objective, independent assessment of weapons program cost, performance and schedule (especially at the beginning of any program), DOD decision-makers have no ability to manage programs with any competence whatsoever.

- A new panel of independent, objective professionals (with no contemporaneous or future ties whatsoever with industry or other sources of bias and self-interest) should be convened by the president to assess

    1. the extent to which DOD programs and policies do or do not fit with current world conditions,

    2. the president's national security strategy, and – very importantly –

    3. a realistic assessment of the reduced budget that will be available for the Department of Defense.

- This panel should provide the secretary of defense his primary advice on how to proceed with DOD program acquisition and management until such time as the military services and the regular civilian bureaucracy have demonstrated sufficient competence and objectivity to re-assert primary control.

- The president should expect strong protest from the advocates of business-as-usual in the military services, the civilian Pentagon bureaucracy, Congress, industry, and "think tanks." Many such individuals cannot now conceive of a U.S. national security apparatus run outside the boundaries of what they have grown accustomed to and what they have advocated. Most will refuse to adapt. Those who can adapt, especially in the military services, should be brought back into the decision-making structure. Those who cannot should anticipate a career outside the Department of Defense.

CHAPTER 1

INTRODUCTION AND HISTORIC OVERVIEW
The Overburden of America's Outdated Defenses

Lt. Col. John Sayen (U.S. Marine Corps, ret.)

"May you live in interesting times." This oft-quoted Chinese curse rings at least as true today as it did when it was first uttered. The latter half of the 20th century and the beginning of the 21st century has indeed proven to be extraordinarily "interesting." Three profound environmental changes have characterized this period. One was the introduction and spread of nuclear weapons. Another was the sudden fall of the Soviet Union and end of the Cold War. The third was the revival and spread of irregular warfare. By irregular warfare we mean wars fought by irregular forces or what the Pentagon describes as "armed individuals or groups who are not members of the regular armed forces, police or other internal security forces."[1]

This anthology is not so much about these changes themselves as it is about the U.S. military's reaction to them. More particularly, its various contributors examine how the U.S. military has reacted to these changes and what, if anything, we can or should do about it.

All of the book's contributors call for reform in a wide variety of areas including finances, procurement, training, tactics, doctrine, organization and military professionalism. The purpose of this introduction is not so much to propose solutions as it is to set forth some of the key and often complex problems that will be tackled by the contributors to this volume.

Most of America's military problems are not new. In the past, they have often been recognized but seldom confronted. We believe that today the need to deal with them has never been greater. Not only does our future military success depend upon it, but our image abroad, influence in the world and our economy, as well as our liberties and the survival of our republic, do as well.

The most important problems can briefly be summarized as follows:

- Our military has broken its constitutional controls. Our Founding Fathers wanted no more than a very limited size and role for a federal military. They feared standing armies not only because they might be used against the American public, i.e. to establish military rule, but also for their potential to involve us in costly foreign wars that would drain our treasury, erode our freedoms and involve us in the "entangling alliances" that George Washington warned of in his farewell address. At that time our armies were composed mainly of state militias that the president needed the cooperation of Congress and the state governors in order to use. Today, we have one large all-volunteer federal Army, which for all practical purposes responds only to the president and the executive branch. It has engaged in numerous foreign wars, involved us in many entangling alliances, drained our treasury and eroded our liberties just as our Founding Fathers foresaw. It has enabled the president to take the nation to war on little more than his own authority. The recent repeal of the *Posse Comitatus* Act of 1878 allows him to unilaterally use the military not only against foreigners, but against the American people as well.

- Our military is inwardly focused. This is to say that it focuses on itself and its internal concerns, rather than looking outward at the world and reacting to what occurs there. This is partly a consequence of domestic politics, which determine the military budget, and partly due to a climate of intellectual laziness and complacency that prefers the glories of the past over the unpleasant realities of the present and future. This has made it very difficult for us either to produce or implement a realistic grand strategy or to adjust to changing realities, particularly the emergence of Fourth Generation War (4GW).

- Our military is very expensive. The "official" budget will soon hit $600 billion per year. This approximates the military budgets of all other nations of the world combined. Some have argued that this amounts to only a few percent of our gross national product (GNP) and that it should be increased. One might reply, however, that the military budget might instead be determined by the military needs of the nation (the determination of which requires looking outward at potential threats) more than an arbitrarily determined portion of its economy. Also, the real budget is much higher than the official one. The official budget does not include the Department of Homeland Security or Veterans Affairs, both of which are really military expenses. The current wars in Iraq and Afghanistan are paid for by offline "supplemental" budgets so they are not included either. If one adds these costs the budget climbs to about a trillion dollars. It absorbs much of the government's discretionary spending and has contributed significantly to the depreciation of the dollar.

- As our military gets more expensive it gets smaller and less capable. Although the current military budget, even adjusting for inflation, is the highest since World War II it buys us only modest forces. At the height of the Reagan military buildup in the 1980s the U.S. Army had 18 active divisions. Yet today, with a higher budget, it has only 10. At the height of the Vietnam War the U.S. military maintained over 500,000 men in Vietnam besides a substantial force in Germany under NATO. It fought an enemy with more than half a million men under arms that had armor, heavy artillery, and even small naval and air forces. The North Vietnamese were also receiving assistance from both the Soviet Union and Communist China. Today, it is all the U.S. military can do to maintain 140,000 to 150,000 troops in Iraq and 30,000 in Afghanistan, where they fight enemies whose combined strength (after Saddam's fall) seldom if ever exceeded 30,000. Unlike in Vietnam these enemies have no air or naval forces, no modern heavy weapons, little or no formal military training, and no outside support. This dramatic decrease in U.S. capabilities should be no less astonishing than the simultaneous increases in the budget. Worse, the strength of the forces we have is eroded by the skyrocketing costs of new weapons. It has resulted in a shrinking inventory of aging weapon systems only a fraction of which can be replaced because their replacements are too costly.

• Our military is not professional. That is to say its officers, especially the senior ones, are poorly educated in the military profession. U.S. Army training in mechanical skills such as flying an airplane or repairing a truck compares very well to similar training in foreign militaries. However, true comprehension of why things are done as opposed to how to do them, is usually deficient. This makes it much harder to deal with the unfamiliar and unexpected. This in turn relates to the military's inward focus already referred to. It is easier to focus inwardly on the familiar than outwardly on the unfamiliar. This follows a long American tradition of commissioning officers at the last-minute (usually when a war is just beginning) based largely on civil education and social status, and then giving them training not unlike that of enlisted recruits. Subsequent promotion depends more on politics, social skills and personal ambition than on military and leadership skills. This has left us with a military that has a leadership that has never really learned to "think" in its own profession. Such leaders find it difficult to devise sound strategy or offer advice to their political superiors that they can clearly explain and justify.[2]

A more detailed elaboration of these main points appears below. Readers should understand that the four points given above are in fact so closely interrelated that to discuss them separately would only lead to confusion. Therefore, I have taken a more chronological approach to describe how these problems evolved and what effect they have on military policy today.

Stuck in Our History: How Our Military Became the President's Own Army

Prior to independence and for many years afterwards the principle defense of North America rested on a citizen militia. This only made sense. Before independence we owed allegiance to Great Britain, who while obligated to protect us, was more than

3,000 miles away. Being an island, Britain relied on its navy for national defense. For home defense it relied on a militia from which ours was later derived. The modern British Army, however, came not from the militia, but from the "New Model Army." This was a force of military professionals that Parliament raised in 1645 to stiffen the militia armies waging a civil war against King Charles I. Militarily the New Model Army was a great success. It defeated Charles' armies, captured and executed Charles himself, chased his son into exile, and then trounced the Scots and the Irish for good measure. Politically, it was a disaster. After dealing with Charles it turned on and overthrew the very Parliament that had created it. It then placed England, until that time probably the freest nation in Europe, under the military dictatorship of its commander, Oliver Cromwell.[3]

Military rule soon became unpopular not only for its repression but also for the high cost of a standing army. After Cromwell's death a reconstituted Parliament and George Monck, one of Cromwell's generals, restored the monarchy in 1660. Parliament and the new king, Charles II, restored the militia and replaced the New Model Army with a tiny national army that, although it gradually increased in size, stayed out of sight and under tight control for many years. The British did not soon forget what an out-of-control military could do.[4]

Our Founding Fathers did not forget it either. The British Army's occupation of Boston also served as a sharp reminder, if any was needed. Nevertheless, Congress soon realized that it could not fight the Revolutionary War with militia alone, and so it raised the Continental Army from militia volunteers. Although the Continental Army never enjoyed the stunning battlefield successes of the New Model Army, it ultimately did what was required of it and then (to everyone's relief) went quietly home. Congress initially retained only a single artillery company to guard stores at West Point. The following year, 1784, it raised a regiment from 700 militiamen to guard posts on the northwestern frontier.[5] Over the next century, Congress gradually increased the U.S. Army's size and responsibilities but as late as 1898 the Army was still authorized only 27,000 men. As for the Navy, Congress sold its last ship in 1785 and only authorized a postwar navy in 1797 after the need for trade protection became imperative.[6]

Congress also established the relationship between the federal government and the state militias with two militia acts passed in 1792. The first gave the president the authority to call out the militia in response to foreign invasion or internal disorder. The second ordered that the militia consist of all able-bodied male citizens between the ages of 18 and 45. Each member would arm and equip himself at his own expense and report for training twice a year. The state legislatures would prescribe the militia's tactical organization (companies, battalions, regiments, etc.). As time went on, however, and the nation grew more secure, militia service effectively became voluntary. Militia units began to resemble social clubs more than military organizations, but even as late as 1898 the militia could field five times more troops than the U.S. Army.[7]

If the president wanted to take the United States to war, he would need a national army that, unlike the militia, could fight anywhere, not just within its home states. Unless the war was to be of extremely limited scope and duration, the regular U.S. Army would be too small. To enlarge it, the president would have to go to Congress not only to obtain a declaration of war, but also the authority and funding needed to call for militia volunteers. Assuming that Congress was forthcoming, the president would then issue a call for volunteers, ordering each state governor to raise a fixed quota of men from their respective militias. These orders were difficult to enforce and during the war of 1812 and the Civil War several governors refused them.[8] However, those that complied would call on the individual companies and regiments of their respective militias to volunteer for federal service. The members of those units would then vote on whether their units would become "U.S. Volunteers." Individual members of units that volunteered could still excuse themselves from service for health or family reasons.

Given that most militia units were below their full strength in peacetime, and that a portion of their existing members would be unwilling or unable to serve, they would need a lot of new recruits if they were to go to war. They would also need time for training and "shaking down." Secretary of War John C. Calhoun in 1818 noted that the United States had no significant continental enemies and was essentially an insular power. Thus, the Navy could ensure that an invader could not land in America before the U.S. Volunteers had time to prepare.[9]

The system certainly made it harder to go to war. In the first 100 years of its existence the United States fought only two significant foreign wars.[10] However, the system certainly had its defects and its critics. Among the most prominent and vocal critics was author and Army officer Emory Upton. Upton graduated from West Point on the eve of the Civil War and greatly distinguished himself during that conflict. By 1865 he was a U.S. Army lieutenant colonel and a brevet major general in the U.S. Volunteers. Upton was appalled at the unnecessary loss of life resulting from the professional incompetence of the United States Volunteer (ex-militia) officers and, unlike his contemporaries, resolved to do something about it. After the war, Army commanding general William T. Sherman sent Upton on a tour of Europe and Asia to study foreign armies, especially the German army, in view of its recent (1871) victory over the French. Upton returned full of ideas about how to professionalize the U.S. Army along German lines. These included the establishment of advanced military schools, a general staff and a personnel evaluation system that included promotion by examination. Upton published an account of his experiences and opinions in his first book, "The Armies of Asia and Europe" in 1878. He also began his second and far more important book, "The Military Policy of the United States." This was a detailed organizational and administrative history of the U.S. Army from the American Revolution forwards. By 1881, Upton (then a colonel) had advanced his narrative to 1862 when he committed suicide at his quarters at the Presidio of San Francisco. Upton is known to have had a brain tumor at the time, and pain or madness from that may have been the motive. However, depression brought on by the recent death of his wife and his own belief that the Army had rejected his ideas probably contributed.[11]

In that last belief, Upton proved to be quite wrong. His second book was highly influential even though it was not actually published until 1904 and only circulated in manuscript form before then. In his book, Upton constantly stressed the folly of entrusting the defense of the United States to ill-trained militia amateurs rather than properly trained military professionals. As a result, soldiers and politicians, many of the latter being Civil War veterans, began to look for ways to either abolish or neuter the militia, or place it under firm U.S. Army control.

The first major clash between the Uptonians backing the professionalization of the Army and traditionalists who defended the status quo occurred in 1898 just before war with Spain. The Uptonians wanted to fight the coming war with an expanded U.S. Army and leave most of the militia on the shelf. However, politically influential militiamen defeated this attempt and forced the government to call out every militia unit that wanted to participate. Together with swarms of individual volunteers, the Army found itself with far more men than it could train or equip, as well as many more than it needed to fight the Spaniards. The result was a logistical disaster that, through privation and disease, killed many more men than the Spanish did. As soon as the war was over the militiamen and other volunteers demanded their discharges and headed home. They had, however, left some important business unfinished.[12]

The peace treaty gave the United States most of Spain's colonial empire. The need to garrison these new territories after the militia went home got the Army the expansion it had sought before the war began. Congress also passed the Militia Act of 1903. This superseded the 1792 acts and greatly extended federal control over the militia, by now increasingly known as the National Guard. The act established a Division of Militia Affairs within the Office of the Secretary of War and vastly increased federal subsidies for the militia. Militia units had to conform to U.S. Army organizational practice and submit to regular inspections. Members had to attend 24 drills and five days' annual training per year. Officer selection and training had to conform to federal standards.[13]

An even greater change came with the National Defense Act of 1916, passed in anticipation of America's entry into World War I. In effect, it transformed all militia units from individual state forces into a federal reserve force. The title of "National Guard" became mandatory for all militia units and, within the War Department the Division of Militia Affairs became the National Guard Bureau. Instead of the state titles that many had borne since the colonial era the former militia units received numbers in sequence with regular Army units. In addition, the act created a U.S. Army Reserve of trained individuals not organized into units and established a Reserve Officer Training Corps (ROTC) in the colleges and universities.[14]

With the passage of the 1916 Defense Act, the Uptonians had won the control they needed to truly professionalize America's armies. The political cost had been high. America now had the large professional standing army (with no counterbalancing militia) that our Founding Fathers warned us against. The president now controlled all of the nation's armed forces in peacetime as well as in war. He would no longer have to beg either Congress or the state governors for troops.

Within a few years he would not have to ask Congress for a declaration of war, either. Yes, Congress still holds the purse strings but, as other chapters of this book will show, it has never gripped them very tightly. Like the New Model Army, the new U.S. Army was effectively accountable only to the executive branch of government. However, it has not enjoyed the New Model Army's unbroken success and especially not since World War II. Although the Uptonians had succeeded in usurping the powers they needed to reform the Army, they largely failed to implement the reforms themselves.[15]

At first there was some excuse. President Woodrow Wilson lost no time in exercising his new powers as armed forces commander in chief. Within a year, well before any serious military reform was possible and completely contrary to his re-election platform he brought the United States into the First World War. (He did at least ask Congress for a declaration.) He even invaded Russia (without a declaration) in 1918.[16] Although the Army had expanded five-fold since 1898, it was still far too small for a European war. Even after all Reservists and National Guardsmen had been called up, the Army would have to expand ten-fold. It needed 150,000 officers but the regular Army, Reserve and National Guard together had only 8,000. Needless to say, the Army cut a lot of corners to get its 150,000 officers and encountered the same problems Upton had railed about regarding the Civil War era U.S. Volunteers. Like the Union Army, however, the American Expeditionary Force (AEF) of 1918 could still tip the military balance in favor of the Allies but the cost was high. Though only in action for about 200 days, the AEF sustained more than a quarter million battle casualties besides many more losses from accidents and disease.[17]

Surely, the problems the AEF experienced would have been fixed in time for the next war. There had been 20 years of peace during which reforms could have been undertaken. Compared to the frantic last-minute mobilization for World War I, the U.S. Army's mobilization for World War II was almost leisurely. It really began just after Germany invaded Poland in 1939 (the Roosevelt administration expected the United States to enter the war sooner or later). Congress had been ramping up the military budget for some years before that. By the time of the Pearl Harbor attack the process was well along, the National Guard having already been called up, the regular Army considerably expanded and a peacetime draft instituted. Furthermore, because of shipping shortages many divisions literally had to wait years to go overseas. Indeed, if not for the organizing genius of Army Ground Forces chief Lt. Gen. Lesley J. McNair much of the Army might not have gotten overseas at all. By the time the bulk of the U.S. Army had entered combat, which was not until well into 1944, the outcome of the war had been largely decided.[18]

Despite all these opportunities to implement them, the reforms never actually happened. Rather than build a truly professional officer corps, the Army chose instead to appoint officers based largely on education and social background. It also appointed far too many officers, for whom it later experienced great difficulty in finding jobs. Officer training was brief and "by the numbers," imparting enough information to solve the problem at hand, but not enough for true understanding. The Army's most important and challenging combat arm, the infantry, received a lot of low-quality officers and recruits because infantry did not require a lot of technical training. Thus, the Army concluded that anyone was fit for it. The Army also neglected its noncommissioned officers (NCOs), making officers out of the best of them and not according much respect or prestige to the others. Emory Upton would have been spinning in his grave.[19]

It has often been argued that the U.S. Army was a citizen force that could not achieve the same professionalism as the army of a more militarized state like Germany, but American "know-how" and initiative would make up the difference. However, when America was rearming, Germany, despite its Nazi government and the fact that its army (like the American) responded only to the authority of a "unitary executive," was not yet a militarized state. The Allies' post-1919 disarmament of Germany had been pretty thorough. Germany had been allowed to keep an active army that, relative to its population, was barely larger than the active U.S. Army and was allowed no reserve forces at all. Germany's rearmament began in earnest only a little sooner than America's and, not having 3,000 miles of ocean to protect it, the German Army had to be able to fight as soon as hostilities began. Yet while Germany would display many shortcomings during the war, even its enemies acknowledged the professional quality of its army officers and NCOs. The Israeli and Finnish armies have used the German methods of officer/NCO training and selection with similar success, but the U.S. Army has rejected them as elitist.[20]

Since World War II, the U.S. military has abandoned its search for excellence in favor of mediocrity. Near-disaster in Korea did produce some reform, and the army that fought in Vietnam was initially much better prepared, but not for the war it was called on to fight. The limited professional education of its leaders left them with a poor understanding of the war they were in and an even poorer ability to explain it to their civilian overlords. Much the same has happened in Iraq and Afghanistan. More recently, the Army has dealt with military reform and excellence as if it had already occurred, describing itself to a wide-eyed Congress and public in the most embarrassing hype ("greatest military on the face of the earth," "that ever existed" and so forth). Mussolini's Italian army did much the same thing.[21]

Also, since the Second World War, the U.S. Army's focus has been far more on itself and its position in domestic politics. This was at least in part a consequence of the Cold War, in which the Army spent a lot of time preparing to fight but not actually fighting a thoroughly studied, conventional and known opponent. However, although they attracted little attention from the U.S. military, major changes in how wars are fought were already taking place.

The Real Threat:
The Rise of Fourth Generation Warfare and the New World Disorder

For the past three centuries or so, most people have lived at least nominally under the rule of a state.[22] The modern state is a European invention dating from the 16th and early 17th centuries. It differed from previous forms of government in that it was a corporate entity (an artificial "person") existing independently of tribe, city or princely house. It also claimed a monopoly on all organized violence and, until recently, it has usually been able to enforce it.[23]

Prior to the state, entities of every kind waged war. They included cities, such as Rome and Athens, and later Florence and Venice. They included tribes or tribal confederacies like those that destroyed Varus' Roman legions. Powerful families, trading organizations like the Hanseatic League and religious orders like the Knights Templar had their own armies and fought their own wars. Bands of mercenaries, such as the White Company of Hundred Years' War fame, which Sir Arthur Conan Doyle later immortalized, hired themselves out to the highest bidder.

In Europe, by the end of the Middle Ages the result was chaos. Not only did armies fight each other, they made war on the civilian population as well. Partly this was because medieval armies had no supply systems or cash, so they looted whatever they needed. Soldiers were also inclined to take revenge on those who resisted them and terrorize even those who did not, knowing that they had little to fear from any legal system.

By the end of the Thirty Years' War in 1648 Europe had had enough. The Thirty Years' War began as a Central European religious struggle between Protestants and Catholics but ended as a purely political contest. Germany in particular was devastated. Europeans wanted order, stability and security, and the Treaty of Westphalia gave it to them. It defined the nation-state as the new governing entity, and decreed that it alone would have the power to make war. All other war-making entities were illegitimate and those who fought for them would be treated not as soldiers but as outlaws. The confinement of lawful violence to states would bring the stability needed for commerce and industry to flourish, learning and science to advance, and for people to feel secure for themselves and their property.

After the treaty was signed, Europe adopted the state system with remarkable speed. The new state armies quickly absorbed the mercenaries or hanged them. With their ability to coin money, levy taxes and organize their people in a way no non-state entity could match, the nation-states soon overwhelmed their non-state competitors. Today in Europe only a handful of tiny pre-state entities, such as Monaco, Andorra and Luxemburg have survived (mainly as banking centers). From Europe the system spread throughout the planet by means of European colonization and imperial expansion. The tribal levies of Africa, the Americas and Asia were no match for the modern, professional state-supported European armies even when they were outnumbered and far from home. By the end of the 19th century, the state system had become so pervasive that few people lived, or could imagine living, under anything else.

At this point it would be well to remind ourselves that at its heart the nation-state, even today, is mostly about violence. Some modern scholars have declared that states should provide not only physical but also social and economic security. This idea was adopted by Otto von Bismarck, Germany's "iron chancellor," but this was two centuries after states had become the norm. Bismarck's social welfare system served to extend his government's domestic power.

Other states did not follow his example in a big way until after the world wars. These wars devastated most of Europe and substantial parts of Asia. Created and waged by states, they undermined public confidence in their respective states' ability to provide the security and stability they promised. Indeed, states such as Nazi Germany and the Soviet Union became as much a menace to the populations they controlled as the most desperate band of pre-1648 brigands had ever been. It was true that some states, favored by geography, superior resources and better strategy, were much more successful at protecting their people. However, the first use of the atomic bomb in 1945 introduced a weapon that no state could defend against. Thus, the primary foundation upon which the state had been built began to crumble.

The world's leading military powers had great difficulty in accepting the fact that conventional warfare between nuclear-armed nations was essentially impossible, but the massive NATO and Warsaw Pact armies that faced each other in Europe never fought. Instead, conventional warfare shifted to the "non-nuclear" parts of the world, but even there it gradually died out. The conventional wars against Iraq in 1991 and 2003 may prove to be among the last.

The reasons for the demise of conventional war go beyond the threat of nuclear weapons. The cost of training and equipping even small conventional forces has become ruinously high. Outside of the so-called "first world" countries, along with Russia, China and India, few nations can afford substantial numbers of modern weapons. Most of the world's poorer armies are now glorified police forces concerned mainly with internal security and politics. They could offer little resistance to a well-equipped invader.

Many states also suffer from the declining loyalty of their own citizens. Post-1945 attempts by many states to buy loyalty (in the Bismarckian style) have fallen short.

This has been especially true in Europe where government ministries dealing with social welfare dwarf the defense ministries. Although the middle classes are unwilling to cause trouble and risk their jobs or pensions, there is a largely unassimilated and foreign-born "under-class" in Europe and America. Barred from the mainstream economy by education, cultural and legal barriers, its members have little loyalty to the states whose welfare systems support them. Their birthrates and levels of violence and unemployment are high. Many feel they have little to lose.

Outside of Europe, North America and the rest of the "first world," the dynamic changes. National governments tend to be new and are often just continuations of the old colonial regimes. Many are kleptocracies or protection rackets, whose rulers enrich themselves by preying on their hapless subjects. Real loyalty in such nations goes to pre-state institutions like tribe, family or religion. Government is merely a source of jobs and patronage, as well as of violence and predatory tax collection.

Four Generations of Warfare

It is this environment that has given rise to the phenomenon called "Fourth Generation War" (4GW). It is the last of four generations constituting a model that describes the evolution of warfare since 1648. The first three generations are of only secondary concern to us here. First Generation War (1GW) reflected the era (ending in the late 19th century) before firearms became technically mature, when close order drill and shock action still had a place on the battlefield. Military ranks, uniforms, saluting and ceremonial drill are all 1GW holdovers.

The Second Generation of Warfare (2GW) was the result of the Industrial Revolution and of firearms technology finally reaching full maturity. The emphasis was on firepower and material superiority with victory invariably going to the "big battalions." Close centralized control (greatly facilitated by telephones and field radios and large staffs) permitted the direction and coordination of the new firepower. The U.S. military is still a 2GW force that relies heavily on its closely coordinated fires and its numerical, material and technical advantages for its success.

The German Army began to evolve Third Generation War (3GW) in 1915. It did this in order to negate the numerical and material advantages enjoyed by its enemies.[24] Also known as "maneuver warfare," 3GW emphasizes decentralization over centralization and maneuver over firepower. Armies using 3GW can defeat stronger 2GW forces by being able to react to situational changes more quickly. American military theorist John Boyd captured this concept in his OODA (Observe, Orient, Decide and Act) loop theory. He had developed it to explain the dynamics of fighter combat but found it applicable to other forms of conflict as well.[25] Under OODA loop theory every combatant observes the situation, orients himself, based on this orientation decides what to do and then does it. If his opponent can do this faster, however, his own actions become outdated and disconnected to the true situation, and his opponent's advantage increases geometrically. The German army's deliberate sacrifice of centralized control to gain faster OODA loops produced many tactical and operational successes against numerically superior opponents. It could not, however, negate the effects of bad strategy, which created for it more enemies than even its 3GW methods could defeat. The Chinese Communists, however, used 3GW against U.S. forces in Korea with great success.[26]

The U.S. Army never adopted 3GW and remains a 2GW force. Although the defeat of 3GW German armies had required an overall numerical superiority of at least two to one, air supremacy, colossal amounts of artillery ammunition and high friendly casualties, the U.S. Army never understood the new methods well and concluded that a 2GW doctrine was good enough.[27] Even near disaster in Korea and failure in Vietnam did not lead to much introspection (the U.S. military still lays the blame for Vietnam upon everyone but itself). A 2GW doctrine was comfortable, conceptually simple and easily taught to the hastily trained "shake and bake" officers who have staffed most of our forces. They remain attractive today, but an army that will not practice at least 3GW levels of decentralization will be at an even greater disadvantage in a fourth generation environment.

Fourth Generation Warfare is in many respects the end of the road because it may mark the end of the state system. The term is often used as a euphemism for guerrilla or irregular warfare, but this is inaccurate. Guerrilla warfare as the irregular war of attrition we know today really began in 1808 while 1GW was still dominant with the uprising by the Spanish populace against Napoleon Bonaparte's invading French army. Unlike 1GW, 2GW or 3GW, 4GW is not about weapons or tactics but about who fights and why. However, who fights and why can certainly influence weapons and tactics. Fourth Generation War is what fills the power vacuum after the state loses its monopoly on violence. It is a reversion to the pre-1648 past. Non-states are fighting wars again and they are beating their state-based opponents far more often than not.[28]

Fourth generation conflicts tend to resemble guerrilla or irregular warfare, and many of the methods used to fight guerrillas still apply. However, the differences created by changes in who fights and why can be large ones. Guerrilla movements aspire to become states themselves (usually by replacing the government they are fighting against or taking part of its territory). They often call themselves states even before anyone recognizes them as such. Fourth generation movements seldom harbor ambitions in this area. Like the FARC in Columbia, for example, their real objectives might be to build a socialist Utopia in the jungle while letting the government in Bogotá (which the FARC had originally been created to overthrow) provide political cover. al-Qaida may indeed want to build a caliphate that would expel non-Muslims from Muslim lands and spread Islam around the world, but sees others, not itself, as ruling it. Chechen rebels fight Moscow for loot as well as for independence. Even when they had a government, they usually ignored it, even as they nominally fought under its banner. Sunni, Shiite and Kurdish groups in Iraq fight each other for land, resources and influence. Some of the Kurds, who are among the United States' few friends in Iraq, also fight the Turks, who are also important U.S. allies. The Sunni, and some Shiites, also fight against the Americans, and (when paid) for them.

Though often few in number, poorly armed and unsophisticated 4GW warriors still present formidable challenges to 2GW and even 3GW opponents. As natives of the region where the war is being fought, they can easily blend with the population. They have no discreet parcels of land or cities to defend. They can neutralize the firepower advantages of a 2GW opponent by denying it targets. Their decentralization (and shorter OODA loops) can exceed even that of 3GW forces. Against foreign invaders these tactics work best of all. The invaders won't know the country, the customs or the language. If they use too much firepower, they alienate the locals, create more recruits for their enemies and dry up their indigenous sources of intelligence. Unless he can supply himself with modern (or relatively modern) heavy weapons, the 4GW warrior will not have the means to face his conventional enemies in open battle.[29] However, in this very weakness lies his strength. His foes so heavily outnumber and outgun him that their inability to destroy him makes them angry, frustrated and embarrassed. His successes make them look foolish. Their successes only make them look like oppressive bullies. In a fight between David and Goliath, who roots for Goliath? Who cheers for the Sheriff of Nottingham over Robin Hood? The 4GW warrior can win just by surviving. Against a foreign 2GW or 3GW opponent it's not a hard job because he can usually decide when, where and how often he fights, thereby regulating his losses. He wears down his nation-state enemies until mounting casualties undermine their morale and political support or the expense bankrupts their treasury.

Erosion of the state system does not just come from the lower social classes and from people whose attachment to the state system was never very strong to begin with. The world's elite, its leading politicians, bureaucrats, bankers and businessmen are quietly undermining it as well. Ease of travel and communication has made these "jet-setters" very cosmopolitan. Like medieval knights and churchmen, they have begun to see themselves as a universal social class, and feel more in common with other members of this class than with their own less exalted countrymen. These elites see an international system culminating in a world government (that they would control, of course) replacing the nation-state as the future provider of stability and security. A world government, reason the elites, would end war because there would be no other government able to fight against it. By imposing a single set of rules and standards it would also ensure fairness. By redistributing wealth, it would overcome poverty and oppression, protect the environment and impose an enlightened version of Aldous Huxley's "Brave New World."[30]

The objections to such a system should be obvious. If national governments cannot command loyalty, what chance has an international government? A world government would be a vast freedom-destroying imperial super state run by largely unelected officials and unaccountable bureaucrats. These ruling elites would see it as a vast tax-subsidized ego trip (not unlike the European Union bureaucrats do), in which the popular will would never be allowed to override the wisdom of their benevolent rulers. Those outside the government (especially in the Third World where the state system is weakest) would see it as a predatory foreign oppressor and, because the international elites tend to be militantly secular, an affront to their religion. Resistance to this super state would pop up everywhere. Everyone would either be feeding off the government or trying to usurp, overthrow or hide from it.

Most of the world's revolutions, notably those of France and Russia, were started by elites who thought they could control the outcome. They soon found out otherwise and many were devoured by the same beasts they had un-caged. Though a world government would probably fail, the chaos that followed its demise would likely destroy much of what remained of the state system. Whether this would eventually lead to anything better is hard to say, but the French and Russian experiences are not encouraging.

The U.S. Military's Response to the New World Disorder

The U.S. military's response to these trends has been an across-the-board resistance to change. It defends its Cold War era weapons and force structure by insisting that an ability to defeat conventional enemies includes the ability to defeat all others, be they fourth generation or otherwise.[31] Even now in the press we read that many in the military begrudge even minor changes to improve the Army's effectiveness against irregular warfare adversaries, because they threaten our "conventional superiority."[32] Advocates of this position even cite Israel's Lebanese fiasco (against a 4GW enemy with the firepower to engage Israeli forces head-on) as evidence of the vital importance of maintaining conventional capabilities.[33] However, no one seems to consider that although the United States has won (or at least been on the winning side of) most of its conventional wars, it has not won an unconventional conflict in nearly 100 years.[34]

The 40-year "Mexican standoff" that characterized the Cold War allowed the U.S. military to focus its war preparations on a single adversary. Except for its disquieting Korean and Vietnam interludes, the U.S. military lived in an intellectually comfortable world of stability and predictability that enabled it to focus its attention on itself. By the time the Soviet Union collapsed, this Cold War status quo had made our military and the industries supporting it highly resistant to change. Change however has come far too rapidly and dramatically for a rigid and internally focused U.S. military to keep up with.

At first perplexed about what to do in a "new world order" (not so very orderly without the Soviet Union), the U.S. military soon found comfort in its ephemeral success in Operation Desert Storm. This seemed to validate the status quo and caused it to spend most of the 1990s in fanciful struggles to justify its Cold War force structure, albeit in an environment where such forces were rapidly losing their relevance. However, status quo advocates point out that the U.S. military must maintain an ability to intervene in the world's trouble spots not only to protect American interests but also to ensure global stability. This, they argue, requires conventional forces as well as the "strategic lift" assets (cargo aircraft, amphibious ships, etc.) needed to get them where they need to go. They also argue that the president requires authority to intervene as he chooses, unfettered by constitutional limits. Hence they applaud the de facto abolition of the militia and the placing of all U.S. military forces under the president's personal control.

But does overseas intervention really work? Officially, our military policy in the world wars and the Cold War were aimed at countering power imbalances in Europe, caused by the rise of first Germany and then the Soviet Union. In fact, these power imbalances, though real, were actually in large measure the products of U.S. meddling. Before the United States entered World War I, the military balance in Europe was just fine. To prove it, the Allies and Central Powers had been beating each other bloody for more than two years with neither side able to gain any advantage. Instead of preserving this balance by brokering a peace, the United States decided to upset it by entering the war on the side of the Allies. This gave the Allies (mainly Britain, France and Italy) a victory that produced the breakup of the Austro-Hungarian Empire, the rise of the Nazi Party in Germany and the Bolshevik takeover of Russia (turning it into the Soviet Union). The European power balance did not stabilize until the Soviet Union fell some 70 years later. Thus, through most of the 20th century, the United States found itself always launching new interventions in order to contain the effects of previous interventions.

Nevertheless, after 1990 and much more so after Sept. 11, the United States began to openly espouse the idea that its own survival and well-being depended on the political and economic stability not just of Europe but the whole world. It saw instability anywhere as a danger with rippling effects breeding existential threats such as nuclear-armed international terrorists.

The sudden fall of Soviet power shattered the simple bipolar orientation that conditioned American strategy and thinking for two generations. It unleashed a muddle of till then suppressed nationalist, ethnic, religious and criminal conflicts. These have produced 4GW conflicts that defy the generalized logic of the Cold War. We now live in a kind of looking glass world in which former allies became enemies and some former enemies became more like allies.[35] However, the looking glass analogy begins to fail when we remember that many of the former friends turned enemies are not actually states or even political movements trying to become states. Earlier, they would hardly merit U.S. attention, but now the United States fights wars with them and finds them much harder to defeat than it had ever imagined.

The Defense Budget and Military Procurement

The current financial state of the Defense Department has its roots in the Cold War. While budgets and the intensity of Cold War politics have waxed and waned between 1950 and 1990, a stable consensus about the Cold War threat produced what amounted to a permanent semi-mobilization. This has evolved a domestic political economy in support of the military that became a vast spider web of defense contractors, politicians, Defense Department bureaucrats (both uniformed and civilian), and a wide array of publicists, lobbyists, academics and journalists. Today, this web of influence has gone well beyond the military-industrial complex that President Dwight D. Eisenhower warned about in his farewell address on Jan. 17, 1961. He had originally described it as a military-industrial-congressional complex (MICC).[36]

Over time, the MICC has increasingly isolated itself from the larger American economy. Naturally, many of the goods that the defense industry produces are irrelevant or illegal in a commercial economy. The market for them consists of only one buyer, but that buyer is a vast entity with supposedly unlimited resources, many stakeholders and a great susceptibility to influences that would not exist in any competitive market economy. This has produced a set of dynamics that has led to an accelerating rate of growth in the technological complexity of weapons as well as in the cost of buying and maintaining them.

Inside these dynamics, however, is a less obvious habitual pattern of bureaucratic behavior made up of deeply entrenched, politically motivated modes of conduct. These modes of conduct, sometimes called Defense Power Games, can be grouped loosely into two complementary bureaucratic strategies: *front-loading* and *political engineering*, which are further discussed in chapters 10 and 11.

Front-loading is the practice of getting a program accepted by downplaying costs and/or exaggerating benefits. Political engineering is the art of quickly building a support network of vested interests to lock in a front-loaded decision before its true costs or performance become apparent. Together, these gaming strategies work like a bait-and-switch operation, creating a pattern of chronic over-commitment. Readers interested in more detailed descriptions of these strategies can download *Defense Power Games* from the World Wide Web.[37]

While the corresponding effects of these power games are apparent in many types of policy-making,[38] they are most evident in the development and procurement of new high-tech weapons. In this case, the most obvious front-loading strategy is the "buy-in," a deliberate low-balling of a cost estimate by a contractor to win a competition, or by a government sponsor to get a program approved, or, more often, both. Whereas front-loading relies on stealth to get the game going, effective political engineering must be palpable and overt. The most common political-engineering strategy in weapons procurement is the art of building a political safety net by spreading subcontracts, dollars, jobs and profits to as many congressional districts as possible before the consequences of the buy-in (i.e., the inevitable cost growth) are felt.[39]

The front-loading and political-engineering gaming strategies have several perni-cious consequences. First, they pack the defense budget with weapons programs more appropriate to the economic needs of the contractors than to the military needs of the nation. Second, they have subtle biases designed to increase weapon-system cost and complexity. "Complexity" can be defined as a subjective quality of the "whole" relating the number and arrangement of its "parts" and to one's ability to compre-hend the "whole." It follows that increasing the complexity of anything makes it less comprehensible. Therefore, the more complex a system is, the easier it becomes to front-load a decision to build it. The greater variety of parts that complex systems require increases the need for subcontractors, thereby making it easier to set up political-engineering operations. Finally, the inward focus of these gaming strategies corrupts decision-making by debasing intellectual rigor and increasing cynicism among those involved.[40]

In addition to packing the budget with too many high-cost programs, defense power games create a powerful structural asymmetry wherein unit costs always grow faster than budgets, even when budgets increase rapidly, as they did in the 1980s. As the cost of the "parts" grows faster than the budget for the "whole," compound inter-est kicks in to make deteriorating trends inevitable. These trends include shrinking forces, aging weapons, reduced readiness, and short-term decision-making to address an endless stream of funding crises.[41]

Although the increasing complexity of weapons and the accompanying cost growth have been the norm since the mid-1950s, these mutually reinforcing trends accelerated during the 1970s and 1980s with the development and fielding of a new generation of post-Vietnam Cold War weapons. Most of these weapons cost far more to procure *and* operate than the weapons they replaced.[42] An even more expensive generation of Cold War–inspired replacement weapons entered research and development in the late 1980s and early 1990s as the Cold War ended and budget reductions began to take effect.[43] The coincidence of tightening budgets with a long-range plan to modernize with an even more costly generation of weapons set the stage for a budget crisis in the late 1990s.[44] America's combat forces shrank faster than their budgets, and inflation-adjusted spending per unit of combat power increased.[45]

As each new generation of weapons enters procurement, the operating costs of existing weapons increase as they age. This in turn eats up the procurement dollars needed to pay for their much more expensive replacements. The predictable result was what former Undersecretary of Defense Jacques Gansler called the "Defense Death Spiral."[46] Its symptoms are declining rates of modernization, aging forces, low readiness and plummeting morale. It is fed by a cacophony of cries for long-term increases in the defense budget. Added to the costs of our wars in Iraq and Afghanistan and our overseas network of over 700 military bases, this has placed the Defense Department on a pathway leading to a domestic political tug-of-war over fiscal resources with Social Security, Medicare and the imperative need to shore up a collapsing dollar.

It was no surprise that the combination of relatively modest budget declines accompanying the end of the Cold War and rapidly increasing unit cost overwhelmed the "savings" from force-structure reductions and reinforced each other to create an "under-funding" crisis by the summer of 2000. The Afghan and Iraq wars, coupled with continued "peacekeeping" and "nation building" in support of the war on terror, have since greatly exacerbated this situation.

The continued acceleration in the growth of complexity is consistent with two conclusions about the roots of paralysis. First, the focus of the MICC is entirely inward. It ignores external threats as it makes the decisions that deform our military. Second, the MICC promotes its own welfare (in the form of using the war on terror, Afghanistan and Iraq to justify business as usual) at the expense of the general welfare.[47]

Why the "Death Spiral" Will Continue

The internal factors described above lock decision-makers into a daily struggle to keep the defense ship financially afloat. They punctuate this struggle with perceived or contrived crises that call for higher budgets.[48] This infuses the defense budget with one bailout after another, and thus saps the political capital and resources needed to change the ship's course.

In the 1990s our military institutions responded to the end of the Cold War with no more than a comfortable modification of past practices. However, they did take advantage of the information revolution to repackage their shopworn ideas into glitzy computerized "visions" – virtual realities – of the threats that would justify their budgets, as opposed to the ones they might actually encounter. It is no coincidence that the "vision-based" future worlds of the 1990s, e.g., Joint Vision 2010 or the so-called future Revolution in Military Affairs (RMA), also protected the *same* internal commercial and political interests creating the cost growth and political rigidity that have been locking the military into its death spiral all along.

While the MICC remains mired in its fanciful struggle to preserve its dying Cold War lifestyle, the real world has moved on. This had led to a widening web of challenges including:

- an outdated 2GW attritional American style of war,
- emerging requirements to address new threats posed by 4GW,
- the unaffordable and growing cost of continuing Cold War business as usual, and
- the political threat of a standing military responsive only to the executive branch.

Until the American military finds a way to escape from its past there seems little chance that it can effectively deal with the challenges of its future.

Some believe that the military can spend its way out of its death spiral. We believe that this makes as much sense as curing a hangover by continuing to drink. Instead, we believe that fundamental change is urgently needed in all three of the basic elements of military power:

1. *People*: recruiting, retention, personnel management, unit cohesion, empowerment and character development.

2. *Ideas*: military theory, doctrine, education, training and organization.

3. *Hardware*: weapons, supplies, infrastructure and technology – at a sustainable cost.

If we can get the changes we need in the first two elements the third should take care of itself.

The purpose of this book is to stimulate debate and identify reforms that can place our military on a healthier pathway to the future. It is not intended to be comprehensive. Most of the essays focus on types of changes needed in the first two categories, and, for reasons of space, personal experience and continuity of exposition, tend to concentrate on ground and air forces. The aim of this introductory essay is to set the stage by describing the nature of change in large institutions and why fundamental reforms are needed for all services in the three categories listed above.

How to Change

What should the American people expect from Congress and the military as the United States begins to adapt to this changing face of warfare?

Military theorist John Boyd taught that effective military systems prioritize the components of which they are composed: people, ideas and hardware – in that order. He responded to the U.S. Army's emphasis on synchronization – the methodical timing of several events in time and space – with the comment, "you can only synchronize watches, not people." He emphasized that "people fight wars, not machines, and they use their minds" and that military systems that give people top priority adapt to changes in warfare more quickly than those that emphasize machines. Boyd defined this in testimony before Congress in April 1991: "There are three basic elements [to win wars] and in order of importance they are: People, because wars are fought by people not weapons. Strategy and tactics [ideas] because wars fought without innovational ideas become ... blood baths winnable or not. Hardware, because weapons that don't work or can't be [produced] in quantity will bring down even the best people and best ideas."

Boyd went on to describe how each aspect is interrelated:

" ... our military needs to be trained in innovative tactics and strategies that will lead to quick decisive victory at minimum cost to American lives... This requires, first, an understanding of conflict. Conflict can be viewed as repeated cycles of observing-orienting-deciding-acting by both sides (and at all levels). The adversary that can move through these cycles faster gains an inestimable advantage by disrupting his enemy's ability to respond effectively... These create continuous and unpredictable change. Therefore our tactics and strategy need to be based on the idea of adapting to and shaping this change faster than the enemy."[49]

To be effective a military system must be able to incorporate these concepts into its culture.

If this is true, then why has the U.S. defense establishment failed to reform itself? Americans love to boast about their innovation, as well as their ability to adapt and overcome adversity. If the current establishment is so out of date, corrupt and slow to adapt to the 21st century, why does no one do anything about it except a few "reformers?"

This book will address changes needed in the defense establishment. By the "establishment" we mean more than just its fighting component. A military machine as large as that of the United States consists of many interrelated institutions. To place even a rifleman on the battlefield, all must work in harmony to ensure that he is well-trained and led, and both physically and mentally equipped for the mission confronting him.

Like an effective combined-arms team, the authors of the following essays represent all branches of the military services, as well as Department of the Defense, its acquisition community and Congress. Some of the authors are retired service members, while others are government civilians. Their motivation is simple. They are patriotic individuals who believe America will lose its next war unless their ideas are adopted by a national security establishment badly in need of change.

ENDNOTES

1   U.S. Department of Defense, *Dictionary of Military and Associated Terms*, Joint Publication 1-02 (JP 1-02), (Washington D.C.) http://www.dtic.mil/doctrine/jel/doddict/acronym_index.html

2   For a further discussion of the issue of generals giving poor advice to politicians see Lawrence J. Korb "Military Leaders Make Weak Advisors," *The Washington Independent*, August 4, 2008, http://washingtonindependent.com

3   For a history of the New Model Army see Ian Gentles, *The New Model Army – in England, Ireland and Scotland, 1645-53* (Oxford: Blackwell Press, 1994).

4 For brief accounts of this period see Michael Barthrop, *The Armies of Britain 1485-1980* (London: National Army Museum, 1980) and Charles Messenger, History of the British Army (Novato, CA: Presidio Press, 1986).

5 Emory Upton, *The Military Policy Of the United States* (U.S. War Department, Washington D.C. 1912), 68-70.

6 Congress did increase the U.S. Army to 55,000 for the post-Civil War occupation of the South, but cut it back to 30,000 in 1870 and then to 25,000 in 1876; official tables of authorized Army strength and organization appear in U.S. Army *Registers* for 1860-1898 (all published Washington D.C. by the Adjutant General). See also Russell F. Weigley, *History of the United States Army*, (Bloomington, IN: Indiana University Press, 1984). For a history of the re-founding of the U.S. Navy see Ian W. Toll, *Six Frigates; The Epic Founding of the U. S. Navy* (New York: W.W. Norton Co., 2006).

7 A reprint of the militia acts of 1792 is available at http://www.constitution.org/mil/mil_act_1792. htm. See also Upton, *Military Policy of the United States*, 54-55. For the size of the organized militia see U.S. Army *Register* and Graham A. Cosmas, *An Army for Empire* (University of Missouri Press, 1971).

8 For examples of this see Emory Upton, *The Armies of Asia and Europe* (New York, NY: Greenwood Press) and *The Military Policy of the United States*, op cit, 61-62 and 227-28.

9 John C. Calhoun, *Reports and Public Letters of John C. Calhoun*, vol. 5 (New York, NY: D. Appleton, 1855), 84.

10 These were the Mexican War and the War of 1812. Much of the latter was actually fought on U.S. territory. The intermittent scuffles with the Barbary pirates in the Mediterranean and with French privateers in the Caribbean, though they got a lot of press, only involved our (at the time) very small navy in its primary role of trade protection.

11 See Upton, *Military Policy of the United States* op cit. See also Russell F. Weigley, *History of the United States Army* (Bloomington, IN: Indiana University Press, 1984).

12 Weigly, 92-110; see also Graham A. Cosmas, *An Army for Empire* (University of Missouri Press, 1971).; Leonard L. Lerwill et al, *The Personnel Replacement System in the United States Army* (1954; repr., Washington D.C.: U.S. Army Center for Military History, 1982, 1988).

13 See 10 U.S. Code Section 311

14 Ibid

15 For further discussion of this point see Vandergriff, *Path to Victory*.

16 He had already invaded Mexico (twice), Cuba, Haiti, the Dominican Republic and Nicaragua, all in his first term.

17 "Report of the Secretary of War" for fiscal year 1925-26, 192-240; this contained the latest revisions of American Expeditionary Force battle casualty figures. See also Leonard P. Ayres, *The War With Germany: A Statistical Summary* (Washington D.C.: U.S. Government Printing Office, 1919), 113-130.; and Lerwill, 213-216. John Mosier in his recent and excellent book, *The Myth of the Great War* (New York, NY: Harper-Collins, 2001) disputes many of these figures. He notes (pp. 12 and 341) that an actual count of AEF war graves shows that some 85,252 American soldiers and Marines are buried in France, though not all of these necessarily died in battle. However, he also cites (p. 365, fn 4) correspondence in the congressional archives concerning the dissatisfaction of key officers with the casualty statistics published by Colonel Ayres, the War Department's chief statistician. It also reveals a War Department insistence on manipulating casualty figures, presumably to protect the reputations of senior officers.

18 Prior to D-Day on June 6, 1944, U.S. forces had been engaged only in limited numbers and in peripheral theater, but the outcome of the war had been largely determined by then. For details of the U.S. Army's World War II mobilization see Shelby L. Stanton, *World War II Order of Battle*,

(New York, NY: Galahad Books, 1986).

19 For the details see Van Creveld.

20 The Finnish army officer corps in 1939 was largely German trained. Many of its senior members had served in the German army's 27th (Finnish) Jaeger Battalion during World War I. Despite its aversion to Nazism, the Israeli army in its early years adopted German military doctrine, even to the extent of using the same map symbols.

21 A good example of military hype is the recent television miniseries "Band of Brothers." Regarding the Italians, see Col. G. B. Jarrett, *West of Alamein* (Northridge, CA: Sentry Books, 1971) for some amusing anecdotes. For background see editors Alan R. Millett and Williamson Murray, *Military Effectiveness Vol. III: The Second World War* (Boston, MA: Allen & Unwin, 1988), 170-72.

22 The Hapsburg Empire might be considered an exception to this, but the empire itself was still a state (if not a nation-state) at least as far as foreign policy was concerned. Its constituent kingdoms can be considered nation- states in most other respects as well.

23 In the non-European Third World nation-states have been much more recently and much less firmly established than elsewhere. In more remote areas, like Afghanistan, states have been much less successful in establishing monopolies on organized violence. However, on paper at least, nearly everyone belongs to a nation-state.

24 For an account of the German army's conversion to 3GW see Bruce I. Gudmundsson, *Stormtroop Tactics* (Westport, CT: Praeger Publishers, 1991).

25 For a biography of Colonel John Boyd and a discussion of his OODA Loop see Robert Coram, *Boyd, the Fighter Pilot Who Changed the Art of War* (New York, NY: Back Bay Books, 2002).

26 The best account of Chinese 3GW success in Korea is Roy E. Appleman, *Disaster in Korea* (College Station, TX: Texas A&M University Press, 1989).

27 For a classic study that compares a 3GW army with a 2GW army see Martin van Creveld, *Fighting Power, German and US Army Performance, 1939-1945* (Westport, CT: Greenwood Press, 1974).

28 Readers can find a compendium of articles on 4GW on the Internet at "Defense and the National Interest," http://www.d-n-i.net/FCS_Folder/fourth_generation_warfare.htm

29 Hezbollah holding off the Israeli army in southern Lebanon in 2006 and Chechen irregulars defeating the Russian army in Grozny in 1995 are proof that 4GW irregulars can take on conventional forces if they are properly equipped. However, these situations are still exceptional.

30 *Brave New World* was copyrighted in 1932 and 1946. One of many editions published since then is Aldous Huxley, *Brave New World* (New York, NY: Harper-Collins, 1998).

31 For an Army doctrinal reference see U.S. Army FM 3-0, Operations (Washington, D.C.: Headquarters, Department of the Army, February 2008).; H. R. McMaster points out in his article, On War; Lessons to be Learned, published online in Survival 50 (February 2008) that the U.S. military sees conventional war as the way it prefers to fight (so it can take advantage of its material superiority and vastly greater firepower) and that this preference is relevant to enemy action, see: http://www.informaworld.com/smpp/content?content=10.1080/00396330801899439

32 For an example, see Gian P. Gentile, "Misreading the Surge Threatens U.S. Army's Conventional Capabilities," *World Politics Review*, March 4, 2008, www.worldpoliticsreview.com/article.aspx?id=1715. The article says that U.S. forces had been successfully practicing counterinsurgency "by the book" and doing so successfully since 2004. If the statistics that the U.S. government has been releasing to the public have any validity, this conclusion is highly questionable. No one did counterinsurgency in Iraq by "the book." No one even read "the book" and the results showed it. Through the first quarter of 2007 (after the "surge" was well under way) the situation in Iraq steadily deteriorated by nearly every conceivable measurement. The "greatest military the world has ever seen" insisted on fighting as if this were a conventional war. Any American soldier could justify killing any Iraqi simply by declaring that he "felt threatened." Crowded urban areas were

heavily bombed or shelled without regard to civilian casualties so that fewer Americans would be placed at risk. Indeed, at the time of this writing the use of air strikes by U.S. forces in both Iraq and Afghanistan has greatly increased, despite its indiscriminate nature and the harm it causes to the civil population (see Anthony H. Cordesman, U.S. Airpower in Iraq and Afghanistan, 2004-07; 2007 Center of Strategic and International Studies, Washington, D.C., http://www.csis. org/media/csis/pubs/071213_oif-oef_airpower.pdf). Indeed, civil-military relations in general, not to mention the provision of sewage treatment, potable water and electricity still get mainly lip service. As for doctrinal and force structure change, this author as chief doctrine writer at the Marine Air Ground Task Force (MAGTF) Staff Training Program, witnessed almost none resulting from Iraq experience. New doctrinal manuals on counterinsurgency were published only recently. Though much better than our old Vietnam-era leftovers, they are poorly written and not widely read. Regarding the "surge" this brief discussion of it is a horrible simplification, but there is simply no space for anything else. According to its originally stated objective of winning a political "breathing space" in which Sunnis and Shiites could address their differences the "surge" was a total failure. In terms of lowering the overall level of national violence, the "surge" appears to have done much better. However, this appears to have been a product of political events that would have occurred even without a surge. The "ethnic cleansing" of Baghdad, largely the work of Shia militias, physically separated many combatants. The willingness of the Sunni tribes to (temporarily at least) accept weapons and bribe money to stop attacking Americans, and Moqtada al-Sadr's decision (quite possibly imposed on him by Iran) to temporarily stand down his Mahdi militia, neither the direct result of American military might (though General Petraeus did have sense enough to use bribery when he got the chance), were both key to the reduction in violence associated with the surge. One notes in passing that although most of the reinforcements associated with the surge went to Baghdad, the greatest reductions in violence occurred in Anbar province.

33 Regarding Israel's ill-fated 2006 Lebanon War, Israel used its air force as its main effort to defeat Hezbollah rather than its ground forces. The Israeli air force would have been least affected by the recent fighting in the Palestinian territories, yet it came up short, killing lots of Lebanese civilians but relatively few Hezbollah combatants. The ground assaults on Hezbollah, conducted mainly with armored and airborne troops, were costly and achieved little. Overconfidence, poor tactics and the fact that Hezbollah had managed to acquire some modern anti-armor weapons seem to have had much to do with this than too much focus on fighting in the territories (see Reuters, "Anti-Tank Weapons Inflict Heavy Losses on Israeli Army," *Defense News*, August 10, 2006, http://www.tau.ac.il/jcss/defensenews100806.html; Efraim Inbar, "How Israel Bungled the Second Lebanon War" *Middle East Quarterly* (Summer 2007), 57-65; and the Wikipedia article on the second Lebanon war, http://en.wikipedia.org/wiki/2006_Lebanon_War

34 Exceptions to this include the War of 1812 and the Korean War, which ended as stalemates. In the two world wars others did the bulk of the fighting on land, though U.S. economic support, and naval and air forces in World War II, were essential. The last guerrilla war in which the United States was successful was the Philippine Insurrection (1899-1916). Some of the supporters of our invasion of Iraq are proclaiming victory over our irregular opponents in that country. This war has in fact become a struggle between multiple entities of which the United States is only one (albeit a powerful one). However, apart from the overthrow of Saddam Hussein (which occurred before the irregular war began), the United States has thus far accomplished none of its original objectives. Its success at bribing the Sunni insurgents (whom it was not able to defeat) and the "ethnic cleansing" of Baghdad (mainly the work of Shi's irregulars though U.S. forces did help), has certainly reduced casualties. In the end, however, all of that may do little more than allow the United States a face-saving exit. At the time of this writing (August 2008), the real winner of this conflict appears to be Iran. Apart from this the United States has succeeded against insurgencies only when it limited its participation to providing arms, money and advisors to the local counterinsurgents (as in El Salvador, Bolivia and Greece).

35 The former Soviet Union and mainland China are two examples of enemies turned friendlier. The Taliban, al- Qaida and Saddam Hussein are examples of former allies turned enemies.

36 For the final version of his speech Eisenhower removed the word "congressional." The speech he actually delivered read, in part, as follows: "Our military organization today bears little relation to that known ... in peacetime, or indeed by the fighting men of World War II or Korea. Until the latest of our world conflicts, the United States had no armaments industry. American makers of plowshares could, with time and as required, make swords as well. But now we can no longer risk emergency improvisation of national defense; we have been compelled to create a permanent armaments industry of vast proportions. Added to this, three and a half million men and women are directly engaged in the defense establishment. We annually spend on military security more than the net income of all United States corporations."

"This conjunction of an immense military establishment and a large arms industry is new in the American experience. The total influence – economic, political, even spiritual – is felt in every city, every state house, every office of the federal government. We recognize the imperative need for this development. Yet we must not fail to comprehend its grave implications. Our toil, resources and livelihood are all involved; so is the very structure of our society."

"In the councils of government, we must guard against the acquisition of unwarranted influence, whether sought or unsought, by the military-industrial complex. The potential for the disastrous rise of misplaced power exists and will persist." (President Dwight D. Eisenhower, "Farewell Address to the Nation," January 17, 1961. *Public Papers of the Presidents: Dwight D. Eisenhower, 1960-61* (Washington, D.C. Eisenhower Center, 1969), 103.

37 Franklin C. Spinney, Defense Power Games (Washington, D.C.: Fund for Constitutional Government, 1990); http://www.d-n-i.net/FCS_Folder/def_power_games_98.htm

38 Two excellent examples of this were how the Clinton administration persuaded Congress to support its decision to deploy peacekeepers to Bosnia, and how the Bush administration sold Congress on its proposed invasion of Iraq. The Clinton administration assured Congress that the Bosnia deployment would only last one year. Likewise, the Bush administration told Congress that the Iraq invasion would be a "cakewalk" lasting no more than a few weeks. There would be very few U.S. casualties, most Iraqis would welcome the fall of Saddam Hussein, and postwar sales of Iraqi oil would cover all the costs. However, it soon became clear that neither venture would end anytime soon, nor stay anywhere near its projected cost parameters. Worse, the Iraqi people proved totally ungrateful for the "liberation" that selfless America had so graciously given them. Some of them even had the impertinence to mount a highly effective guerrilla campaign against their "benefactors" that still continues with no end in sight. It seems hardly necessary to mention that Iraqi oil revenues never even began to cover the costs of the war, and that American casualties ran into the tens of thousands. But America had committed its prestige to both operations (and to the invasion of Afghanistan which, though it began well, has since become as much a donnybrook as Iraq). Their promoters have not ceased to argue that any decision to pull out would destroy U.S. "credibility."

Perhaps the classic example of political engineering is the current F-35 program. It ropes in not only hundreds of congressional districts but foreign allies as well. Naturally, the cost has been unbelievably front-loaded as well.

40 An example, though a few years old, amply illustrates the illogical cynicism that now permeates every defense budget debate. On Feb. 25, 2000, the Defense Department Inspector General identified $2.3 trillion of unsubstantiated accounting adjustments during his annual audit of DOD's bookkeeping system. Based on this finding, he issued yet another disclaimer of opinion saying that "DOD internal controls were not adequate to ensure that resources were properly managed and accounted for, that DOD complied with applicable laws and regulations, and that the financial statements were free of material misstatements." (http://www.d-n-i.net/FCS_Folder/budget.htm) Nevertheless, six months later, on Sept. 14, 2000, the CBO's Daniel Crippen did not explain to the Senate Budget Committee how CBO analysts could reliably determine that

there was a $50 billion per year shortfall in the Pentagon's budget, when the Pentagon's inspector general had determined that the DOD's bookkeeping system was un-auditable. See http://www.cbo.gov/showdoc.cfm?index=2399&sequence=0&from=7

41 Franklin C. Spinney, "Defense Spending Time Bomb," *Challenge: The Magazine of Economic Affairs*, (July-August 1996), 23-33. This report illustrates the general point with a case study of air force tactical fighter aviation. It shows how the long-term effects of behavior that drives up costs faster than budgets leads to smaller and older forces and continual pressure to reduce readiness. Finally, it gives the reader an idea of the magnitude of the adjustment now needed to fix the current aging crisis. See http://www.infowar.com/mil_c4i/defense.html-ssi

42 Promises of lower life cycle costs have not materialized because the increased reliance on computer diagnostics increased both the variety and quantity of depot-repairable repair parts, requiring a more sophisticated logistics management system to keep track of the growing number of individually accountable items in the supply pipeline. Moreover, by displacing a greater percentage of repairs in space and time from the point of activity, it became more difficult to determine the appropriate mix for war stockpiles. This led to an increasing dependence on wartime workarounds, such as "cannibalization" to support peacetime operations. All this translates into more money. If, for example, one compares the M1 tank to the M60A3 it replaced, official DOD budget data indicates unit procurement costs increased by a factor of 200 percent, and operating costs per mile increased by 70 percent to 180 percent for the M1 and M1A1 respectively. A similar comparison of the F-15 to the F-4 reveals an increase of 240 percent in unit procurement costs, and a 53-percent increase in operating and support cost per flying hour. All comparisons have the effects of inflation removed and include the appropriate allocation of depot and replenishment spare costs using official service budget factors. With a few exceptions (e.g., A-10) the overwhelming majority of other weapon categories exhibited a similar pattern of cost increases.

43 Obvious examples include the F-22 fighter, F-35 fighter-bomber, V-22 tilt-rotor, Littoral Combat Ship (LCS), SSN-21, the NSSN, the Army's "Future Combat System," and the Marines' "Expeditionary Combat Vehicle."

44 In the case of tactical fighters, for example, the Air Force and Navy made deliberate decisions to rush the F-22 and F/A-18E/F into engineering and manufacturing development in 1991 and 1992 before constructing a fiscally realistic plan to modernize their entire inventory of tactical fighters over the long term. These decisions led directly to the aging-readiness crises of the late 1990s and the subsequent addition of a huge and potentially unaffordable budget bow wave to pay for the required addition of more than 2900 Joint Strike Fighters during the first two decades of the 21st century. See Franklin C. Spinney, "JSF: One More Card in the House," *Proceedings* XXIV. No. 3 (Annapolis, MD: U.S. Naval Institute, September 2000), 96.

45 Comptroller data indicates that defense budgets declined by 37 percent in inflation-adjusted dollars between the Reagan peak in 1985 and the Clinton low in 1998. On the other hand, most combat forces (e.g., ships in the navy, tactical fighters in the air force, maneuver battalions in the army, nuclear platforms) declined by 40 to 50 percent.

46 *Defense Daily*, September 3, 1998.

47 James Madison, *Federalist* No. 10 (originally titled "The Same Subject Continued: The Union as a Safeguard Against Domestic Faction and Insurrection," *New York Packet*, November 23, 1787).

48 For example, the bomber gap in the early 1950s, the missile gap in 1960, the "window of vulnerability" in the late 1970s, and the inability to prosecute two major theater wars simultaneously in the late 1990s. Now, of course, there is the war on terror and the threat of a Chinese "superpower."

49 As quoted in a thesis of Maj. Jeffrey L. Cowan, U.S. Air Force, "From Air Force Fighter Pilot to Marine Corps Warfighting: Colonel John Boyd, His Theories on War, and their Unexpected Legacy" (U.S. Marine Corps Command and Staff College, 2000), 14.

CHAPTER 2

SHATTERING ILLUSIONS
A National Security Strategy for 2009-2017

Col. Chet Richards (U.S. Air Force, ret.)

> War no longer exists. Confrontation, conflict, and combat undoubtedly exist all round the world … and states still have armed forces which they use as a symbol of power. None the less, war as cognitively known to most non-combatants, war as battle in a field between men and machinery, war as a massive deciding event in a dispute in international affairs: such war no longer exists.[1]

The new administration will take office in January 2009, inheriting a budget for the Department of Defense that will exceed $600 billion dollars per year, roughly equal to the rest of the world put together.[2] Because we are not facing the possibility of armed conflict with the rest of the world put together, it is clear that some adjustment is appropriate.

In theory, such adjustment is straightforward. The administration considers trends in the world situation and devises a national security strategy to deal with those trends. It then examines the capabilities of our current military forces, identifies areas where our forces are either deficient or superfluous and proposes a plan to rationalize them. As part of the planning process, the administration considers various combinations of forces, facilities and new programs until it settles on one that provides the requisite level of capability at a risk and for a cost that the president considers acceptable. The risks and costs may be domestic – political – as well as strategic.

What is a "National Security Strategy" and Do We Need One?

Some would argue that producing a "national security strategy" is a wasteful exercise because the process must take too many unknowns into account. The result, in this view, is little more than a public relations gambit to sell decisions that were made through domestic political trade-offs or by inertia. Others might take the position that although a strategy could be useful, divulging it would be dangerous because its dissemination would alert our enemies.

Before proposing a strategy, therefore, it is useful to consider what it is that we want such a strategy to do. The most basic question is why we need a formal strategy at all. Why not, in other words, just "wing it"? This means that at any given time, for any particular problem, the administration takes the action that appears most likely to accomplish its objectives. Why wouldn't this work?

Ad hoc strategies

As we know from our everyday lives, "winging it" often produces acceptable results, despite aphorisms like "if you don't know where you're going, any road will take you there." At less than the top levels of tennis, for example, a good strategy is to keep the ball in play and let the opponent make the first mistake – hit the ball into the net or set up an easy winner. Some of the greatest strategists have recommended similar approaches to warfare. Sun Tzu told commanders, for example, to prepare their troops and then let them exploit the current situation.[3] Instead of detailed battle planning, Rommel relied on the training of his troops and his own mental agility to find a means to victory in the unpredictable action of combat.[4]

A closer examination of these examples, however, reveals that in both Sun Tzu and Rommel were addressing the tactical level of warfare, fighting and winning battles. National leaders, on the other hand, must be concerned with more than tactics.[5] Otherwise, the country will have a *de facto* strategy of concentrating our energies at the tactical level with the hope that victory on enough battlefields will force an acceptable solution on the opposing government or whomever we are fighting. Unfortunately, there are too many examples, from Pyrrhus in ancient Greece to Cornwallis during the American Revolution to the German Army on the Eastern Front, to the United States in Vietnam and Iraq, where tactical victories did not produce the desired strategic results.

There is a missing element in all of these, a layer of strategy that would link the efforts expended on the ground to the results that national leaders want to achieve. This layer is usually known as *grand strategy*. Ideally, a grand strategy would integrate all elements of national power to secure our vital interests against today's and tomorrow's opponents. It would of necessity operate for decades, carefully matching means to ends and assuring that national strength is conserved for future generations.[6]

Although the need for a national or grand strategy stated in this manner may appear obvious, there are practical problems applying it to a republic like ours. Perhaps the most limiting is that we have a political revolution every four years and therefore external priorities are a reflection of the domestic political realities of the moment, or, at its most farseeing, the next election. One does not have to be a strategic Luddite to question the role of more formal strategies in our national life.

Domestic political considerations aside, it is debatable whether human beings have the wisdom to construct such far-reaching structures. As the influential blogger "Fabius Maximus" observed:

> Even if the people of a developed State could agree on a goal, an ambitious grand strategy remains a chimera for a global power.

> It is hubris to believe that any person or small group has sufficient information to develop a plan on a global scale. There are too many complex, unknowable

factors. Social factors, such as ethic and religious dynamics. Plus economic, military, and political factors. We lack the understanding to process the data into accurate patterns – a plan. That requires a science of sociology developed to the degree of modern chemistry, so that we could reliably predict results of our actions. Unfortunately sociology is at the stage of chemistry in the Middle Ages, when it was called alchemy. In fact, the yearning for a grand strategy is the equivalent to the search for the Philosopher's Stone.[7]

Such warnings should be heeded, but they are too pessimistic when taken as absolute prohibitions against high-level strategy. The British, for example, were successful for nearly two centuries with a grand strategy that included maintaining naval superiority over any competing power in Europe and using all elements of power to ensure that no single state came to dominate the continent. One can contrast their success, however, with British efforts since 1914 and German and Japanese grand strategies in the first half of the 20th century. Grand strategies, in other words, are useful and arguably necessary, but they are not sufficient for national prosperity. So we need to be careful what we ask of national or grand strategy – and this chapter will horrify purists by using the terms interchangeably – recognizing its value but remaining realistic and somewhat humble about our ability to create and implement one.

Preparation

If we adopt a national posture of opportunism-of-the-moment, despairing of better, then we forgo what even an imperfect strategy could provide. When choices must be made – when resources are not sufficient to accomplish every objective – there must be a basis for picking some courses and rejecting others. In a democracy, furthermore, some critical mass of the population must agree with, or at least acquiesce in, why the administration is spending their money and lives. Otherwise the national leaders formulating the strategy risk unemployment at the next election.

It is important to reach a widely-shared view that the stated basis is appropriate because conditions of military superiority do not emerge suddenly or swiftly and they are never permanent. Without a strategic roadmap to guide decision making, national power – economic, cultural, military and eventually political – slips away. Weapons systems – whose development spans several administrations – are not developed or are late and unsuited for the task,[8] personnel systems train people to fight the last war, tactics and doctrine focus on enemies, like the Soviet Union, who no longer pose a threat, and military operations do not produce the results that the country was promised.

Over the last two administrations, we have experienced the effects of poorly conceived strategy at the national level. The result has been an accelerating erosion of our strength as a nation, with stagnant incomes, declining health standards, soaring prices for the most basic ingredient of our well-being – energy – and the evisceration of our military, burdened by a worn-out and anachronistic inventory of weapons and a cadre of soldiers, sailors, Marines and airmen overstressed by repeated deployments to Iraq and Afghanistan.

On the balance, therefore, the United States will benefit from a national security strategy that avoids the trap of predicting or programming the future, yet enunciates a clear strategic purpose for the use of military and other elements of national power (including when not to use them). Such a grand strategy will determine the place of the United States within the international system – reassuring allies, attracting the uncommitted, and giving pause to potential opponents, which is a fair trade-off for alerting them – and it will also help solve some of the problems inherent to all democracies, that of letting internal politics drive the nation's involvement with the military forces of other countries.

A National Security Strategy for the United States

Perhaps our diplomacy of the first five decades of this century, and our reactions to the very different problems that have assailed us since 1950, both reflect realities much deeper than our responses of either period: namely, the lack of any accepted, enduring doctrine for relating military strength to political policy, and a persistent tendency to fashion our policy towards others with a view to feeding a pleasant image of ourselves rather than to achieving real, and desperately needed, results in our relations with others.[9]

This chapter represents an executive summary of a national security strategy as might be presented by the new administration to the 111th Congress. It is intended to provide all the security that military force can, while reducing the burden on the American taxpayer and thereby freeing resources for citizens to spend or invest as they see fit.

The elements of this strategy, or any national security strategy, are:

• The endstate – what the United States should look like and wants to achieve inside the international system. Devising a new analytical framework that helps policy-makers and senior military leaders to define and routinely reevaluate the purpose, method and endstate for the use of American power must be a top priority if America is to avoid unnecessary conflicts and stop squandering its wealth and power.

Defining the endstate is the job of the highest political leadership of the country speaking on behalf of the American people who elected them. It is an entirely political task that must precede and therefore lies beyond the scope of national security strategy. The new National Defense Strategy adopts this approach, repeating the political objectives of promoting freedom, justice and the spread of democracy within a stable system of states that can control insurgencies and transnational violent groups within their borders.[10] The next administration must consider whether such an open-ended, if laudable, goal represents a viable endstate.

- The dynamics of the world situation, including the major security challenges to the United States and the directions they appear to be taking. Nobody has an infallible crystal ball, so precise forecasts are specious. The general outlines, however, of any major military threats would be visible today.

- The administration's philosophy on the relative importance of these threats to the United States and the tools we have for dealing with them, which may range from confronting them to containing them to ignoring them. It is in this section that the administration should address the utility of military force.

- The direction the administration intends to take, given the situation, the status of U.S. forces, and its philosophy on the usefulness of the means available. The direction must balance between being too general, so that it offers no guidance, and too specific, so that it becomes irrelevant before it can be promulgated.

- The first steps it intends to take. So if an element of the administration's approach is to reduce spending on Cold War-era weapons programs, there should be a statement, "As our initial step, we will cancel the ..." A statement like this, which will be elaborated in the details of the strategy, signals to the American people that this is a strategy the new administration intends to implement.

Although the theory is straightforward, the formulation of strategy can be tortuous because people will disagree on the elements and defend their positions for personal, philosophical, political or bureaucratic reasons to the point of obstruction. A trillion dollar annual expenditure,[11] whether justifiable analytically or not, brings along a potent constituency, people whose prosperity, livelihood, or in the case of wounded veterans, for example, even survival depend on this flow of money.

Because a strategy that does not lead to feasible plans is both worthless and wasteful, the administration should make an estimate of what is possible. If Congress, for example, is not going to allow cancellation of major programs or the demobilization of substantial parts of the force structure, then the administration should not build these elements into its proposals. Even without this level of change, the administration can rationalize defense by eliminating overhead, support and bureaucracy duplicated among the services – the "four air forces" situation providing just one example, the fact that it has persisted for so many years testifying to its intractability. A coherent national security strategy can provide the basis for making these decisions and for selling them to the American public, bypassing the entrenched special interests who are now keeping them alive.

If the administration defines a logical strategy – including an attractive endstate – and sells it consistently, then what is impossible today may become possible or even inevitable in three or four years as the country's economic position changes (either for better or for worse).

The World Today

The new administration should begin by describing the trends in military threats to the United States. Although the process for deriving the points will be complex and even convoluted, if the administration expects the American people to buy into the results, they must be presented in terms that make sense to the average citizen.

Here is one view of the world; the administration's may differ but should be explainable in about the same space:

- The number of countries that possess nuclear weapons – now assumed to be nine[12] – will not decrease and may increase. The Center for Defense Information lists 35 countries that have some sort of civilian atomic energy program,[13] and several states in the Middle East are improving their knowledge of nuclear technology under the guise of developing stable sources of power for their populations.[14] Even those that are under the supervision of the International Atomic Energy Agency may attempt to hide their weapons programs or they may renounce the treaty and expel the inspectors. No country with nuclear weapons has ever been invaded, much less occupied, a lesson not lost on any number of national leaders.

- Several states are improving their conventional (non-nuclear) military capabilities, including Russia, China and India. These efforts will bolster their regional capabilities but do not present any direct threat to the United States or its allies.

Figure 1

Country	Potential Internal Conflicts	Miles of Border
Russia[15]	Chechnya; far eastern border areas	12,487
China	Tibet, Taiwan, Uyghurs (potential Muslim separatists)	13,743
India	Naxalite and other Maoist guerrillas; separatist movements in Assam, Kashmir, and Nagaland; sectarian violence	8,763

As shown in Figure 1, all three of these countries have, for example, long borders with potentially hostile states and all face significant threat of internal conflict:

By comparison, the United States faces no military threat in the foreseeable future from along its 7,478 miles of border with Canada and Mexico and no internal conflicts where military force must be employed. Comparisons of military spending between the United States and other countries with significant military capabilities must therefore be made with caution.

• All major conventional powers also possess nuclear weapons or are allies of the United States or both, and this situation will continue.

• The United States could become involved in a conflict if an ally were attacked by another country. It is not clear whether this possibility is becoming more likely, and the national security apparatus of the new administration should spend some time examining this question.

• There are any number of states that do not have functioning governments regarded as legitimate by their citizens. Although the potential for armed conflict within and between these countries will remain high, none of them poses a threat to the security of the United States.

• There are transnational, nonstate organizations that can do damage. Because these organizations do not possess military forces of their own, they are most appropriately regarded as criminal cartels. As is the case with fighting international piracy on the high seas, the military can provide assistance. The ultimate solution, however, as with all criminal enterprises, lies in the emergence of local governments that create environments hostile to criminal organizations.

As noted, the new administration's list may differ, but its analysis should encompass these same categories: nuclear war, major conventional war, "brushfire" war, stability operations, and non-state armed conflict or what is also called "Fourth Generation" warfare.[16]

Tools of Policy

Although some commentators, particularly on the left, decry the creation of an American empire and a perceived drive for global hegemony, the fact is that the United States has a surprisingly limited capability to influence events around the world. We are straining, for example, to keep fewer than 200,000 troops in Iraq and Afghanistan,[17] of which perhaps 40-50 percent are patrolling or otherwise in combat roles (the rest perform support functions). Should a significant fraction of the 55 million people living in these two countries decide to do so, they could certainly drive us out. Such a possibility remains.

Another factor that constrains our options is financial. The purchase of American debt by countries such as China and Russia is well documented and in such quantities that it would be difficult to continue operations in Iraq and Afghanistan without it.[18] Yet, unlike most previous empires, the United States is not likely to emerge from Iraq and Afghanistan with any improvement in its national wealth. That is, the results of our occupations of Iraq and Afghanistan are not likely to generate wealth sufficient to pay back those who have loaned us the money to conduct them and also to increase the prosperity of the people of the United States in general, although the fortunes of certain sectors, such as defense contractors, may improve immensely. We are, it seems, the first imperial power to be paying for the privilege, with estimates of the total cost of the war running in the $3 trillion to $5 trillion range.[19]

Given constraints such as these, the new administration should describe the utility of military force to deal with the trends it identified.

Employing the military tool

How should we procure and operate military forces in the 21st century to accomplish the national goals as set out in the Constitution and elaborated by the new administration? Following Sun Tzu's famous admonition that to win without fighting is best, a superior national security strategy would minimize the number of people who want to confront us violently and deny even these adversaries the ability to accomplish much in the way of disruption.

It is impossible, of course, to eliminate all threats to our well being, and attempting to carry our quest for security to unreasonable levels does our opponents' jobs for them:

> The culture of fear is like a genie that has been let out of its bottle. It acquires a life of its own – and can become demoralizing. ... We are now divided, uncertain and potentially very susceptible to panic in the event of another terrorist act in the United States itself.[20]

Most of the means for reducing the threat of violence do not involve military forces and rely instead on trade, diplomacy, commerce, intelligence, law enforcement, tourism, educational exchange and so on.[21] In a world populated by human beings, however, there will be times when amicable agreement is not possible, when religious fervor or nationalistic feelings or pride or ego combined with miscalculation of the odds of success leads to the use of armed force.

So there is need for military force, even if the administration were to adopt an isolationist national posture. To answer the question of how much, the administration will need to consider a set of issues that relate military force to national objectives. Specifically:

1. What role should military forces play in the national security of the United States?

2. When is it appropriate to use military forces for missions other than defending the United States from attack? In particular, when is it appropriate to use such forces outside the borders of the country?

3. Given our answers to questions 1 and 2, how many tanks, fighter aircraft, aircraft carriers and other forces for large-scale, non-nuclear combat do we need?

The next three sections will illustrate how the new administration could address these questions.

As Far as the United States is Concerned, What is the Role of Military Force in the 21st Century?

To help citizens and members of Congress grasp why the nature of national defense is changing, and so why its organization and funding must also change, the national security strategy should supply the historical context. The rest of this section provides an outline.

After winning its independence, the new country faced many potential armed threats, from rebellion to depredations by Indians along the frontier, but the founders felt that most of them could be dealt with by the state militias.[22] In fact, there was a heated debate over whether to have an army, which explains the curious language in Article I, Section 8, of the Constitution authorizing Congress to raise and fund an army, language not applied to the Navy.

Although few argued that military force was anything but necessary – there were major wars in Europe, for example, every generation or so – for more than 150 years the standing U.S. Army was quite small. It would be augmented with volunteers when necessary, but then shrink back to its normal size.[23] So George Armstrong Custer, who had been a dashing major general of cavalry in the Civil War, died 11 years later wearing a lieutenant colonel's silver leaves.

This arrangement worked so long as the country observed George Washington's warning to avoid foreign entanglements.[24] For 130 years, this was not difficult: The new nation was absorbed with spreading across the continent, subduing its original inhabitants and incorporating millions of new ones, a destiny that was manifest to all but the original inhabitants. Until 1917, we saw little need to engage the nations of Old Europe on their home territory.

Time and technology march on, however, and by the early 20th century, our ocean moats had shrunk to a week's steaming and it was clear that in a few years, the Atlantic and Pacific would join the English Channel in the list of barriers that could be crossed in hours or even minutes.

After World War II, the argument was made that because our oceans no longer shielded us, we needed a capable defense structure available on very short notice. For this reason, post-war administrations decided to maintain a standing military comparable in size to the largest anywhere, ready to defend the country from threats from any direction, and to form alliances whose members we would assist in defending themselves from threats from any direction.

Types of Military Threats

These threats consisted of three broad types, and this classification is important for explaining the proposed changes in defense policy. First, there were the conventional forces – the tanks, airplanes, soldiers, ships, and so on like we faced in World War II. They could wreak enormous damage and kill huge numbers of people – fatalities in the 50 to 70 million range are often cited for World War II – but they took some time to do it. Because they needed large numbers of trained troops and vast supplies of expensive weapons, they made up (and still make up) the majority of the world's defense budget.

Then there were the nuclear forces. They were relatively cheap, in comparison to conventional forces.[25] Like conventional weapons, nukes could cause considerable damage, but they could do it in seconds. By the mid-1960s, there were enough of these in the arsenals of the major nuclear powers that the survival of the human race itself was doubtful, should they ever be used.[26]

After a brief skirmish over which service would monopolize the nuclear advantage, nuclear power reinforced the traditional individual-services way of war that dominated the Cold War. The Goldwater-Nichols Act had created the combatant commands, such as Central Command and Pacific Command, and had given them operational control of the forces in their areas of responsibility, but the money – and along with it the power to determine how the forces would train, equip and fight – remained with the service bureaucracies that, for the most part, were not motivated by the needs or desires of the combatant commanders.

Finally, there was "none of the above," the "unconventional" threats, primarily insurgencies, that manifested themselves in "low intensity conflicts." The militaries of the developed world tended to ignore them at least as far as spending money on "special forces" to engage in them, on the grounds that "if we can lick the cat, we can lick the kitten."[27] As one Army officer recently put it, the U.S. military considered insurgencies "ephemeral anomalies."[28] Because we did not put any great emphasis on the subject, and although special forces are highly trained, there are very few of them (hence "special"), and because they needed little in the way of expensive hardware, they were cheap.

Thus the Cold War. Then over the space of a few months, the Soviet Union fell and the Cold War ended.[29]

In the shadow of Soviet conventional and nuclear attack, Cold War defense budgets had seldom been challenged. Thanks to a compliant and supportive Congress, the admirals and generals would design their acquisition programs to counter a set of predictable but potentially devastating threats, threats that no one in Congress was willing to challenge. The end of the Cold War constituted a tectonic shift in international relations that required innovation, creativity and a real understanding inside the Armed Forces.

Unfortunately, it has hardly made an impact. The experience of direct assault on the American homeland on Sept. 11, 2001 had surprisingly little influence on the structure, thinking and modernization of America's air, ground and naval forces. To cite a recent example, combatant commanders' urgent requests for armed vessels capable of operating in the riverine or coastal environments have met with lukewarm responses.

When is the Use of Military Force Appropriate?
In the Pentagon, downsizing did not raise the questions that should shape the armed forces' destiny – questions such as, whom and where do we fight? How should we fight? And, most important, what is the strategic purpose – the desired endstate – for which we will be required to fight? All of these questions help answer the larger question of when the nation should bear the costs of using its military forces.

Because we face no conventional military threat to our survival in the early post-Cold War period, any use of non-nuclear military forces by the United States will be voluntary, in "wars of choice" or "cabinet wars" as they are sometimes called. They would represent the "continuation of policy" by other means, in the words of the U.S. military's favorite strategist, the early 19th century Prussian aristocrat Carl von Clausewitz.[30]

The new administration must decide whether such wars are appropriate for the United States. When, in other words, should U.S. military forces be used for missions other than the immediate defense of the United States, which requires only nuclear deterrence and a very few conventional ground, sea and air forces? How the new administration answers this question will determine the size and composition of U.S. military forces.

Can we run on autopilot?
Before examining potential uses for military force in the 21st century, it should be acknowledged that some people would pick an arbitrary percentage of the U.S. gross

domestic product, usually 4 or 5 percent, and spend that amount on something every year. The logic often provided is that we have spent that percentage at times in the past.[31] This rationale, however, neglects the world situations at those times, including the existence of major threats in the Soviet Union and the People's Republic of China.

The constant percentage argument also overlooks the enormous growth in the U.S. economy since the 1970s, which would increase spending on a constant percentage basis even if all other nations eliminated their weapons, and it does not account for other priorities in the early 21st century, including the fall of the dollar, rise in energy prices, and impending retirement of the baby boom generation.

Examined in this light, the arguments for holding defense spending at a constant percentage of GDP appear designed more to ensure a money flow to the defense industries than to improve the security and well-being of the rest of our citizens. It is important, therefore, that the new administration conduct a legitimate examination of our defense needs and make recommendations accordingly.

Potential uses for military force

Although the Soviet Union is gone, there remain potential uses of conventional military forces in the 21st century. These include, in rough order of potential severity (as contrasted with likelihood):

1. A major conventional conflict between the United States and a "near-peer" power, usually hypothesized as either China or Russia, but which could represent the emergence of another as yet unspecified conventional threat.

2. Wars between allies of the United States and other states. These might include proxy wars between our ally and that of another major power. The word "ally" is used in the loose sense of any state that the United States would feel compelled to assist, regardless of formal treaty obligation. Thus, Kuwait was such an ally in 1990, and Saudi Arabia is today.

3. Invasion and occupation of a developing country by U.S. military forces. This option also includes assistance to an insurgency, which, like an invasion, involves the use of U.S. military power against the government of a foreign country. Oddly, the National Defense Strategy (NDS) fails to consider aid to insurgencies.[32]

4. Counterinsurgency (COIN), where the military forces of the United States assist a friendly government in suppressing an attempt by indigenous rebels to overthrow it or to replace it within a region of that country. This is the only

type of irregular operation considered by the NDS, placing that document in the mainstream of nearly a century of policies backing rulers clever enough to convince us that they were supporting American interests at the time.[33]

5. Law enforcement, where U.S. military forces suppress nonstate groups other than insurgents. Piracy is an immediate example: some 95 percent of U.S. exports/imports continue to move by sea. Today, any interruption in the flow of goods and commodities into and out of American ports would have serious consequences for American economic stability and prosperity.[34]

6. Stability operations and peacekeeping, where military forces are used primarily for nonconflict roles.

The new administration should carefully examine these potential missions, looking at the circumstances under which they might occur, the costs and risks if they did, and the options for mitigating them, including non-military means. This analysis must be "zero-based," that is, conclusions must be justified on the basis of the unfolding world situation and not merely as a continuation of U.S. policy. Regaining the strategic immunity once provided by the oceans and our fleets may be impossible, but it is not impossible to restore most of it through the prudent use of rational diplomacy and limited military power.

The next several sections will outline some of the issues involved in structuring forces to deal with each of these categories of conflict.

War against a "near-peer"

During the 1990s, a few strategists came to an epiphany, recognition of which unites these writers like no other issue.[35] That insight is that major nations are not going to wage war on each other, except by means of analogies as in "trade war," and so military force is of diminished utility in the modern world. With the nuclear weapons of the major powers checkmating each others' conventional as well as nuclear forces, our oceans have become moats again. We have returned to where we were at the founding of the republic and where we stayed until after World War II. Can we rationalize or even downsize our conventional forces as we did for so many years before World War II?

As noted above, forces for a large-scale conventional war are expensive and will dominate the budget of any alternative where they are included. Under what circumstances would including large conventional forces in our planning make sense? Because it is difficult to imagine a conventional attack on the United States, the only way we could wage a real war against a substantial opponent would be if we brought our military to them. This means that we must hypothesize an opponent who:

1. Does not have nuclear weapons.

2. Or, if it does, has agreed that they will allow themselves to be defeated without using them. Otherwise our engagement would not be "war" in the usual sense, but some type of military sparring match, filler for the 24-hour news operations.

3. Is not a NATO ally or in some other alliance with the United States.

4. Has managed to acquire suitable weapons in large numbers, evolve effective doctrines, and recruit and train forces in their use.

5. Could, by means of conventional military actions alone, represent a threat to the quality of life of the people of the United States.

A look at the collection of states fails to reveal any immediate candidate. China and Russia have significant conventional capabilities, but as the opening of this chapter noted, they also face security challenges both along their long borders and internally. It should be noted that since the end of the Vietnam War, attempts of both of these to project military force beyond their own borders have been rare and not particularly successful except against very weak opponents.[36]

Alternatives

The NDS observes that "the predominant near-term challenges will come from state and non-state actors using irregular and catastrophic capabilities."[37] This raises the obvious question of why they should be the only ones. Rather than trundling our military forces around the world to replay the Battle of the Bulge, there are better alternatives for dealing with errant conventional forces, as the Vietnamese, Afghans and Iraqis have shown the world.

The next administration should study how we can make these proven irregular techniques work for us as 21st century alternatives to the slug-it-out-on-the-battlefield tactics of previous generations. We know that the Chinese are doing exactly that kind of planning should they ever have to confront U.S. forces in their vicinity.[38]

Implications for force structure

In summary, the notion that the United States and her allies would engage another major power in large-scale conventional combat is more a fantasy than a scenario and should not affect the sizing of American military forces.

The next section will consider scenarios more likely to bring major conventional forces into conflict.

Proxy wars and other wars supporting allies

The first Gulf war, the Korean War and the Vietnam War were of this type: The United States itself was not directly threatened, but believed that it must intervene on behalf of a third party that may itself be supported by another major conventional power. An example of a future war of this type might be a Serbian incursion into Kosovo backed by Russian tactical air in order to relieve beleaguered Serb communities. A proxy war ensues when the ground forces of European NATO states supported by American ships and warplanes intervene on behalf of the Kosavars.

The important point about all such wars to date is that the United States did not intervene alone but formed an alliance that helped counter the attack.[39] As is the case with confrontation with a near peer, the international community has options other than intervention with conventional forces, including diplomacy, economic sanctions and, as we did against the Soviets in Afghanistan, covert support to resistance forces.

Implications for force structure

The imponderable in this scenario is unanticipated escalation that would present the best opportunity for major conventional powers to confront each other on a battlefield. Considering the potential for escalation into nuclear conflict, whether by miscalculation or emotion, the focus of U.S. policy regarding such confrontations should be on avoiding them, rather than viewing them as tools of policy. An appropriate strategy for the United States, therefore, is to maintain a level of conventional military force sufficient to act in concert with our allies to remove any temptation to settle international disputes through the use of military force.

The other chapters of this volume will make specific recommendations that can serve as starting points for the new administration as it undertakes this analysis.

Invasion and occupation: Is occupation realistic?

In the late 20th and early 21st centuries, the two outcomes that wars of choice have had in common is that they turned out to take much longer and they cost considerably more in lives and money than their proponents promised. The NATO-Serbian War (March 24-June 10, 1999) was supposed to last three days, but dragged on through 78 and ended only when the NATO alliance cobbled together the credible threat of a ground invasion and dropped demands that Serbia abdicate its sovereignty, and when the Russians withdrew their support for the Milosevic government. The miscalculations involving the Soviet occupation of Afghanistan, the American invasions and occupations of Iraq and Afghanistan, and the Israeli invasion of Lebanon in 2006 are too numerous and well known to merit further discussion here. The conclusion is that in an increasingly populated world, highly networked and awash in light weaponry, any group of people can, if it chooses, make occupation by any other group highly unpleasant.

Given the events of the last generation, the United States, her allies and other members of the developed world should be skeptical about the costs and potential benefits of such occupations. We must abandon the mindset of overt interventionism, at least without the support of our closest and most long-standing allies and give thought to when intervening is a reasonable option. The United States, in particular, should consider whether, if a substantial fraction of our NATO allies are not willing to join us, our proposed intervention is appropriate. Such an attitude might have served us well in the run up to the second Gulf War.

This seems like a strange requirement, because we are the only superpower standing and should be able to go anywhere in the developing world we want without any risk. This is true, we can. However, the problem we've never been able to solve is, "What then?" Unless we're invading Monaco, the Vatican, or some South Pacific island, our initial numerical advantage over any Third World military, particularly when one factors in air power, will turn into a huge numerical disadvantage relative to the population. In Iraq, the occupation involves 160,000 combat troops trying to control a country of some 20,000,000 (excluding the Kurds), few of whom share a common language, religion, or cultural heritage with us.

The problem is complicated by the fact that the fighting in Iraq is not so much an insurgency against an established government as a multifaceted civil war where various armed groups and militias jockey for power, vie for support from outsiders such as the United States, Saudi Arabia and Iran, and position themselves for the day that the occupation forces leave. This is a common situation when a state fails, and history shows that since the end of World War II, armed force by outsiders has been of limited effectiveness in resolving it.[40]

Will COIN theory make occupations possible?

There are claims that counterinsurgency theory has proven itself in Iraq and so can solve the problem of other occupations. It may be early, however, to start claiming success for COIN doctrine in that country, which appears to be evolving into a religiously conservative state dominated by Shiite clerics and politicians friendly to Iran. These were not among the goals the president enunciated before launching the 2003 invasion.[41]

What is usually meant by "success" in Iraq is the recent decrease in U.S. casualties – also not one of the goals the president originally set out for the war. Even this decrease, however, has a variety of causes, the most significant of which is the decision by Moqtada al-Sadr to suspend operations by his al-Mahdi Army. Another factor in the decrease in casualties was the drawdown of ethnic cleansing operations in Baghdad as this once multiethnic city has become a maze of walled ghettoes. In any case, the tempo of violence in Middle East civil wars ebbs and flows – one might recall Lebanon – and as this chapter is written, we are far too close to events to make any reasonable judgment on the eventual effect of U.S. actions.

Perhaps the strongest argument against future invasions, even if an insurgency against the occupation were somehow to be contained, is that nobody knows how to rebuild destroyed societies. Anyone who has driven across the northern end of the Gulf coast, from New Orleans to Mobile, can see this first hand. Even the area often cited as a success story, the former Yugoslavia, is an economic and social mess:

> However badly run Kosovo may be at the moment, and however much gang-sterism and ethno-nationalism have flourished there under the haphazard stewardship of the so-called international community. ... Bosnia is falling apart again; Macedonia still looks fragile.[42]

The upshot is that most interventions, and practically all occupations, will turn out badly in the 21st century, unless brutal force to the point of depopulation is used to coerce the inhabitants into submission.[43] If we wish to keep such interventions as policy options, we would need to greatly expand the U.S. military establishment and correspondingly increase spending in order to attempt to fight insurgencies around the world, with no expectation of success.

A corollary lesson is that whenever ideology defines the military objective, the result is usually a demand for military action that defies strategic logic. Justifying the ideology locks the orientations of senior leaders so that lack of success is interpreted not as evidence of poor strategy but as failure to try hard enough or long enough. Hitler's meddling with *Wehrmacht* operations on the Eastern Front after 1942 is often cited in this regard.[44] In the end, the operation fails because its aim is to fulfill an ideological purpose, not accomplish a strategic military requirement.[45]

This does not imply that the new administration should adopt an isolationist posture but that our interaction with the world must rest upon other than military means. U.S. and Western national security policy must resolve to live with developing countries without invading them, or if we do, to go in fully aware of and realistically assessing the likely costs and consequences. Military leaders charged with executing military action need to understand the strategic limits of what they can accomplish while reacting to pressure from politicians to execute open-ended, ill-advised and sometimes ideologi-cally-driven missions. They should also be realistic in advising these same politicians about what military force can reasonably be expected to accomplish.

Implications for force structure

If this strategy is adopted, the forces we maintain for use in conventional operations with our allies will suffice for the rare interventions we take as a group into develop-ing countries. If we continue with an interventionist foreign policy that leads to the occupation of more countries, there is no way to estimate how many additional forces will be required.

Counterinsurgency of the traditional type

There is considerable controversy on whether counterinsurgency by outside forces – a mission sometimes known as "foreign internal defense" – is possible. The record of such attempts is not good, El Salvador being the only recent success by U.S. forces.[46]

The focus of counterinsurgency is on establishing a legitimate government, and tanks and fighter aircraft have at most a limited role to play. As RAND researchers David Gompert and John Gordon IV concluded in a major new study of counterinsurgency prepared for the Office of the Secretary of Defense:

> Like traditional insurgencies, this new type is essentially a contest for the allegiance of local populations. Consequentially, to counter it, foreign military forces are no substitute for effective and legitimate local governance, including critical public services and indigenous security forces. Indeed, data from some 90 insurgencies since World War II reveal that insurgencies nearly always fail against governments that are representative, competent, and honest in the eyes of their citizens.[47]

The issue in counterinsurgency is whether foreign military forces can contribute to the legitimacy of a threatened government. Gompert and Gordon note that the presence of foreign troops tends, instead, to diminish the legitimacy of a government:

> Consequently, when an insurgency reaches the point that only foreign intervention can save the state, the insurgency tends to grow stronger and bolder, and the chances of defeating it decrease rather than increase. This is borne out by historical data, which reveal an inverse relationship between large-scale foreign intervention and successful COIN.[48]

Implications for force structure

Regardless of the theoretical utility of military forces in counterinsurgency, or of its lack, they will not be a large contributor to the defense budget. A counterinsurgency mission may, however, affect the composition of U.S. forces. Several chapters in this anthology address forces for counterinsurgency.

Law enforcement

Armies will be replaced by police-like security forces on the one hand and bands of ruffians on the other, not that the difference is always clear, even today.[49]

Our invasion of Afghanistan in our unsuccessful attempt to capture Osama bin Laden is one such example. The expedition against Pancho Villa in 1916-17, the confrontations with the Barbary pirates (1801-1815), and today's anti-piracy operations at sea are others. Much of what is hypothesized as "Fourth Generation Warfare" – state versus nonstate groups or "transnational insurgencies" – falls into this category and so does not represent a new form of warfare so much as an evolution of crime. Our opponents in these conflicts are not organized military forces or even insurgent units fighting to overthrow a government, but have more the form of transnational criminal cartels, albeit sometimes with an ideological or religious veneer. Al-Qaida fits this description as do many narco-trafficking cartels and even evolved street gangs such as MS-13. Our purpose in using military force would be not so much to wage war as to conduct extraterritorial law enforcement, and future administrations will have to be careful not to follow this path into another occupation of a foreign country.

Like most of our probable opponents, these criminal organizations have neither the means nor the desire to confront our tanks and combat aircraft in conventional battle. Instead, they will move aside and blend into the population. Once this happens, military forces become a minor facet of the law enforcement efforts because they will rarely be able to distinguish members of the criminal organization from ordinary civilians. As van Creveld noted, the populations of developed countries do not like to see their military forces inflicting severe damage on civilians.[50] Military forces can assist in support roles, such as by sealing off an area, enforcing martial law, providing logistics and operating high-tech equipment.

Implications for force structure
The conclusion as far as force structuring is concerned is that this mission will have little impact. Few people would argue for increasing the military budget so that we can enforce martial law in parts of Bolivia.

Stability operations and peacekeeping
Although the history of such operations does not give cause for optimism, the alternative – to do nothing – may not be acceptable to the populations of the developed world who sometimes demand that their military forces achieve high moral purposes, such as stopping genocide, that have nothing to do with defense of their own nations. As with all incursions into the Third World, however, the stopping part may be simple compared to what follows. What is required is establishing legitimate governments and functioning economies and their integration into the world's economic and political systems. Unfortunately, as the quote above regarding the Balkans indicates, and our experiences in Iraq, Afghanistan and Haiti reinforce, these are the very things we don't know how to do.[51]

Implications for force structure
To date, we have participated in these operations only as members of international organizations, such as NATO or the United Nations. Although peacekeeping (as con-

trasted with "peacemaking") might be an important component of sizing forces for smaller members of these organizations, it typically only requires a small fraction of U.S. military capability, on the order of a brigade (5,000 troops).

There is also a large question about whether this is really a mission for military forces at all. Stability operations and peacekeeping do not require much of the traditional military skills of defeating capable opponents in combat. Instead, they require different competencies, more akin to law enforcement or engineering. History suggests that militaries that engage in these activities lose the ability to be effective combat forces.[52] Israel was given a rude reminder of this in the 2006 war with the nonstate group Hezbollah.

So while the goals of stability and peacekeeping are undoubtedly worthy, it is not at all clear that military forces as traditionally defined should be performing them. The missions that do apply – logistics, communications, intelligence, etc. – are support roles and will have little impact on force structure.

Conclusions

The next administration will have the opportunity to find a new strategic formula for America's national security. This new formula needs to be a better fit for the American people than our current mobilization-based military designed to re-fight World War II. The new formula should also reconsider our political ideology of exporting democracy through long-term military occupations and should not assume that we have found a formula for occupations.

It is debatable whether, given its costs and the uncertain nature of its outcomes, war should ever have been considered a tool of policy. In the early 21st century, the presence of nuclear weapons at the high end of the military operations spectrum combined with the demonstrated inability of Western military forces to achieve desired outcomes in Third World countries suggests that there is no longer room for debate. Framed this way, the question of national security policy for the 21st century becomes: In a world where virtually all of the threats to a nation's well-being are self-inflicted – economic performance, distribution of wealth, pollution, infrastructure, immigration, education, health care, discrimination against ethnic minorities, etc. – where should military force fall in the priority list of things to spend money on?

For the new administration, the cardinal rule should be: *Military forces should be funded only for missions that only the military can do.* To use them for other purposes risks diluting their unique capabilities, and they probably won't be very good at them.

The new administration should review the roles and sizes of our military forces under this conclusion. Here are several elements that might go into their recommendations:

1. Keep our nuclear deterrence credible against any conceivable combination of opponents. Deterrence depends not only upon the number of warheads but on

the survivability of the force and its ability to be effective. The administration should be wary of establishing a goal of total nuclear disarmament, however. Without nuclear weapons, large-scale conventional war between major powers becomes not only possible again but inevitable. The world would resume where it was in July 1945, before the Trinity test showed that nuclear weapons could be built.[53]

Although disarmament is neither practical nor desirable, considerable rationalization of and ultimately reduction in our nuclear force is possible; materials made available by the Center for Defense Information and its associated World Security Institute address alternatives.

2. Propose a plan for rationalizing conventional forces and then obtaining better value from the resources we devote to them. This plan should include:

   a. The ultimate size and composition of a conventional force to cooperate with allies where the employment of such forces is required. There are several chapters in this book that describe such a force. This force would be adequate for all other uses of conventional military force by the United States.

   b. A drawdown schedule for transitioning from our current force to the target force.

   c. A program for mitigating the economic and social dislocations this will cause.

Chapters three through 11 address alternatives for realigning our conventional forces and their budgets to the realities of the 21st century.

3. Land and air forces that the administration wishes to retain but that are not trained or equipped for overseas employment with allies should be transferred to the National Guard and placed under the control of the states. The administration must carefully consider how to rationalize the Navy and Coast Guard to best perform the range of maritime missions, which covers the full spectrum from nuclear warfare to law enforcement to rescue at sea.

4. For law enforcement, insurgency and COIN: Retain some portion of our naval, Coast Guard and special operations forces to provide assistance for international law enforcement, counterproliferation, anti-piracy, hostage rescue and other activities in conjunction with our allies. Such forces may also participate in allied/international ventures to change regimes that have threatened their

neighbors or committed abuses of human rights so egregious that our politicians feel they cannot be ignored, although the natural tendency to resist occupations must be taken into account. Counterinsurgency is not a reason to fund conventional military forces because experience shows that governments that rely on foreign forces to protect them from indigenous guerrilla movements forfeit the very legitimacy they need to survive.

5. Think long and hard about the intelligence function. The first step toward the formulation of a new policy is to understand the realities of the Middle East as it is now.[54]

    Providing the information that underpins that understanding is the job of intelligence, and it needs to take a much stronger role in national security policy than heretofore.

    The last administration has experienced intelligence debacles on several levels, and failure to determine their causes and fix them will render the rest of our national security program meaningless. A brief survey illustrates this:

Figure 2

Event	Result
The Sept. 11 attack	Three thousand American deaths; incalculable cost to the nation in other ways
Failure to capture Osama bin Laden	Al-Qaida survives to plan further attacks, inspire a new generation of "ideological insurgent"
Failure to predict Iraqi reaction to prolonged occupation	Another 4,000 Americans killed, many thousands more severely injured, rejuvenation of al-Qaida, enhanced reputation of Iran, costs that will probably exceed $3 trillion
Failure to understand Afghan reaction to prolonged occupation	Rejuvenation of the Taliban, explosion in opium cultivation, establishment of a Taliban / al-Qaida base area in northern Pakistan

Intelligence failures can occur at three stages of the understanding process, and the administration must conduct a zero-based review of each. First, we may not be collecting enough information or we may not be collecting the right information. Second, we may not be effectively converting information into intelligence, that is, interpreting the data we collect, sorting through its contradictions, filling in the missing areas and assessing what it means.[55] Finally, senior government officials including the president may not appreciate the intelligence product or, if it conflicts with strongly held beliefs, may choose to disregard it.

There are many oxen to be gored in this review and it will take a strong and experienced individual to lead it. It should also be process-driven, not organizationally driven. The question, in other words, is not: How do we fix the CIA? It is how to provide intelligence that is more accurate and timelier than what we have today and how to make better use of it. This review should consider fundamental changes going beyond the updating of Executive Order 12333 that the administration issued in July.[56]

6. Exploit the creativity and innovation of the private sector. The next administration must avoid the temptation to let the well-publicized debacles involving contractors in Iraq and Afghanistan sour the country on harnessing the power of private enterprise. As they have in all modern wars, efforts by private industry will be important elements in any future conflict and will be crucial to our response to another attack on the scale of Sept. 11. No plan to increase the resiliency of our states and cities against attack can succeed without drawing on the private sector. Private enterprise brings decentralized decision making – the bureaucracies of even the largest companies pale in comparison to that of the federal government and those of most states – and an agility that comes from thousands of people and companies who use their creativity and initiative to solve their immediate problems.

    Although most people would agree that the private sector is the engine of progress, the engine is not the vehicle. The issue is how better to employ the private sector to serve the national security of the United States.

    Again, this analysis must be as free of assumptions as possible. The critical need is for the government to become better at regulating and managing contractors in the public interest. No function that contractors are now performing, or not performing, should be off the table. It should be always kept in mind that many of our future opponents are not the uniformed militaries of some state. As this chapter as tried to show, those are a fairly minor threat to U.S. national security. For the most part our future opponents are already privatized.

These points should not discourage the next president and his secretary of defense in the least. Arguments that fundamental change is too costly in political, military and monetary terms do not hold up to closer scrutiny. The reformed Prussian army that defeated Napoleon in 1814 and 1815 was certainly no more expensive than the unreformed one Napoleon humiliated in 1805. Programs designed to rationalize force design and doctrine save money. What is more important, they change the standards and expectations of military performance. This reorients thinking, behavior and action and is the path to success in conflict and prosperity in peace.

The remainder of this book provides recommendations for implementing a national security strategy consistent with what has been presented here. The purpose is to illustrate in hard numbers that the new administration has options that will provide for the national defense at an acceptable level of risk and at a cost that is affordable even in the constrained budgetary environment that the administration will face.

ENDNOTES

1   Rupert Smith, *The Utility of Force, The Art of War in the Modern World* (London: Penguin, 2005) 1.

2   Estimates of total U.S. spending on defense vary depending on what is included. Adding other items directly related to national security, such as Homeland Security, Veterans Affairs and interest on the debt to pay for defense-related items could bring the total to nearly one trillion dollars per year. For further information, see the *Military Almanac 2007* (Washington, D.C.: Center for Defense Information), 87, 110-111.

3   Sun Tzu, *The Art of War*, trans. by Samuel B. Griffith (Oxford: Oxford University Press, 1963).

4   Douglas Fraser, *Knight's Cross* (New York: HarperCollins, 1994).

5   Sun Tzu addressed all levels of warfare, not just tactics, and he made clear distinctions of the levels of war that concern political and military leaders, respectively.

6   In this sense, the new National Defense Strategy (NDS) announced by the Department of Defense on July 31, 2008 rates as the military component of a grand strategy because it addresses the matching of elements of national power to achieve long-term political objectives. *National Defense Strategy* (Washington, D.C.: Department of Defense, June 2008).

7   "Fabius Maximus," "The Myth of Grand Strategy," January 1, 2006, http://fabiusmaximus.wordpress.com/2006/01/31/myth

8   Lockheed, for example, won the right to build the F-22 fighter during the George H.W. Bush administration. The program actually started in former President Reagan's first term in office. Tom Christie addresses systemic problems with defense procurement in Chapter 10.

9   George F. Kennan, *American Diplomacy* (Chicago: University of Chicago Press, 1984).

10 *National Defense Strategy*, p. 1.

11 The total U.S. spending on all elements of national defense, including military forces, intelligence, homeland security, medical and other care for veterans, border security, and interest on past defense-related debt will total roughly a trillion dollars in 2008. See, for example, Robert Higgs, "The trillion-dollar defense budget is already here," The Independent Institute, March 15, 2007, http://www.independent.org/newsroom/article.asp?id=1941; Robert Dreyfuss, "Financing the imperial armed forces: A trillion dollars and nowhere to go but up," *Tom Dispatch*, June 8, 2007, http://tomdispatch.com/post/174793/robert_dreyfuss_the_pentagon_s_blank_check

12 These are the United States, Russia, United Kingdom, France, China, India, Pakistan, Israel and North Korea. (Center for Defense Information, *2007 Military Almanac*, p. 26) Israel, India and Pakistan have not signed the nuclear nonproliferation treaty, and North Korea has withdrawn from it.

13 Bruce Blair, "Primed and Ready," *The Defense Monitor*, XXXVI (3), May/June 2007, 1-5.

14 Marina Ottaway, Nathan J. Brown, Amr Hamzawy, Karim Sadjadpour, and Paul Salem, *The New Middle East* (Washington, D.C.: Carnegie Endowment for International Peace, 2008) 19.

15 Russia also faces increasing internal security challenges as a result of its declining population. "Transcript of Remarks by Director of the Central Intelligence Agency, Gen. Michael V. Hayden,

at the Landon Lecture Series, Kansas State University," Central Intelligence Agency, April 30, 2008.

16 For discussions of Fourth Generation Warfare, see Thomas X. Hammes, *The Sling and the Stone* (St. Paul, MN: Zenith, 2004) and the various works of William S. Lind archived at http://www.d-n-i.net; Martin van Creveld has stated that his notion of "non-trinitarian war," as described in his *The Transformation of War* (New York: Free Press, 1991), is essentially the same as Fourth Generation War. Theorists like John Robb are examining conflict by groups so distributed, yet networked, that some have proposed a "fifth generation" of war. See Robb's book, *Brave New War* (New York: Wiley, 2007).

17 Andrew J. Bacevich, "Surging to Defeat: Petraeus's strategy only postponed the inevitable," *The American Conservative*, April 21, 2008; "No US troop increase in Afghanistan without deeper cuts in Iraq: Pentagon," Agence France-Presse, May 7, 2008.

18 The latest U.S. government figures are provided at http://www.treas.gov.tic/mfh.txt. They show that, as of February 2008, China holds approximately half a trillion dollars of U.S. government securities, and the "oil exporters" (i.e. the OPEC nations and others) account for another $150 billion. Some experts consider these numbers to be understated because nations can buy these securities through private brokers, and many regard the size and composition of their reserves as state secrets.

19 Linda J. Bilmes and Joseph E. Stiglitz, "The Iraq War Will Cost Us $3 Trillion, And Much More," *The Washington Post*, March 9, 2008. Three trillion dollars roughly equals a $10,000 burden on every man, woman and child in the United States.

20 Zbigniew Brzezinski, "Terrorized by 'war on terror': How a three-word mantra has undermined America," *The Washington Post*, March 25, 2007.

21 The Department of Defense recognizes the "DIMES" model: diplomacy, information, military, economic, and societal-cultural factors. Walter Pincus, "Irregular Warfare, Both Future and Present,"*The Washington Post*, April 7, 2008.

22 For a summary of these arguments, see Alexander Hamilton, "The Powers Necessary to the Common Defense Further Considered," *Federalist* No. 24.

23 In the Civil War, more than 90 percent of the officers in the Union Army were U.S. Volunteers. Regular U.S. Army officers often got commissions in the U.S. Volunteers several grades higher than the ones they held in the U.S. Army. When the war ended and the Volunteers went home they would resume their U.S. Army commissions.

24 From George Washington's 1796 "Farewell Address" to the people of the United States: "So likewise, a passionate attachment of one nation for another produces a variety of evils."

25 Just to cite one example, according to the Center for Defense Information's *2007 Military Almanac*, pp. 98-99, the cost of a Trident II submarine-launched ballistic missile, capable of destroying any city on earth, is about half that of a single F-22 tactical fighter aircraft.

26 This lesson took a while to sink in. Until about 1960, the United States considered "tactical" nuclear weapons as ordinary tools of war. See: Walter Pincus, "Eisenhower Advisers Discussed Using Nuclear Weapons in China," *The Washington Post*, April 30, 2008.

27 People will someday appreciate that facile phrases are a highly dangerous substitute for thought.

28 Robert M. Cassidy, *Counterinsurgency and the Global War on Terror* (Stanford, CA: Stanford University Press, 2008) 3.

29 Putting the end to another facile phrase, popular on the political right, that communism was a mortal threat because "no country had ever successfully thrown off communism."

30 Because the German word for "policy" can also be translated as "politics," his formula also fits "wag the dog" wars waged for domestic political reasons.

31 For a typical list of justifications for spending 4 percent, see the Heritage Foundation's white paper, "Providing for the Common Defense: Why 4 Percent?" The Heritage Foundation, April 2, 2008, http://www.heritage.org/Research/HomelandDefense/wp040208.cfm

32 It could be argued, interestingly enough, that by funding and arming the Sunni "Awakening" movements in Iraq, we are siding with future insurgents against a Shi'ite government allied with Iran.

33 For many years, the policy was anti-communism and today it is anti-terrorism, both leading to our identification with unpopular rulers throughout the developing world.

34 With the predicted rise in Chinese and Indian energy consumption, it is likely that Asian states will be more dependent upon oil traveling by sea. Reasoning by analogy is often misleading, but access to the sea was a major cause for Japan's entry into World War II, a fact not lost on India or China, both of which maintain sizable fleets.

35 Two of the best known, William S. Lind and Thomas P. M. Barnett, agree on little else and have called each other "evil" in print.

36 China against Vietnam in 1979, and Russia (as the Soviet Union) against Afghanistan, quasi-internally against Chechnya (1994 to the present), and the recent conflict with Georgia.

37 *National Defense Strategy*, p. 22.

38 The best known example is *Unrestricted Warfare*, by Qiao Liang and Wang Xiangsui (Beijing: PLA Literature and Arts Publishing House, February 1999), also known as the "Chinese colonel's paper." The fact that it was intended for the international readership should not detract from the validity of its message.

39 Even in Vietnam, we were supported by units from Korea, Australia, New Zealand and the Philippines.

40 The many-sided nature of the fighting in Iraq and its implications are well-documented and analyzed in Bruce R. Pirnie and Edward O'Connell, "Counterinsurgency in Iraq," *Rand Counterinsurgency Study 2* (Santa Monica, CA: RAND Corporation, 2008). The recent ineffectiveness of military force in solving what are largely political problems is documented in Patricia Sullivan, "War Aims and War Outcomes: Why Powerful States Lose Limited Wars," *Journal of Conflict Resolution* 51, no. 3: 496-524.

41 These included democracy and freedom for the Iraqi people, defeat of Islamic terrorists in that country, and of course, elimination of Saddam's weapons of mass destruction.

42 "The Case for Clarity," Economist.com, February 21, 2008.

43 For a discussion on the need for coercion in maintaining modern occupations, see Martin van Creveld, *The Changing Face of War*, (New York: Ballentine, 2006) and Sir Rupert Smith, *The Utility of Force*.

44 Today, neoconservatives are making the same argument: "Recent suggestions in Washington that reductions could begin sooner or proceed more rapidly are premature." Frederick W. Kagan, Kimberly Kagan and Jack Keane, "The New Reality in Iraq," *The Wall Street Journal*, July 16, 2008.

45 Geoffrey Regan, *Great Military Disasters. An Historical Survey of Military Incompetence*, (New York, NY: Barnes & Noble Books, 1987), 14.

46 U.S. assistance in El Salvador (1981 to 1992) was limited to advice, training and financial assistance. For a detailed examination of U.S. actions in El Salvador, see: Steven Metz, *Counterinsurgency Strategy and the Phoenix of American Capability* (Carlisle, PA: Strategic Studies Institute, U.S. Army War College, 1995). For an extensive discussion of counterinsurgency since the end of World War II, please refer to Chet Richards, *If We Can Keep It* (Washington: Center for Defense Information, 2008), particularly Chapter 4.

47 RAND, "Countering Insurgency in the Muslim World, Rethinking U.S. Priorities and Capabilities," Research Brief, February 2008, describing the conclusions in David Gompert and John

Gordon IV, *War by Other Means* (Santa Monica, CA: The RAND Corporation, 2008). Insurgencies may also fail against brutal, incompetent dictatorships, of course.

48 Gompert and Gordon 2008, 34. See also Richards, *If We Can Keep It*, 50-52.

49 Martin van Creveld, *The Transformation of War* (New York: Free Press, 1991), 225.

50 "To kill an opponent who is much weaker than yourself is unnecessary and therefore cruel; to let that opponent kill you is unnecessary and therefore foolish," "Why Iraq Will end Like Vietnam Did," http://www.defense-and-society.org/creveld/why_iraq_will_end_as_vietnam_did.htm

51 To illustrate, one way to jump start an economy is for the developed world to begin buying things from it. Initially, these will often be agricultural commodities. Unfortunately, such a policy runs into opposition from domestic constituencies and leads to a variety of obstacles including agricultural tariffs and subsidies, "Buy American" provisions, and the desire of senior politicians to reward American contractors. For a discussion, see Thomas P. M. Barnett, *Blueprint for Action* (New York: Putnam, 2005), 244. Note that dividing a country along ethnic lines – sometimes offered as a solution for problems in developing countries – may exchange a single repressive and incompetent government for a set of them.

52 Martin van Creveld, *The Sword and the Olive*, (New York: Public Affairs/Perseus, 2002).

53 The new administration may come under some pressure to consider a goal of nuclear disarmament. Several figures of the foreign policy establishment from both parties, including Henry Kissinger and Sam Nunn, are advocating such an approach. See Carla Anne Robbins, "Thinking the Unthinkable: A World Without Nuclear Weapons," *The New York Times*, June 30, 2008.

54 Ottaway 2008, 4.

55 Information reports, particularly raw reports of the type so often cited in the neoconservative press as evidence of Saddam Hussein's nuclear weapons or his close cooperation with Osama bin Laden, are notoriously unreliable. On any given day, for example, there are hundreds of reports of flying saucers, space aliens and Bigfoot. It is the job of intelligence to find the nuggets of legitimate information in the mound of reports that stream in.

56 "Executive Order: Further Amendments to Executive Order 12333, United States Intelligence Activities," Office of the White House Press Secretary, July 31, 2008. The term "update" was used by the press secretary in the "fact sheet" issued with the executive order.

CHAPTER 3

LEADING THE HUMAN DIMENSION OUT OF A LEGACY OF FAILURE[1]

Col. G.I. Wilson (U.S. Marine Corps, ret.)
and Maj. Donald Vandergriff (U.S. Army, ret.)

"Take away my people, but leave my factories, and soon grass will grow on the factory floors. Take away my factories, but leave my people, and soon we will have a new and better factory." – Andrew Carnegie[2]

Summary: A Legacy of Failure

The end of the Cold War brought changes to our national defense strategy and force structure. Yet, we remain hobbled by an archaic and dysfunctional personnel system that fails to recognize the new realities of leading our human resources. The most serious of these realities is that the demands on our active duty, reserves and retired recall personnel differ greatly from those of the past. Institutional failures are abundant in the management of military human resources.

Eliot A. Cohen and John Gooch's book, "Military Misfortunes: The Anatomy of Failure in War," describes three kinds of institutional failures: failure to learn, failure to adapt and failure to anticipate. This chapter contends that the military legacy of human resource failure encompasses all three types by incorporating flawed mental constructs – including lack of imagination, faulty assumptions and analysis paralysis – compounded by lack of risk awareness, preference for the status quo and organizational factors such as institutional-think, "turf" battles and bureaucratic arrogance.

All large organizations have similar needs for managing their human resources. Therefore, DOD's legacy of human resource failures can legitimately be evaluated from a business perspective. For example, a recent economics conference conducted by The Brookings Institution in Washington, D.C., to ascertain whether American industry could raise productivity by changing the way it pays its employees reached the conclusion that productivity may be boosted more by changing the way workers are treated than by changing the way they are paid.[3] In line with that finding, the late Peter F. Drucker, perhaps still the most respected writer on leadership and management in the United States, concluded "most of our assumptions about business, technology and organizations are at least 50 years old.[4] They have outlived their time." Drucker went on to identify a number of personnel management assumptions that are no longer valid:

- There is only one right way to manage people.

- People who work for an organization are subordinates expected to do what they are assigned to do and not much else.

- People who work for an organization are dependent on the organization for their livelihood.

Drucker also made a number of suggestions about the management of people that seem to be relevant for any service human dimension as well:

- Employees must be managed as if they were volunteers.

- Many employees are knowledge workers who must be managed as if they are associates, not subordinates.

- Employees need a challenge. They must know and believe in the mission.

- Employees have to be managed as partners whose goals are aligned with the goals of the organization.

- Maximize the performance of people by capitalizing on their strengths and their knowledge rather than by trying to force them into molds.

As technology spreads around the world, the only competitive advantage the United States can hope to have is the productivity of its knowledge workers.

It is evident after studying Drucker and other scholars of business leadership that today's military personnel management (vice human resources leadership) is based on invalid assumptions, including requirements for mass mobilization, equity, a surplus of pseudo-command qualified officers that drive centralized management, individual evaluation systems, and the "up-or-out" personnel promotion system. These will each be described in detail below. If these assumptions are no longer valid, then the direction for a solution is clear: Develop a human resources leadership model that is adaptable and focused on developing leaders earlier and that places people where they best serve the military and the nation, while providing units to accomplish full-spectrum missions.

Foundation: Leading Human Resources and the Future Force

We predominately use Army case studies, nevertheless, all the services and the Department of Defense will find that much of what we present can be extrapolated and applied with great fidelity. To date, the Army's efforts to uncover the human resource requirements of the future force have generated projects like the "Pentathlete," conducted by the U.S. Army War College task force in 2005, as well as studies conducted by the Army Officer Personnel Management System (OPMS) 2005-2006. The Army Training and Doctrine Command (TRADOC) has recently released a detailed and far-reaching study called the "Human Dimension in the Future 2015-2024" that also calls for reforms to the current personnel system and how the Army develops and trains its soldiers. Concerns drawn from these works include:

- The Army must promote adaptability in the Army and encourage innovation.

- The Army must recognize the fragile nature of the all-volunteer force and never take it for granted. The Army, too, must maintain constant vigilance for signs of personnel "hollowness," understand the balance between enlistments and the civilian labor market, and keep watch over significant indicators. In 2015, for example, the Army will have a smaller pool of potential recruits than it does today.

- The Army must continue to focus on quality and seek to determine how much it will pay for this attribute in light of how much it can afford.

- The Army must focus on human resource to sustain a quality force. If that means placing more recruiters in the marketplace in order to obtain quality soldiers who are willing to go the distance in the Army, so be it.

Additional insights about the military's environment from these various studies include domestic business trends as well as the Joint Operating Environment (all the services working together as a unified force):

- The domestic U.S. environment will continue its shift from industrial age to information age. In a parallel manner, adaptability and innovation – and their inherent human characteristics – will continue to play a larger role in the Army's success.

- Intuition is becoming recognized as a powerful leadership and management tool.

- Adaptability is only a buzzword in the U.S. military, but it is resident in business and government organizations. In regards to the latter, proposals have been made to collect and categorize the traits and attributes of each individual to best use that person to meet the needs of the military while balancing with the needs of the person.

- Multiple environments will also present challenges to the Future Force Human Dimension (human resource) strategy.[5]

It is fair to conclude that among all the services, the Army recognizes the need to change with the times and has an idea outlined in its own "Human Dimension in the Future 2015-2024." While many of the ideas in this study remain to be implemented into the personnel management system, the Army is taking on new approaches to education and training.

A Centralized Beer Can Personnel System

As John Tillson states in the paper "Reducing the Impact of Tempo," "A conflict exists in the Army."[6] The same holds true for the Marine Corps as well. The services, particularly the Army and Marine Corps, must manage individuals and they must manage units. We see what we call "beer can personnel management": The operant idea is to reach into the stack (i.e. human resources) of cold beer sitting in the refrigerator, grab one, slam it down, crumple up the beer can (i.e. the individual), toss it out, and reach for another. The cycle is repeated over and over taking an irreparable toll on individuals, the personnel systems and operations.

To be sure, the Army and Marine Corps do a good job of developing the individual skills and building the motivation of their members. Marines and soldiers in the future will be imbued with a warrior ethos and discipline and be physically and mentally hardened for combat. They will possess perseverance, competence and, most importantly, the will and means to win. Additionally, they will be sophisticated in the use of emerging technologies and trained for a full range of operations. Furthermore, they will have the "moral determination to kill our enemies as readily as alleviate the suffering of innocents."[7]

To manage individuals, the Army moves them from place to place in accordance with both its defined need for trained individuals and its concept of the jobs a successful career should encompass, but with little or no concern for the impact of these moves on the readiness of the units to which these individuals are assigned. To ensure the readiness and capability of units, however, the Army must constantly train and retrain units primarily to make up for the constant exchange of untrained individuals for trained individuals caused by the personnel system.[8]

Army and Marine Corps leaders recognize that they hurt unit readiness and capability when they move individuals from unit to unit and from job to job. For that reason, the Army moved to a unit stabilization program, where it rotates divisions to and from Iraq, beginning with an Army Chief of Staff policy letter signed November 2003 (part of this is the aligning of battalion and higher command tours with the rotation). Army and Marine Corps leaders, however, still believe that the movement of individuals under the Individual Replacement System (IRS) is necessary to fulfill their need to manage individuals. The Army is unable to resolve this core conflict because there are a number of questionable assumptions that drive Army personnel policies, practices and measures.[9]

Here are two examples.

The first assumption is that individuals must be managed by a centralized personnel system. This assumption was built into the Army personnel management system in the early 1900s when the War Department modeled its personnel management system on that of the Pennsylvania Railroad. It was strengthened during World War I and World War II when the size of the military increased dramatically and centralized control seemed essential for success. It was further reinforced in the 1950s when American corporations espoused the virtues of centralized control. Centralization continued into the 1970s and 1980s with the centralization of promotions of most officers and noncommissioned officers (NCOs), as well as the centralization of command selection.[10]

The second assumption is that the personnel system must provide a surplus of qualified Army officers in the middle grades in order to support a future total mobilization similar to the mobilization experienced in World War II. At the end of World War II, the Army, having participated in the total mobilization for World War I and World War II, concluded that it was necessary to maintain a surplus of qualified officers to support a total mobilization that would create entirely new units to meet the needs of a future, multiyear war with the Soviet Union. Accordingly, the Army designed a personnel management system that would provide a surplus of qualified middle-level officers. Key to maintaining this surplus was an up-or-out requirement and a 20-year retirement that would create a large number of middle-level officers but would get them out of the Army before they became too old.[11]

These assumptions have been "hard wired" into the system over many years and most officers, even most personnel experts, seem to be unaware of their existence.[12] Over the years the Army has found ways to mitigate some of the effects of these assumptions. For example, the new Army personnel policy calling for some officers to become specialists – in contrast to its longstanding emphasis on producing "generalists" – can be seen as a way of finding equitable solutions for excess officers. This policy has the added benefit of reducing the number of more senior officers, all generalists, who must become "command qualified." These changes can be seen as an implicit effort to mitigate the impact of the mobilization assumption.[13]

The generalist assumption has been a part of American military culture since the late 19th century and early 20th century, when the United States rejected Emory Upton's efforts to create a professional Army and general staff whose officers were rigidly selected and trained in technical areas. This generalist concept was enhanced at the end of World War II with the reforms of the Officer Personnel Act of 1947 (OPA 47). The Officer Personnel Act of 1947 enshrines this thinking and was institutionalized by the Defense Officer Personnel Management Act of 1980 (DOPMA). Continual adaptation by the personnel system has retained its core legacies.[14]

In the early days of the Cold War, the Army continued to evolve a personnel system to meet the needs of a future war. This system, which was promulgated in OPA 47, was strongly influenced by the determination that, in a future total mobilization, the services must not have the problems they experienced at the start of World War II.

The Army, in particular, had had two major problems in expanding from fewer than 200,000 regulars in 1936, to 1.6 million in December 1941, to 8.3 million in May 1945. First, the Army did not have enough trained officers at the middle and upper levels to take on the responsibilities of a much larger force. Second, it had too many older senior officers. During the war the Army responded to these problems, first by centralizing authority to compensate for the lack of experienced officers and, second, by forcing many older officers to retire.

The post-war solution to the first problem was to create a bulge of middle-grade officers who were "qualified" to take on the additional duties associated with a large-scale expansion of the force. This policy was built into OPA 47, under which it became the responsibility of the centralized personnel system to ensure that officers were qualified to meet mobilization demands. Given the uncertainties associated with mobilization, this translated into a demand for "generalists."[15]

Individual Evaluation Systems

The Army has embraced some form of written evaluation since the early 1800s, and in subsequent years this report has proved to be the only tool used to evaluate the performance and potential of officers. There have been attempts to broaden the basis of promotion, however. In 1881, upon the founding of the School of Infantry and Cavalry, the future Command and General Staff College, at Fort Leavenworth, Kan., reformists, known as "Uptonians" after Gen. Emory Upton, surfaced who attempted to implement the use of formal and objective examinations using the Prussian military as a model.

This move to establish professional standards was severely resisted by most of the officer corps. The hue and cry was the practice was "undemocratic" and unfair. In reality, it was because the majority of officers, except for graduates of West Point, were largely uneducated, especially in the art of war. Examinations would expose the weakness of the officer corps and the Army in the knowledge of their profession to Congress as well as the public.[16]

This cemented the tradition of resisting professionalism and intellectual achievement. It remained dominant until after World War II, and resistance is still seen today, where the only personnel tool-of-comfort for evaluations is subjective and easily controlled, manipulated and massaged by centralized promotion boards. Those serving on that board ultimately fall prey to picking those who most resemble the board members.

As one Army colonel put it, Army selection and promotion boards are "selecting those who they feel most comfortable with; those who are like you." Remember those on the board got promoted by the very same system, so if it was good enough for them why change it? This does not just happen in the Army either.[17]

The pernicious and persuasive impact of subjective selection undermines the Army's (and the other services') ability to become adaptive and to participate in constructive change. Personnel managers, unlike human resource leaders, only know how to react to change. Human resource leaders, by contrast, leverage change, adjusting the first decision with their second decision and so on.

As the 21st century opens, change remains the bane of personnel managers while human resource leaders view change as opportunity. Roger Martin writes in the Harvard Business Review about leaders and what it takes to stay a leader: "Part of the challenge is changing with the times and looking inward as well as outward." Human resource leadership is about change and grasping what Marshall Goldsmith considers an essential principle of "What got you here, won't get you there."[18]

Personnel-Comfort Tool: Officer Evaluation Report (OER)

The Officer Efficiency Report (OER) Series 67 was standardized in July 1947, in line with the reforms being pushed by Gen. George C. Marshall that would culminate in OPA of 1947. The Army has gone through 10 versions of the OER from 1947 to present. Because of its purpose of supporting an up-or-out promotion system, the OER has always been prone to inflation by officers wanting to project their subordinates as the best, or because the raters or senior raters did not have the moral courage to face their officers with average or below average OERs that would destroy the careers. The OER fits perfectly into a culture of management science that stresses equity, where generalist officers are measured by how well they pleased the boss because it is their superior or raters who make or break their careers.

The OER was and is now used as the main tool on promotion and selection boards. As the OER continued to gain strength, it came to be used in one of two ways. In a negative sense, it could be used to damage an officer's career or even end it. An officer with strong character who posed a threat to a commanding officer could be sabotaged. The other way was to advance a favorite of the "brass" rapidly up the ranks or into the right job. In both cases writing an OER became an art to the career-minded officer who learned how to employ the right words in the right places to make a point.[19] Today, every assignment has to receive a perfect OER in order to get an officer selected for battalion, higher command and for special assignments such as graduate intern programs.

The result of the OER façade as a tool of careerism, which does not create professionalism, has become apparent to the members of the officer corps. "There is now a total disbelief in the system and a concomitant question regarding the integrity of all of us who continue its use."[20] The use of the OER reflects poorly on the ethical strength of the officer corps because officers cannot fairly assess performance and potential. Every officer is caught up in the scandal. With a large officer corps operating under an inflated evaluation system, anyone who tries to use the system to fairly assess his officers would destroy his officers.

Up-or-Out Promotion System

OPA 47's provisions were also based on the belief that the best way to prepare for war was to make every officer a generalist. Gen. George Marshall and succeeding chiefs of staff of the Army directed personnel managers to formulate Army policies that moved officers around frequently so they would become experienced in numerous positions, always emphasizing the need to prepare for more responsibility at the highest levels of command. They also sent instructions to promotion and selection boards to look for a wealth of experience in numerous positions and duties. Their purpose was to ensure that officers would be prepared to lead the new units that would be created when war came with the Soviet Union, and the services once again expanded as part of a total mobilization. This generalist theory was also popular in corporate management at the time. It should be noted that recent Army changes in the personnel system could be seen as an implicit effort to mitigate the effect of this assumption.

The generalist assumption is also tied to the assumption that the Army must provide equity. Following World War II, a number of officers were sent to the best business schools in the country where theories of "career equity" were taught. This concept rested on two suppositions: 1) the creation of a corporate generalist, who developed via a series of short assignments to a large number of different positions, and 2) the idea of treating all corporate members equally or fairly. This was not "equal opportunity," but "equity" in which everyone was treated the same by the centralized personnel management authority.[21]

The officers brought these business concepts back to the Army, where the concept of passing large numbers of people through critical jobs fit well with the OPA 47 concepts calling for a large number of trained middle-grade officers all managed by a centralized personnel bureaucracy. This concept also fit well with the centralized "one size fits all" policies that the 1999 8th Quadrennial Review of Military Compensation (QRMC) identified as a problem for the Army today.[22]

Another key assumption is that Army members must be interchangeable – "beer can" personnel management. This assumption is a product of the reforms introduced in the early 1900s by Secretary of War Elihu Root. One of his "modern management concepts," drawn from the Industrial Revolution, viewed individuals as identical component parts that could be created on an assembly line. This concept led the Army to change from a unit-based system for replacing casualties to the individual casualty replacement system it used in World War I, World War II, Korea and Vietnam. Under this system, soldiers resemble replacement parts and have a set of identical skills that can be defined by a Military Occupational Specialty (MOS). The Army's "one size fits all" personnel policies may also derive in part from this assumption.[23]

The up-or-out system underwrites the "Peter Principle," in which individuals are promoted to their level of incompetence. Officers then get mired in jobs because there is no way to advance, and, because the holders are not competent, the assignments are not performed well. Sadly, the Army does not generally take steps to move personnel back to a level where they can function effectively. Where the Army runs into problems is when it uses promotion to reward short-term performance. These two concepts – performance-competence and leadership potential – need to be separated in the promotion system.

Personnel: Changing the Wrapping, Not the Substance

The OPMS (formally OPMS 3) task force attempted in 2005-2006 to once again fix the deficiencies of the culture, which was caused by the Officer Personnel Act of 1947, the Defense Officer Personnel Management Act of 1980 and the Army's own rigid management policies, by continuing to try to fix something with small adjustments that requires a complete overhaul. OPMS continues its process of specialization of the officer corps for the future, yet within existing cultural boundaries set by centralized management and the up-or-out promotion system.

The benefits of OPMS are yet to be seen, but the potential exists to put the officer corps back on the right track. The OPMS emphasis on specialization within the bounds set by OPA 47 and DOPMA ensures that fewer officers will get "an opportunity to command." This will be a small price to pay for the benefits of specialization, and arguments that more former commanders are needed for mobilization ignore the ability of staff officers and junior commanders to learn from good examples. The larger benefit of the OPMS proposals is the continual strengthening of critical staff and "soft skills" specialties throughout the Army, such as the foreign area officer (FAO). Excellent officers not selected for command can pursue successful careers through repeated assignments in one of the above fields.

The long-term goal of OPMS is to have well-qualified specialists selected as general officers, destroying the myth that command experience is essential to high-level advancement. More importantly, the Army would run well without the influence of entrenched civilian bureaucrats, of obvious benefit to the functioning of units in combat. OPMS changes are a step in the right direction, yet more remains to be done outside its boundaries, such as addressing the problems caused by the up-or-out promotion system, a bloated officer corps, the all-or-nothing retirement system, and a lack of a unit personnel system.[24]

OPMS has, in reality, only guaranteed that the competition will be "fair." By moving many out of the old command track, which is now the operational field, into the three other fields, as well as promising that everyone can attend ILE (Intermediate

Leader Education), formally known as Command and General Staff College (C&GSC), it can once again promise all starters who reach the grade of major an equal chance to win. In this way the Army can continue to feed the up-or-out promotion system and fill the numerous jobs mandated by law. It can also assure that few competitors will become prematurely discouraged in the race for status. As mentioned, under OPMS, the symbol of status will swing somewhat away from the need to command and the generalist career pattern. It continues the trend of providing "many roads to the top" by increasing chances for promotion and promising all majors attendance to ILE, which was a career discriminator if an officer was not selected to attend. OPMS continues to streamline fairness by remodeling the façade of the personnel system's customary mechanism for maintaining the tractability of the officer corps.

All is not positive with OPMS, however. It continues to manifest the competitive ethic caused by the up-or-out promotion system and a bloated officer corps. OPMS allows the organization to extract deference through competition. As did the earlier three OPMS systems (1971, 1984 and 1997), the new system uses competition more than ever as a lever to control the career soldier. Under the culture of management science, from the very day officers receive their commissions the Army impresses upon them the importance of remaining competitive. Thus, the Army encourages officers to compete against each other to survive in the up-or-out system. It uses the "competitive ethic" in an explicitly coercive manner. To become noncompetitive is to risk exclusion from the Army officer profession altogether. Officers have and continue to feel compelled to give careful attention to the institution's performance cues, despite the demands of the ongoing wars in Iraq and Afghanistan.

The Army's officer system under OPMS will continue to use competition, theorizing the "best" will rise to the top, when in fact it corrupts and creates an unhealthy strain that no officer can elude. The preference inherent in most offices to adhere to the profession's ethical code eventually yields to the grinding realization that the officer must also satisfy the institutional demand to remain competitive, if only out of self-preservation.

On balance, looking at both positive and negative aspects, one could argue that given the strict boundaries imposed by the laws that govern our officer system and the culture, the reforms under OPMS are perhaps the best that could be given to the officer corps. The problem remains, though, with broader issues, including the fear of mass mobilization and an undying belief in management science. Before any changes can really be termed reforms, issues that generate careerism and undermine readiness must be openly discussed. Unfortunately, OPMS's downfall, as it was with the previous three OPMS "reforms," is that it leaves careerism unaffected due to the emphasis it places on the competitive ethic, which despite specialization, will remain.[25]

On the whole, however, our prognosis is positive. Perhaps by recognizing the limitations of personnel management science, as well as the compulsion to maintain policies around a personnel system developed for mass mobilization, OPMS can become more than a short-term fix that will soon become another of the series of evolutionary fixes. Instead, OPMS might best be viewed as a bridge to more and better reforms in the near future. The Army will eventually create its own military version of a new, flatter organization with the inherent officer personnel policies revolving around the unit policies that must accompany it. As a result, the Army will reintroduce professionalism to its officer corps.

Professionalism: Thriving on Change

The current war is forcing the Army and the other services to examine a new doctrine that emphasizes increased responsibility for lower ranks. At the same time, the Army must struggle with embracing and integrating new technology through the Future Combat Systems (FCS). The Army, therefore, has no choice but to be bold and create a new institutional culture. This new culture will create, nurture and promote human resource leaders who thrive on change in general and, in particular, on the increased demands that doctrine writers are advocating and, most importantly, the future challenges our foes create.

This is a different culture from the one we have now. We cannot continue to write glowing documents advocating adaptability, yet subtly support peacetime politically correct practices that shore up bureaucratic qualities rather than combat leadership qualities. Unfortunately, when leaders come up for promotion and selection, the out-of-date system too often selects out the most creative and dynamic of leaders and subordinates.

To prepare leaders for the Army in the 21st century, we must:

- Continue to replace the individual personnel system with a unit personnel system. Revolve all personnel policies around a modular, unit-based system and move to an Army force structure that can be supported by a unit replacement system.

- Eliminate the up-or-out promotion system and replace it with an up-or-stay promotion system using tougher accessions.

- Replace the specific branches such as Armor, Field Artillery, Infantry, Aviation, Quartermaster, Transportation, etc., and place officers on a track or category system at the captain (O-3) or major (O-4) level. Retain NCOs in their branches until they reach master sergeant or first sergeant (E-8). Make personnel management more flexible by setting up a database system that lists a person's attributes and traits in order to put that person in the place where they best can serve the Army and nation.

- Revise the officer evaluation system to involve a narrative Evaluation Report (ER) on character with a periodic examination to enter the officer corps, as well as attendance at the Command and General Staff College. Add the 360-degree evaluation system with the ER as one part of that system.

- Revise the education system, using the Adaptive Leader Methodology (ALM) (the new leader development model using experiential learning) as the core to the leader development for officers, NCOs and civilians at all levels (the Army is moving to ALM).[26]

The purpose of these reforms is to change the incentive system. It is time to usher in human-resource leadership. Human-resource leaders must seek to reward strength of character, especially as manifested in a willingness to set priorities (i.e. in the order of people, etc.), make decisions, take action and penalize those who simply go along to get along, get by while doing nothing and passionately embrace risk avoidance.

It does no good to call for promoting the risk-takers when the incentives all work the other way. Once strength of character is rewarded, then loyalty to the nation, the Army and unit can be established over loyalty to self, which is the centerpiece of to-day's personnel management science. It is the reasoning behind the personnel system's advocacy of the individualist focus "be all you can be," and it underlies the belief that people must be constantly moved and promoted, as well as make-work opportunities hyped, to give the appearance of it-happened-on-my-watch promotion points.

The "OODA Loop": Change as a Component of Strategy

The important 20th century strategist, the late U.S. Air Force Col. John Boyd, con-tended that there is a direct relationship between strategy and change. The purpose of strategy is to improve our ability to shape and adapt to circumstances, so that we, as individuals, groups, cultures or nation-states, can survive on our own terms. In business and national security it is vital to stay ahead of adversaries. Those who ignore change often find themselves unequal to its challenges.[27]

The pace and challenge of change since the end of World War II have surpassed anything our military faced in the preceding 170 years, where with the exception of skirmishes with Native Americans in the late 1800s, the presumed foe was always a military establishment similar to our own. During the last 60 years, however, we have found ourselves fighting an assortment of Third World militaries, insurgencies and, most recently, terrorist networks. To deal with such periods of rapid change and un-predictable opponents, Boyd developed the concept of "operating inside an opponent's Observe Orient Decide and Act (OODA loops)."[28] It is a formula for, in the words of business consultant Tom Peters, "thriving on chaos." As an associate of Boyd's, retired U.S. Air Force Col. Chet Richards, describes it in his book, "Certain to Win":

You are simultaneously observing any mismatches between your conception of the world and the way the world really is, trying to reorient to a confusing and threatening situation, and attempting to come up with ideas to deal with it. It is the "quickness" of the entire OODA Loop cycle and the time it takes to transition from one orientation state to another, which keeps you up with the pace of changing events.[29]

It would not be overstating the matter to conclude that real human resource leaders use "OODA loop thinking" to anticipate and rely on change, unlike the personnel tool-of comfort approach.

Nonetheless, despite the recognition by human resources leadership professionals of "What got you here, won't get you there now," personnel comfort tools still hold a death grip on our personnel system, robbing it of agility and quickness to meet the changing needs of the Army. Jack Welch, former CEO of General Electric, implored his people to face reality and change each morning, for each morning is different from the last. Welch continually insisted to GE management that what was important yesterday might no longer be important today. Welch was not afraid of going back on something and giving new direction. He exhibited a willingness to change and saw it as leadership strength.[31] So, we will strive to this end and begin with a brief case study to explore the dominant personnel comfort tool, the written personnel evaluation known officially as the Officer Evaluation Report (OER).

DOPMA: How Many Officers?

The first ingredient in the reforms to prepare the leaders and the Army for combat in the 21st century is to unload a force structure that must be manned by a top- and middle-heavy officer corps. Surprisingly, the Army still employs a similar table of organization and equipment (TO & E) to the one derived in World War II (in historical doctrinal terms, we are still operating similar to Napoleon's *corps-de-armee* concept). The Army's primitive structure, despite this era of e-mail, faxes, telecommunications and faster intelligence gathering and assessment systems, still consists of industrial-age hierarchies, which means many layers of supervisors, or colonels and generals, all practicing perfection in a bureaucracy brought on board by Elihu Root in 1903. What makes it worse, despite our modern age of automation, is the percentage of the officer corps, which comprises 14.3 percent of the entire force. This is as bad as it was at its height during the Vietnam War.

The Army has the worst officer-to-enlisted ratio ever, 1 to 6. At the same time, the number of senior officers – especially at the middle and general officer level – has become bloated, with one field grade officer for every junior officer and one general for every 1,006 soldiers. This is not simply a matter of inefficiency or the Army's preoccupation with mobilization. When there is a surplus of officers, officers must frequently be assigned to "make-work" jobs that are not relevant to warfighting and in which military skills atrophy. Personnel turnover and competition increases as officers fight for moves from "make-work" to critical "branch qualifying" jobs, such as company command for captains, battalion operations and executive officer jobs for majors, and battalion command for lieutenant colonels. In addition, an officer surplus leads to centralization, as officers at more senior levels create work for themselves by pulling decisions up to their level and creating work for their staffs producing an incredible number of PowerPoint briefing slides.[32]

While the theory behind maintaining a large officer corps was readiness for mobilization, what in fact occurs is the opposite. As we have noted, the current up-or-out promotion system and the idea of a large officer corps evolved from Marshall's experience with the problem of maintaining a force ready in peacetime to respond to the unique demands of war. This system rests on two principles. First, if the system works properly, there will always be more officers qualified for promotion than there are vacancies available. This permits selectivity, the selection of the "best qualified." It was also theorized that exposure to numerous jobs could apply in a meaningful way to senior leadership positions. As a result, officers are forced through the ranks very quickly, often with too little time to learn the ropes, not being able to gain the confidence and respect of the troops: "Future Force (Future Army) would work fine if officers were given the time in one position to learn the how the technology, techniques, tactics and procedures involved in the new doctrine work."[33]

The unneeded inflation of officers at the middle grades of major, lieutenant colonel and colonel, and at the senior levels of general officers, contributes to the "swollen middles of American command bureaucracies – which themselves sometimes exist only to give a two- or three-star general a place to hang his hat."[34] There are, for example, commands consisting entirely of Military Intelligence battalions and brigades – commands that exist for command reasons alone and do not have a battlefield function. There are the redundant commands of Recruiting and Cadet. Then there are the numerous acquisition and testing commands and area commands such as U.S. Army Japan. Most of these commands themselves have under them numerous positions filled by senior officers and their staffs. Thus, we have positions in unnecessary commands that must be filled by personnel managers. These numerous commands with bloated staffs, with each officer occupying a position behind a computer generating more work under the demands of a "perform-now" evaluation system consists of "too much overhead, too hierarchical, too much middle management, and too slow."[35]

The experience an officer gains in the current environment – be it in the halls and the cubicles of the Pentagon, or in one of the many large headquarters – is contradictory to the demands of the global battlefield, which calls for decisive action when dealing with the "friction of war," unless we have really led ourselves to belief that technology will eliminate the fog and friction of war. A gradual reduction of the officer corps at major and above by 50 percent, while reducing the entire officer corps to 3 to 5 percent of the force, is necessary to eliminate the competitive ethic, bureaucratization and centralization. Reducing the officer corps vastly extends an officer's time as a platoon leader, company and battalion commander or primary staff member, allowing officers to gain more experience in their duties and to take more time to learn the art of war.

The challenge for the Army (and the entire military because everyone falls under DOPMA) is to prioritize which positions are important, and which are unimportant, those unrelated to combat or the structure necessary to support combat units, and to go to Congress and ask them to change the multitude of laws that mandate the use of officers, i.e., requirements for officers to train the National Guard under Title XI, and Joint Duty under the Goldwater-Nichols Act.

The Army needs to ask Congress to go back and revise DOPMA, tailoring the law to the needs of each service. The Air Force, for example, is more technically and individually oriented, whereas the Army's polices should revolve around its emerging unit manning and modular unit system. A unit personnel system would:

- Increase the collective training and maintain the "band of excellence" longer,

- Ease Operations Tempo (OPTEMPO) or how much units are deployed in relation to their personnel turnover that counters cohesion or unit stabilization,

- Reduce personnel costs,

- Create a larger pool of readily available units for immediate deployment, and

- Diminish the need to pour massive amounts of money into "surge" training in anticipation of or at the start of a conflict.

Future warfare of the type envisaged by think tanks and doctrine writers will rarely involve anything like the initial drive of Operation Iraqi Freedom (OIF) to Baghdad, where the Army, the 3rd Infantry Division, received by default the personnel cohesion it needed because its decrepit and incompetent opponent allowed it six months to build up and train up. Future operations will more likely consist of rapid deployment and entry operations (pre-emptive offensive operations), where success depends on initial surprise and penetration achieved by the units at the forefront of the operation, supported by units that come in later to protect their flanks from counterattacks. Precision fires and sensors would sweep any future battlefield where an opponent dares to fight the U.S. Army in the open.[36]

Most operations in the foreseeable future will take place in urban-suburban environments, where the stress of combat will require the highest levels of unit cohesion. For this reason, the Army must continue its evolution from dependence on physical mass to adaptability, which will be at a premium in urban operations. Past attrition doctrine requires mere numbers and massive firepower, while today's future operations require quality in the very best units, able to use selective firepower and do more than just fight. The doctrine emerging in FM 3-0, or Army warfighting doctrine, is supported by a unit-focused, decentralized culture that produces a unit system based upon a Brigade Combat Team (BCT) package configured under modularity.[37]

Modular BCT System

This second part of a unit system, building on a revised DOPMA, is a brigade combat team-type modular and replacement system that enables battle-tried BCTs to be pulled off the line and reconstituted in unit packets from a division depot. This latter part, of course, requires what many analysts in the upper echelons of DOD and those advising Congress would view as extra or uncommitted BCTs as part of Army Generating Force (ARFORGEN).[38]

Unlike COHORT,[39] an earlier attempt at unit manning, where the individual personnel system was divorced from the unit because of concerns for leader career opportunities, under a modular BCT system, all personnel – officers and enlisted – are permanently regimentally assigned and seconded from their division. Divisions become administrative or horizontal headquarters as part of ARFORGEN located in various locations throughout the country, with specified brigade-level units such as those that compose the logistical branches covering broader areas and overlapping those of BCTs. BCTs rotate through three phases through a three- or four-year cycle. The first and third phase falls under a division for training and rebuilding phases. In the first phase the modular brigade gathers and trains for combat at the individual and team levels, and in the final phase, it draws down and its members form a cadre to conduct many missions including post support, advisors to reserve units that also constitute BCTs within the division, and a host of duties that are normally filled by borrowed military. During the second phase, or the deployment phase, the modular BCTs fall under a vertical or command headquarters of a joint task force for operations in the field or actual combat missions.

Up-or-Stay Promotion System

The new officer management law should eliminate the up-or-out promotion system and replace it with an up-or-stay system. The up-or-out promotion system drives personnel policies that minimize the probability that officers will have the time to develop the abilities to rapidly grasp changes in situations and conditions, as well as exercise initiative by independently planning. Leaders continue to spend their career on a treadmill. It also develops the anxiety about getting promoted in leaders and thus forces them to adhere to the competitive ethic.

The new promotion system will have to become more decentralized. In contrast to the Army, American corporations have given up the concept of centralized personnel management. According to the 1999 8th Quadrennial Review of Military Compensation (QRMC), the changes in corporate personnel systems came about because "traditional systems did not meet organizational needs in the new environment and older policies and practices often worked at cross purposes with other initiatives."[40]

The QRMC report also explained the changes in corporate practices as follows: "As organizations' operating environments became more complex, larger, and more diverse, organizations began moving from the rigidity of 'one size fits all' systems toward human resource management systems designs tailored to achieve the strategic objectives of the different operating units." Finally, the QRMC identifies the current status of corporate personnel management today: "It is rare today for large corporations to centrally manage all human resource practices and insist that all business use all the same pay practices, the same pay systems, the same training packages, the same selection tools, and so on."

The key principle of promotion should be that only those who know the leaders under consideration could do the promoting and selecting. This means that division boards will have to be established to view fewer officers for longer periods of time. With commanders remaining at their positions longer, they will be able to better assess, on a first-hand basis, which officers deserve to be promoted or selected for attendance at a staff college. BCT and division commanders should be empowered and trusted to appoint boards to promote officers up through the rank of lieutenant colonel. With the field narrowed by a smaller officer corps, centralized boards could then decide who gets promoted to the rank of colonel and higher, and select officers to command brigades and larger formations.

All boards at all levels will use multiple tools – a 360-degree evaluation system in which an individual evaluation report is written solely in regards to the leader's character, an examination taken yearly and the personal conduct of the officer in front of the board – to determine promotions and selections. The bottom line in using such stringent tools is the implication that leadership and professionalism are too important to either rest on the 60-second consensus opinions of disinterested officers serving a political agenda or promoting someone based on stacks of reports.

The causes of poor morale – career anxiety, the emphasis on the competitive ethic, and the transformation or elimination of bold personality types – are the reasons to rid the Army of the up-or-out promotion system. This is particularly troubling for the type of Army officer and organizations required to carry out high-tempo operations in conditions that will require us to fight outnumbered and win. We invariably lose our warrior-leaders and our innovators. Only an up-or-stay, "perform or out," system based on objective measuring tools can create the type of leaders the Army deserves.[41]

In an up-or-stay promotion system, if a leader wants to get promoted, he or she will ask for it. The patterns for career management will change to support the number one priority, a unit personnel system. An officer will still enter the officer corps from one of three commissioning sources, but accessions (entry) will be more selective than ever before with a smaller officer corps, while NCOs will continue to use the system they have now for promoting and selecting their leaders.

All potential officers will serve a minimum of two years with a National Guard or Reserve unit (similar to the Simultaneous Membership Program (SMP) employed in conjunction with ROTC programs now).[42] Officers will then have experience working with the Reserves. Next, the mission of the commissioning sources is selecting and strenuously preparing their candidates to become officers. Filling quotas should not be a concern of the commissioning sources, only having candidates meet standards, quality not quantity is what the sources should strive for and meet. Prior to becoming commissioned, officers will have to pass a comprehensive entrance exam. Those who pass examination will then serve their initial four-year tour with a BCT. Branches for officers will be eliminated and replaced by combined arms, logistics and specialists. An initial tour in a specific area will not determine the officer's path for the rest of his career. Officers may move from one area to another throughout their careers or remain in that one area as long as they perform admirably.

At the end of this first tour, which aligns with the four-year/three-phase life of a BCT, accession into the professional corps will occur based on how well the new officers scored on their second entrance examination, performance in the regiment and a decentralized selection board examining the above mentioned tools. The board will also determine the specialty of the officer into one of three tracks: tactical, operational or technical, while serving in one of the three areas of combined arms, logistics or specialist. Under this system, the Army would be able to spend substantial time on the development, assessment and evaluation of its officers, instead of the "60-second" perusal officers currently get on promotion-selection boards for the search for the one "discriminator" in one's file. Instead, the use of a multitude of evaluation tools and a smaller officer corps will enable the Army to become more objective in its personnel decisions with the nation, with both the Army and the officer benefiting from the system.

Specialties

The following paragraphs briefly touch upon the reorganization of the officer management branches and officer specialties. The Army will have to "recode" several military occupational specialties to align with the new, broader fields.

Tactical track

The tactical track ensures officers will remain at the company, battalion, BCT or division level the rest of their careers. After selection to the tactical track, officers will attend the Basic Officer Leader Course (BOLC) II and a course specific to one of the three branch-replacing areas mentioned above using the Adaptive Leader Methodology (ALM) currently being accepted by the Army. The ALM constantly puts students in difficult, unexpected situations, and then requires them to decide and act under time pressure. ALM takes students out of their "comfort zones." Stress – mental and moral as well as physical – must be constant. War games, map exercises and free-play field exercises must constitute the bulk of the curriculum, while proficiency in drill and ceremonies are not important.

Higher command levels overseeing leader courses must look for high dropout and expulsion rates as signs that the job is being done right. Those leaders who successfully pass through the schools must continue to be developed by their commanders; learning cannot stop at the schoolhouse door. Once passing the ALM, leaders may rotate from positions within one of the tactical levels to instructor positions and back. This track includes all units from both combined arms and logistical units involved at the tactical level. Officers may remain in this track, with the option of being promoted to the level of colonel, and thus with the possibility of commanding a brigade.

Operational track

Those officers who score in the top 15 to 20 percent of the entrance examination to the professional force and demonstrate outstanding performance in front of the board will be admitted to the operational track. Additional requirements to the operational level will include an understanding of the art of war, as demonstrated on the entrance exam, and proficiency in a foreign language.

The operational track will consist of officers who become the operational experts of the Army. They will rotate between command and staff assignments at the divisional or higher levels and back to the Army or Joint Staff. These officers will attend a combined version of intermediate level education (for mid-level officers) (ILE) and the School of Advanced Military Science (SAMS) – a two-year version of graduate school in the art and science of war. These officers become the institutional cradle for proficiency in the art of war at the operational and strategic levels.

Technical track

The technical track relates to the specific technical abilities inherent in the more technologically advanced Army and the management of the tables of distribution and allowances, or TDA army. (This part of the army, TDA, provides the support structure for the combat units i.e., Training and Doctrine Command, Recruiting and ROTC commands, which as noted above, need to be drastically consolidated or reduced.) This field involves far more than the medical and law professions, but includes all positions that require graduate-level, civilian-related education or technical training such as acquisition corps, academic instructors, operations research system analysis, comptrollers, computer programmers, communications specialists and facilities managers.

Officers in this category could remain captains, with pro-rated pay, but would have to continually demonstrate their proficiency with periodic examinations combined with reviews of their evaluation reports. Officers could opt for promotion as the technical experts at division or higher levels, while the appropriate higher-level ranks would correspond with higher headquarters and responsibilities.

Training and Education System

The education system as touched upon earlier will dramatically change as well. A true education is much more than the learning of skills or the acquisition of facts. Rather, it means acquiring a broad understanding of the art of war, its ideas, principles and history. This true education must also give a thorough grounding in the warrior/leader culture, with heavy emphasis on making decisions and welcoming responsibility.

To conduct maneuver warfare, which is needed to facilitate the reductions in force structure and manpower cited above, a shift is needed from mere mental "training" to truly educating Army leaders. A shift is also needed away from the current practice of giving all branches, regardless of their relationship to the battlefield, "equity" in attending ILE or sending favored officers so "they can make contacts." A maneuver warfare Army demands leaders with a particular mindset, a culture that rewards audacity, tempo and creative decision-making. As a people, Americans possess the requisite skills to be successful in maneuver warfare, but our military professionals also require a military education that will encourage and develop boldness and mental agility.

Instead of forming the repositories for innovative, thorough training and education, most intermediate service schools remain Cartesian in their methods – mired in memorization and adherence to formulas; advancing immutable formats, principles or processes that, if properly learned and applied, will supposedly bring victory. Schools emphasizing such rules, reinforced with the properly formatted quantitative decision-aids and tables, serve only to numb creativity in leadership.

Making military education relevant to future war, with its myriad of changes and challenges, will not be easy. Already, the missions in Iraq and Afghanistan demand that leaders understand the political and strategic implications of their actions, particularly in light of the impact of new, real-time media. With rules of engagement (ROE) that impose limitations on their operational and tactical capabilities, the officers of the next century face unique challenges.

Because the officer corps will be relatively small and there will be fewer in the operational track, ILE should come soon after the officer is selected for the operational track. War college should also come sooner, perhaps as early as after 10 to 12 years of the officer's service, with selected officers from both the tactical and operational fields attending. There, the curriculum would be dramatically refocused. All officers would also be encouraged to get an education from new universities, such as the American Military University offered online, that provide unique educational opportunities from "cradle to grave" in the military art and sciences.[43]

How should the curricula at the schools that remain be refocused to effectively fight in the high tempo, nonlinear environment of projected future warfare? The answer is that our officers, commissioned and noncommissioned, and civilians alike must be educated in the classical sense through the Adaptive Leader Methodology (ALM) model that the Army is now grasping. Their education must be grounded in the art of war, but also in aggressively challenging their instructors, questioning a status quo that, in fact, no longer exists. The professional must understand why principles evolved and where they are best used and amended. This demands training that provides not set-piece scenarios, but chaos that is inherent in the nature of war.

Classroom education is still necessary, but it must be focused on the case study, demanding critical analysis of historic examples. Leaders must move beyond mere rote memorization of techniques to experimentation with unorthodox solutions. Using interactive tactical decision tools similar to those already available in the civilian sector, they should formulate, discuss and debate imaginative solutions. As they progress through the curriculum, they should increasingly encounter the often-missing combat intangible of simulation – a living opponent, possessing his own will with an incentive to win.

Free-play wargaming

Force-on-force, free-play wargaming provides the best available training for leaders and decision-makers. Free play exercises should be taken to their natural conclusion, allowing for a clear winner and loser. Such exercises provide leaders with invaluable learning and the context-based experience necessary for the development of cognitive and intuitive skills. Additionally, they identify those who fully understand the intricacies of command as well as possess the intuition and innovativeness for success.

These must be more than exercises pitting school-trained leaders against similarly trained leaders. There must be an enemy who is asymmetrical in experience as well as armament and weaponry. Here our ability to integrate "reach-back" technology and unorthodox opponents can provide a distinct advantage. A young, former gang member from Los Angeles, for example, can teach our most senior leaders more about modern warfare in an urban environment than most might want to admit. While not skilled in the military art, such opponents offer the conventional soldier a means to assess the challenges of those surviving through instinct. Certainly, our Army could have used this before we occupied Baghdad. Augmenting aggressors by employing and training with local Guard and Army Reserve, and/or foreign area experts (military or academic) familiar with a given area and culture, can also enhance the learning of 21st century students. In the case of the Reserve, this is a win-win situation regarding training and preparedness.

The advantages of this type of competition-based education are found in history. We are all aware of the successes and innovations of the *Militärische Gesellschaft,* the Prussian Army in the early 1800s, and its successor, the Prussian/German general staff. Less well-known, likely because of a lack of national institutionalization, was Gen. Al Gray's reformation of Marine Corps education in the late 1980s, as well as former Brig. Gen. Huba Wass de Czege's establishment of the School of Advanced Military Studies.

All three initiatives recognized that leader development programs dominated by principles and formulas were outmoded. All three instituted programs to develop leaders with a higher degree of intelligence, possessive of a favorable attitude toward change and innovation, and perhaps most importantly, with a propensity to assess and, as needed, undertake risk. All three also challenged their students to approach problems realistically, rewarding decisions and judgments that demonstrated their ability to incorporate innovation, tactical logic, situational awareness and boldness – essentially "out-decision cycling" their respective competitor. Their mastery was determined not by methodical application of predetermined school solutions, but by their ability to win. The ACM/ALC model will best prepare our leaders for the battles ahead.

Selection criteria

Selection for attendance at these reformed warfighting schools must also be reconsidered. Advanced readings assigned to specific tracks must be accomplished well before attendance to formal school. Officers must clearly demonstrate, at the appropriate level, a capacity for decision-making beyond their current grades. Whether by mentor/board evaluation (as in defense of a thesis) or by examination, officers should be carefully screened prior to selection for attendance. The program of instruction should be arduous and demanding.

Faculty

Finally, to reform our school system, the Army has to change personnel priority for assignments to the faculty at Army schools. As the last drawdown demonstrated, the first officers at the middle grades to be cut were instructors at the service schools. In most Western armies, by contrast, the top officers are selected to be instructors at their service schools. This also occurred in the Army in the 1930s and 1920s with C&GSC and the War College where top-performing officers rotated back to the schoolhouse to teach.

Officers and academics selected for service school faculty must be among the best and well-schooled in their military subject areas. Besides command, no assignment should be more sought after than instructing and teaching. We must institutionalize this mindset among the officer corps, and inculcate our juniors with the desire to become instructors and help shape our officer corps. This is not currently the case and, while change is coming, it needs to be expedited.

The Time is Now, the Future is Too Late

Effectiveness for the Army is not an option; it is imperative. The new culture needed to execute the type of missions imagined in the future is *sine qua non* to the effectiveness of the Army. Many officers and civilian leaders believe technology makes the difference, but as John Boyd said, people make the difference, especially when there is effective leadership. The personnel system is the linchpin that will directly affect combat effectiveness, doctrine and a host of other critical issues pertaining to the Army of the future. The culture must adjust its course before the Army can execute the high- tempo and rapidly changing warfare of the future.

The fundamental reason for instituting serious reform is that our national security construct, from our national security strategy down to the smallest military organization and how we manage our personnel, is not keeping pace with the rapid changes in the world today. The military's personnel system is an outdated adjunct to an officer personnel system designed for the Cold War. Most leaders are uncomfortable with our system; they know that it is not sufficient to meet the challenges that are clearly coming, that something's lacking. They feel this way because officers understand that our current culture is founded on the very organizational model used almost a hundred years ago to reform the War Department (today's Department of Defense).

We would be among the first to agree that much of the current system that is dysfunctional is the result of good intentions that have had unintended consequences. The people who are upholding the culture of personnel management science for the last 100 years and who put these systems in place were trying to do the right thing. Their only fault is that they have ignored the bad results of their implementations – the use of individual replacements in World War II, Korea, Vietnam, and to a certain degree in Iraq and Afghanistan, and the maintenance of an up-or-out promotion system in an age where specialization must occur not only in a given field, but also at a given rank. Other examples of well-intended practices that have had unpleasant outcomes:

- A larger than necessary officer corps at the middle and senior levels in order to prepare for mobilization of the Army to fight World War III employing an attrition doctrine. In June 2008 the Army added five more generals to its already bloated population of 308 generals.

- Fairness, transparency, objectivity are all good things, but they have led to a system that causes OERs to be "scored," making quantitatively commensurable things that should not be.

- The personnel system is simply a part of the larger constellation of management science, which in addition to the personnel bureaucracy gave us the program bureaucracy – operations research and cost/benefit analysis.

Instead, the Army and Marine Corps personnel system has become a weighted organization with its own logic, tradition and inertia. The implementation of new doctrinal and unit organizational, as well as educational and training reforms will take a long time given the current way of doing things and the Army bureaucracy's thick hide, its resistance to taking risks and making change. The journey will be worth the effort, however, as reforms replace DOD's, specifically the Army's and Marine Corps', personnel management science culture that is negatively focused to one that is human resource leadership focused, professional, and steeped in trust.

Conclusion: Where Have All the Mavericks Gone? Long Time Passing

In forcing this implementation, the Army needs to follow the lead of Army chief of staff, World War II and Korean War hero, Gen. Matthew Ridgway, who said, "My greatest contribution as chief of staff was to nourish the mavericks." To paraphrase the famous folk singers, Peter, Paul and Mary: "Where have all the mavericks gone? Long time passing."

Mavericks lead with courage, creativity, boldness, vision, and at times irreverence. The services must understand it is acceptable, even admirable, to have a love quarrel with the institution that they serve while still remaining loyal. The Army and the other services must adapt an organizational model and personnel system that will nourish the mavericks and keep them from leaving, thereby nurturing the innovators and not the saboteurs.

It is time the services paid attention to their officer corps and the need to become true professionals. True professional soldiers who are not popular in peacetime must be kept around because the art of war is best learned through the course of several campaigns. They will defend us in our old age, and more importantly, defend our progeny. No utopian, brave new, politically correct, gender neutral, nonlethal, high-tech-clean-war generation is stepping forward to replace the hard chargers now abandoning the Army, and none is going to.

It is time that we now lay the blame where the fault lies for this conversion of our Army to something less than it needs to be, and use the "L" word: leadership. Human resource leaders know that embracing change does not mean seizing upon every idea or opportunity. "Civilization didn't get this far by embracing every idea that came along; it got this far by accepting certain changes that were inevitable and certain others that were demonstrably beneficial, and by opposing, sometimes violently, changes that would have imperiled the species. Interesting, some think a good leader has to be a change killer as well as a change agent."[44]

In deciding what to keep and what to replace or reform, leaders of the Defense Department must always focus on the probability that in the future, wars may be very short and intense, requiring rapid and important decisions by many different levels of command. Much depends on proper planning and preparation to ensure that leaders and their units can perform in the best way possible during the critical initial days of combat. The Army, the military and nation may not have three years to prepare.

The Army, or any service for that matter, may not have sufficient time to organize to organize, so the Army (and DOD) needs to be ready beyond what technology can provide us. Such complex change requires leadership by extraordinary civilian and military leaders possessing vision. Our leaders must provide the beginnings to a revolution of change that is even more dramatic than the ones conducted by Elihu Root and George Marshall. Indeed, we need a generation of mavericks.

No one makes a better case for military mavericks than Secretary of Defense Gates and retired Col. Mike Wyly, U.S. Marine Corps. Gates and Wyly recognize the brilliance of one of DOD's most stellar mavericks, the late Col. John Boyd. Wyly wrote in the *Armed Forces Journal* of July 2008 of how Gates, inspired by "Genghis John" Boyd, called upon a gathering of young uniformed officers to be like the irreverent Boyd. Gates, using Boyd's own words, challenged these young officers to be principled, creative and reform-minded leaders who "want to do something, not be somebody." Wyly notes that for a defense secretary to quote the maverick Boyd, who left the Air Force as a pariah in the minds of some, was an incredibly bold and risky step. Nevertheless, Wyly lays bare how, today, we need brilliant mavericks throughout all the services with the abilities "to overcome bureaucratic resistance and institutional hostility."

ENDNOTES

1   Background for this paper began in 1998 with research for the book *Path to Victory: America's Army and the Revolution in Human Affairs* (Presidio, 2002), and continued with the self-imposed study "Raising the Bar: Developing and Nurturing Adaptability to Deal with the Changing Face of War," (March-May 2005), which in turn formed the foundation for the book by the same name (Center for Defense Information, Washington, D.C., November 2006).

2   Friedman, T. L., *The world is flat: A brief history of the twenty-first century* (New York: Farrar, Straus and Giroux, 2006).

3   Alan S. Blinder, *Paying for Productivity* (Washington, D.C.: The Brookings Institution, 1999), 13.

4   Peter F. Drucker, "Management's New Paradigms," *Forbes Magazine*, October 5, 1998, 152.

5   Officer Personnel Management System, "Council of Colonels 25-26 Oct 06," unpublished briefing, (Washington, D.C.: Department of the Army (October 2006), 213-214.

6   John Tillson, "Reducing the Impact of Tempo," (Alexandria, VA: Institute of Defense Analyses (IDA), 1999), S-3.

7   Rick Mustion, "Personnel Strategy Considerations," briefing, (Carlisle, PA: U.S. Army War College, 2001).

8 The authors would like to thank Mr. John Tillson, of the Institute of Defense of Analyses (IDA), and now a senior executive working with the Army in Germany for his insights and assistance. Tillson, "Reducing the Impact of Tempo," S-3.

9 Rickey Gibbs, "Determining the Appropriate Force Size Paradigm for the Army," Strategic Studies Institute, (Carlisle, PA: Army War College, 2004), 11.

10 Vandergriff, *Path to Victory*, 45-57.

11 Ibid.

12 Tillson, "Reducing the Impact of Tempo," 8.

13 Tillson, "Reducing the Impact of Tempo," 9.

14 Vandergriff, *Path to Victory*, 35.

15 Donald E. Vandergriff, "Culture Wars," *Digital Wars: A View from the Frontlines* (Novato, CA: Presidio Press, 1999), 78.

16 For a thorough assessment of OPMS 71, see William Hauser, "The Peacetime Army: Retrospect and Prospect," in Robin Higham and Carol Brandt, eds., *The United States Army in Peacetime* (Manhattan, KS: Military Affairs/Aerospace Publishing, 1975), 217. Also see, David McCormick, *The Downsized Warrior: America's Army in Transition* (New York, NY: New York University Press, 1998).

17 Harry J. Bondy, "Postmodernism and the Source of Military Strength in the Anglo West." *Armed Forces & Society* 31, no. 1 (November 2004).

18 Ibid, p. 3.

19 Lt. Col. Harry J. Bondy, "New Regiments, New Specialist Corps, and a New General Staff." *Journal of Military and Strategic Studies*, Canadian Defense and Foreign Affairs Institute, (Winter 2004): 3-5.

20 Interview with Major David Hunter, June 2, 2007.

21 Col. Stephen Jones, "Improving Accountability for Effective Command Climate: A Strategic Imperative," Strategic Studies Institute, (Carlisle, PA: U.S. Army War College, September 2003) p. 5.

22 Tillson, Reducing the Impact of Tempo, 19.

23 Author e-mail correspondence with Lt. Col. Harry J. Bondy, Canadian Army, April 2005. Also see: Harry Bondy, "New Regiments, New Specialist Corps, and A New General Staff." pp. 3-5. Available at http://www.jmss.org/2004/winter/articlesbody5.htm. Bondy and the author have shared many facts and ideas over the last few years. Many of the factors that affect the U.S. Army also affect the Canadian Army.

24 Colonel J.B. Burton, "Command's Feedback on Officer Critical Skills Retention Bonus," downloaded from the internet, (Iraq, 1st Cavalry Division, May 24, 2007).

25 U.S. Army, "OPMS Council of Colonels," unpublished power point presentation, (Alexandria, VA: Human Resources Command, October 2006), 4-5.

26 Vandergriff, *Raising the Bar*, pp. 77-79; while I call it Adaptive Course Model in the book, the Army has changed it first to Adaptive Leaders Course (ALC), then in December 2007, to Adaptive Leaders Methodology (ALM). Except for the name, nothing has changed.

27 John Boyd, "A Discourse on Winning and Losing," (unpublished briefing, Washington D.C.: August 1987), pp. 5-7. Available at http://www.d-n-i.net. We are also indebted to Col. T.X. Hammes, William S. Lind, Franklin Spinney, Col. G.I. Wilson and Greg Wilcox for their insights into 4th Generation Warfare

28 Boyd defined the "OODA loop" as a system of knowledge generation and decision-making whose components are observation, orientation, decision and action. See Boyd's "Discourse" for further explanation.

29 Chet Richards, *Certain to Win* (Philadelphia, PA: Xlibris, 2004), 61.

30 G.I. Wilson, *Business is war*, (1997) Retrieved November 21, 2007, from www.belisarius.com/modern_business_strategy/wilson/boyd_symposium_1997.htm

31 R. Slater, *Jack Welch and the GE way* (1st ed.), (New York: McGraw-Hill, 1999) 97.

32 Lisa Burgess, "Army Captains Offered up to $35,000 to stay," *Stars and Stripes*, September 19, 2007, http://www.military.com/features/0,15240,149817,00.html

33 Chet Richards, *A Swift, Elusive Sword: What if Sun Tzu and John Boyd Did a National Defense Review*, (Center for Defense Information, May 2001)

34 James Bennett, "So Many Officers Too Little to Do," *Washington Monthly*, (Washington, D.C.: Washington Monthly, February 1990), 4. Though this article was written 18 years ago, unfortunately, nothing has changed.

35 U.S. Army, "OPMS: Issues and Answers," (unpublished briefing, Washington, D.C. U.S. Army Human Resources Command, February 2006), S-2.

36 Donald E. Vandergriff, "An Invisible Revolution Sparked 3rd ID's Success," *Voice of the Grunt*, (October 2003)

37 http://en.wikipedia.org/wiki/Brigade_Combat_Team

38 U.S. Army, "Army Force Generation," *Army Knowledge Online*, http://www.army.mil/aps/07/addendum/h.html

39 U.S. Army, "The COHORT System: Is it meeting the Army's Needs?", (Washington, D.C. U.S. Army, June 6, 1988), 3. This was the last Army effort at unit manning at the company and battalion level from 1980-1990. "In its basic form, COHORT model sought to create an environment in which soldiers would feel a more genuine attachment to their fellow soldiers and to their units." Though considered successful by those who participated, and by the results of unit performance, the U.S. Army abolished the program at the end of the Gulf War citing that it was too difficult to maintain.

40 John Tillson, "Impact of Tempo," pp. 13-15.

41 Mark Lewis, "Time to Regenerate: A GenX Response to Dr. Wong's Monograph," (Arlington, VA: November 2000).

42 http://www.shsu.edu/~mls_www/Opportunities/smp/smp.html

43 http://www.amu.apus.edu/

44 R. A. Lutz, *Guts* (1st ed.), (New York: John Wiley and Sons, Inc. 1998), 196-197.

CHAPTER 4

MANEUVER FORCES
The Army and Marine Corps After Iraq

Col. Douglas Macgregor (U.S. Army. ret.)
and Col. G.I. Wilson (U.S. Marine Corps, ret.)

During the Cold War, the U.S. Army and Marines were designed to deploy and fight from bases in the United States, from allied territory or from the sea to protect U.S. vital strategic interests. Over time, Army and Marine forces evolved into single-service warfighting structures organized, trained and equipped to defeat enemies like those America fought in World War II, with occasional, unrewarding excursions into so-called low-intensity conflicts.

Today, those warfighting structures have reached block obsolescence. The strategic conditions that created them no longer exist. Today's single-service structures are too rigid and too complex to provide maneuver forces with the strategic agility they need to operate in settings where combatants and noncombatants are mixed, where the destruction of infrastructure and cultural assets is unacceptable, and where critical, time-sensitive, informed decisions must be made on the spot without waiting for permission from generals remote from the scene of the action.

These rigid, anachronistic force structures have created serious problems inside the Army and Marines that additional manpower and more money will not solve. These problems arise from single-service, World War II-style organizations for combat, inventories of aging, broken equipment thanks to unaffordable and mismanaged modernization programs, heavy operational dependence on fixed bases in Iraq and Afghanistan, disjointed rotational readiness policies, and, most importantly, an exodus of young talent out of the ground combat formations.

The situation inside the Army and Marines is made worse by a lack of leadership from the Department of Defense and Congress on defining genuine threats to America's vital strategic interests. Since 2001, basically anything could be and was claimed as an existential threat to the United States when none existed – China, Iran, Venezuela, Cuba, Islamist terrorists, and, more recently, a resurgent Russia. The next administration must clearly define what it sees as real threats and determine the right mixes of military capabilities to deal with them. Once those two steps are taken, the administration will find it must move the Army and Marines away from long-term occupations of foreign territory – operations that locals and the rest of the world see not as counterinsurgency, but as colonial warfare – and toward expeditionary warfare with defined, attainable *military* objectives, and homeland defense.

This paper argues that the nation needs maneuver forces organized and equipped to expand the nation's range of strategic options – forces capable of conducting joint, mobile, dispersed warfare operations against a mix of conventional and unconventional enemies.[1] No potential adversary of the United States will wittingly concentrate its forces to present U.S. strike assets with the target sets for which they are optimized. But to fight effectively in the environment of mobile, dispersed warfare that will include weapons of mass destruction (WMDs), the maneuver forces will need a new organization for combat within a new joint command and control structure along with a new approach to acquisition and modernization.

Fielding a maneuver force for the 21st century is an organizational marathon, not a sprint; and, one that holds flag officers and political appointees accountable for results. This means a reduction in spending combined with a laser-like focus on *people*, *ideas*, and *things* in that order.

These points not withstanding, if the next administration postpones fundamental reorganization and reform opting instead to harvest short-term savings by cutting big-dollar defense programs, nothing of importance in the Department of Defense will change. The entrenched Cold War institutions and force planning constructs that operate independently of any new national military strategy will ensure the nation's maneuver forces remain expensive tributes to the past. In time, these hugely expensive Cold War forces will both bankrupt the taxpayer and perpetuate anachronistic military organizations; weapon systems and ways of thinking that undermine U.S. national security by preparing soldiers and Marines for wars we shouldn't fight while preventing us from preparing for wars that may well be thrust upon us.

Strategic Confusion

The George W. Bush administration urged the leadership of the Army and the Marines to view operations in Iraq as the warfare of the future implying that the most dangerous adversary soldiers and Marines will have to fight is a weakly armed Muslim Arab rebel whose only hope of inflicting damage on U.S. forces is to engage in an insurgency directed against an unwanted U.S. military occupation.[2] But why would the United States ever willingly seize control of another Muslim country, occupy it and then fight a rebellion (insurgency) against the U.S. military's unwanted presence in that country?[3] American military occupation seems to aggravate the problem of Islamist terrorism rather than solve it.[4]

The American military experience in Southwest Asia reinforces the importance of employing means other than raw military power to cope with Islamist terrorism. The 21st century Islamist terrorist lives anywhere and everywhere; connected by the Internet. He is known more by his ideology than by his race, color, creed, national origin or geographic location and he is defined by his affinity for destructive ideologies or intents. To the contemporary terrorist, the structures and institutions of globalizing influence are high-value targets. The terrorist thrives in the midst of resistive populations making the use of destructive and lethal force difficult, if not impossible in most cases. In this environment, actions to disenfranchise, disarm, dishearten and demoralize the Islamist terrorist and his potential recruits promise to achieve more success than brute force.

This is why the idea that hundreds of thousands of conventional American combat troops with some combination of better counterinsurgency tactics and massive economic investment could create a Western-style democratic nation-state where none exists in Iraq or Afghanistan was delusional. It ignored the fact that the foundation for liberal democratic institutions in the rump of Germany under Allied control was already in place before U.S. forces occupied it in 1945. German reconstruction after World War II was an exercise in Allied supervision of re-emergent indigenous German institutions of self-government and economic development that predated Hitler by over 150 years.[5] In Japan, the U.S. occupation authorities worked within a similar pre-existing institutional framework legitimated by the Japanese emperor and reinforced through the deliberate U.S. restoration of control of the Japanese economy in 1947 to pre-war Japanese business and political interests.[6]

Thus, trying to export democracy at gunpoint with masses of U.S. ground troops is delusional. Large conscript ground forces are rarely well-trained or effectively commanded, and although capable of great carnage, it's often the ground forces themselves, in the form of half-trained and ill-led troops that blunder into war's meat grinder. This was often the case in both World Wars, in Korea and Vietnam. And Americans have seen some of the same behavior in Iraq. In fact, unless American military occupation forces are prepared to slaughter the occupied peoples in the style of the Roman legions or the Mongol armies, Western armies in developing countries will always fail to overpower what is fundamentally a historically conditioned, internal, bottom-up, self-organizing evolutionary, cultural process: nation-building.[7]

These points suggest that intervention in so-called failed states is usually counterproductive. Unless the failure presents a direct security threat to U.S. and allied interests, intervention is an opportunity to waste blood and treasure on the scale seen in Iraq and not much more. The American military experience in Southwest Asia argues against the kind of brute force employed in Iraq. Actions to disenfranchise, disarm, dishearten and demoralize the terrorist and his potential recruits offer far better means to overcome this enemy than brute force whether it comes in the form of massive air strikes or large conventional forces.

None of these insights make predicting when and where Army and Marine forces will fight any easier. The truth is history is littered with wars nobody thought would happen.

For instance, a sudden North Korean meltdown is a real possibility that would demand the rapid occupation of North Korea by forces from the Republic of Korea. U.S. ground forces might well be needed to sortie into the collapsing communist state in order to secure control of its nuclear facilities, an operation that might well include some stiff conventional fighting along the way. Similar events could occur in Pakistan where nuclear weapons could fall into very dangerous hands indeed.

In the competition for energy resources, yesterday's ally could become tomorrow's opponent. Army and Marine forces might well be employed in joint operations to facilitate, and if necessary guarantee, U.S. access to energy resources. The growing competition between energy and food markets offers a glimpse of future conflict that will stem from the convergence of resource depletion, intractable, uneven global economic development and large-scale cultural change. Inside the United States, a future biological attack could result in the commitment of U.S. Army forces to quell food and water riots while the troops quarantine large urban areas.[8]

Defense spending in adjusted dollars is now higher than at any point since the end of World War II. After Sept. 11, 2001, the massive flow of cash into the Pentagon made tough decisions regarding these matters impossible, but the decline in American economic performance may finally compel unity of effort through more effective integration of capabilities across service lines.[9] The question is: How to do it?

What is to be done?

In the 21st century, military power is no longer based on the mobilization of the manpower and industrial resources of the entire nation-state. The requirement today is for highly skilled, lethal professional combat forces that are capable of rapidly responding to military contingencies on short notice. Compensating for existing deficiencies in Army and Marine warfighting structures by binding ground forces more tightly within networked systems won't work and it's prohibitively expensive. Networking thousands of single-service command and control (C2) nodes is no substitute for a new joint operational architecture tied to a joint operational concept that integrates maneuver, strike, and information, intelligence, surveillance and reconnaissance (IISR) and sustainment across service lines.

The point is Cold War single-service command structures have too many echelons; too many nodes and they are too slow to act.[10] Configuring divisions in smaller pieces under the guise of modularity changes nothing in the way ground forces operate; they do not reduce or eliminate echelons of unneeded C2, nor advance unity of effort (*Jointness*).

As a result, closing the gap between the Cold War force with new equipment the generals want, the maneuver force the United States needs and the maneuver force the American people can afford is the problem that must be solved. Solving this problem requires the next administration to impose some realistic thinking on the Army and Marines.

- Mobile dispersed warfare has replaced warfare with defined, continuous fronts as the dominant form of combat for the foreseeable future. Ubiquitous strike capabilities and the proliferation of WMD make the concentration of large conventional or unconventional forces very dangerous, if not impossible.

• Surrounded on two sides by the world's largest oceans, 95 percent of all U.S. exports and imports move by sea, making the maintenance of U.S. naval and aerospace supremacy a precondition for American prosperity and survival.[11] This strategic condition constrains the size of maneuver forces in expeditionary warfare, Army and Marine.

• Any enemy attempting to defend a beach will be targeted and destroyed from the air. The more likely scenario involves area denial operations that capitalize on sea mines and unmanned systems to protect critical approaches from the sea, while dispersed enemy forces (nonstate or state actors) defend from positions inland. Thus, the Marines are much more likely to conduct operations like the Army than they are to re-enact an Inchon landing.

• In the 21st century "adaptive hybrid opponents" employing both conventional and unconventional organizations and tactics with access to sophisticated technology are causing Army and Marine missions and organizations to converge. Where it makes sense to do so, American defense planning should capitalize on the convergence. This includes the use of maneuver forces in homeland defense.

• The single-service command and control structures of the past along with the maneuver forces' tactical organizations for combat – Army/Marine Corps Expeditionary Force, division, brigade and battalion – are not strategically relevant. "Flattened" integrated, Joint C2 is vital if initiative has any chance of working at the lower end of complex modern military organizations.[12] Every additional link in the chain of command reduces the effect of an order by the process of transferring information; and by the additional time needed to pass it on.

Centralized, single-service, top-down controlled maneuver forces on the WW II model will not defeat decentralized conventional or unconventional forces organized for mobile dispersed warfare.[13] (Figure 1 on the next page.) Mobile dispersed warfare, whether waged by guerilla fighters in Afghanistan or Latin America or conventional forces from Asia or Europe demands Joint C2 structures that accelerate decision cycles and integrate the functions of maneuver, strike, IISR, and sustainment across service lines on the operational level of war. What is not needed is the kind of convoluted C2 Americans have in Baghdad – roughly one general officer, plus his staff and security detail, for nearly every maneuver battalion in Iraq.

Figure 1.
The problem: too many single serve C2 echelons, too slow to decide,
too expensive to modernize, too vulnerable to WMD

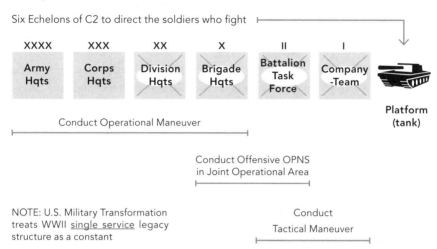

NOTE: U.S. Military Transformation
treats WWII <u>single service</u> legacy
structure as a constant

In the years since World War II, the greatest institutional obstacle to this understanding and the emergence of a new integrated, joint warfare paradigm is the division
echelon, a formation that is undeserving of its sacred status as Brig. Gen. Richard
Simpkin pointed out 30 years ago.

> Before looking at future force structures in any detail, we need to rid ourselves
> of a sacred cow – the division. This is in fact no more than another step down
> an evolutionary path marked out by technological advance. The "division" is
> an ancient and important tactical concept, but the idea of the division as the
> key organizational formation ... does not seem to go back much beyond the
> middle of the nineteenth century ... the more recent the tradition, the hotter
> and more irrational the defense of it.[14]

Many of the changes in the structures and decision-making processes found in
the American commercial sector have reached similar conclusions about the role of
management and the locus of decision-making.[15] Business and military theorist, John
Boyd, contended there is a direct relationship between strategy and change. Thus, the
purpose of strategy is to improve our ability to shape and adapt to circumstances, so
that we (as individuals or as groups or as a culture or as a nation-state) can survive
on our own terms.[16] In business, changing shape and perpetual fluidity in response
to market demands is vital to survival.[17]

Jack Welch, former CEO of General Electric, implored his employees to face reality and change each morning for each morning is different from the last. What was important yesterday may no longer be important today. Welch was not afraid of going back on something and giving new direction; Welch sees "willingness to change" and constantly looking at things anew as a leadership strength.[18] The same applies to forces engaged in mobile dispersed warfare.

In mobile dispersed warfare, the word modular translates as stand-alone. The current regimental and brigade formations inside Army and Marine divisions cannot stand alone, which is why they continue to be dramatically reinforced for operations in Iraq and remain acutely dependent on division, corps and Army echelons for direction and support. Thus, any new formation that replaces the brigade or division must be modular and, of necessity, integrate the command element, the desired capability and the support element into stand-alone force packages. Fortunately, disassembling Army and Marine divisions and reorganizing them into mission-focused force packages that can be assembled like Legos into larger joint operations forces is not difficult and it has been done before.

During World War II, the Army's armored divisions followed the German military example and reorganized their fighting forces into two combat commands of roughly 5,000 men each inside divisions. A brigadier general commanded each. What kept the division command echelon in the fight was the inability of World War II communications technology to routinely link higher commanders to their subordinate elements over large distances. Today, this is no longer an obstacle to change. Further, new technology confers the ability on Army and Marine ground forces to combine maneuver and strike capabilities in ways that create more options for commanders on the operational and strategic levels, ways that pose more complex threats to new kinds of enemies.

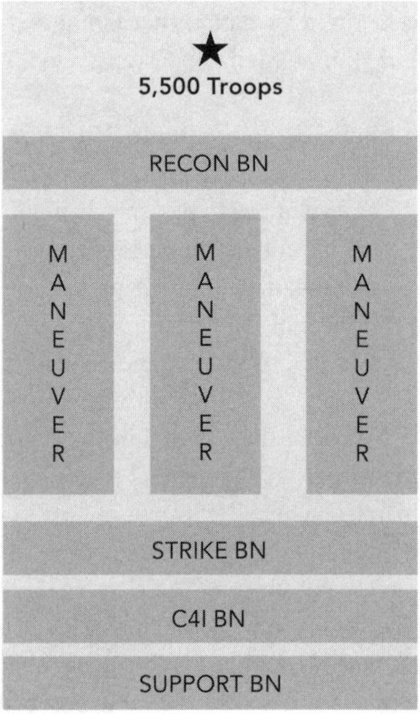

Mimicking the combat commands of long ago means compressing regiments, brigades and divisions into a new fighting echelon of 5,000 to 6,000 man combat groups or battle groups organized functionally as maneuver, strike, IISR, or sustainment formations. (Figure 2.) The resulting formations become specialized modules of

Figure 2.

Figure 3.
Integrated C² Structure for a Combat Maneuver Group

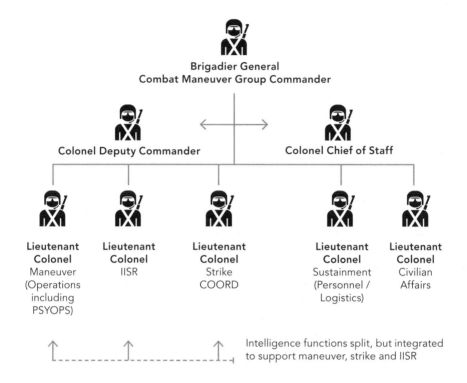

Intelligence functions split, but integrated to support maneuver, strike and IISR

combat power that have the capacity for self-contained, dispersed tactical operations on land reminiscent of the way ships operate at sea. With the kind of Joint C4ISR connectivity that exists at division levels introduced into the functionally organized combat groups, the new formations can plug directly into joint command and control structures. (Figure 3.) At current force levels, the Army and Marine Corps could easily field 42 to 44 5,500-man combat groups (manned at 6,000 men) for close combat (252,000 men).

Compelling the Army to adopt the naval rotational readiness model for expeditionary warfare will also improve unity of effort and rationalize the training, modernization, deployment and reconstitution of its forces in coordination with the maneuver, strike, IISR and sustainment forces inside the Navy, Marine Corps and Air Force. Reorganizing Army and Marine forces along these lines would provide a ready, deployable combat force of 60,000 soldiers and Marines including 35,000 troops, trained and equipped inside six combat maneuver groups for close combat.19 The additional

25,000 would come from a pool of 125,000 troops consisting of supporting groups organized for sustainment, IISR or strike operations depending on the mission.

Of course, committing a 60,000 man expeditionary force to a regional unified command within 30 to 45 days from the moment the national command authorities determine to use it requires the nation to provide the sealift and the airlift to move it. But knowing the size and capabilities of the ground maneuver force does provide a concrete target for the construction of ships and aircraft to do the job, something that is missing from current defense planning.

Surging additional forces to a regional unified command from the pool of Army and Marine forces in the rotational readiness system could commence as soon as the air and naval assets to move them were available. Within 90 days, an expeditionary maneuver force of 120,000 soldiers and Marines could be deployed and ready to fight in any of the regional unified commands. If required, the expeditionary force could be relieved in another six months by a similar force of 120,000. Or a second force of 120,000 could be deployed to yet another theater if conditions warranted it.

The 298,000 soldiers and Marines not assigned to the pool of 377,000 soldiers and Marines inside maneuver forces on rotational readiness would be available to man the training, administrative and support structures in the United States and the regional unified commands. The Army National Guard and Reserve could also be reorganized to mirror this organizational paradigm in rotational windows that make sense for citizen soldiers and ensure their readiness to conduct expeditionary or homeland defense operations if needed.

Building Joint C2 while trimming unneeded overhead

The idea that a Marine flag officer or an Army general could command the forces of the other service is anathema. Both services seem to have forgotten that in World War I when Gen. John J. Pershing had to replace the Army major general who commanded the Army's 2nd Infantry Division, a division that also contained two brigades of Marine infantry, he selected Marine Corps Brig. Gen. John Archer LeJeune for the command. LeJeune commanded the division with distinction and went on to become the Marine Corps commandant after the war. Returning to this kind of jointness demands an integrated joint C2 structure that compels officers from different services to cross service lines to be effective. Fortunately, the standard for a joint force-capable headquarters is well known.

A joint force headquarters must have the capability to command and control integrated joint operations to accomplish missions in a defined joint operations area. This capability demands the ability to employ assigned and attached forces, including multinational forces, as well as coordinating and integrating intergovernmental and nongovernmental organizations and multinational partners' support.

For joint C2 to be meaningful, flag officers must be drawn from all services, not just the Army or the Marines. Adding joint plugs and liaison officers to redundant and expensive single-service division, corps and Army headquarters is not the answer. It is nothing more than premium platinum layering.

Joint C2 must focus on integrated force design and a universal command web. The operational driver is the streamlining and integration of systems, service headquarters, and operational elements, NOT the proliferation of them. It is difficult, if not impossible at times to share information and intelligence due to single-service interface issues, politics, and physics. Our single-service mindset often witnesses the hoarding of intelligence and information rather than it being put to use. So too the cloak-and-dagger aspects of classification across the services overtake the fundamentals means of exploiting information and intelligence. This unwittingly preempts integrated maneuver.

The organizing imperative must be the integration of maneuver and strike assets through a flatter operational architecture empowered by new terrestrial and space-based communications. With the right collaborative tools and systems architecture, there is no reason why a joint force command (JFC) cannot effectively command a joint expeditionary force of soldiers and marines plus routine operational control of available air and naval strike assets. Ideally, a JFC should be a lean entity along the lines envisioned by Lesley McNair for World War II corps headquarters, and it should be prepared to take on whatever combat power is assigned.

The mission to implement this operational concept inside the JFC falls to the lieutenant general or vice admiral in the JFC. (Figure 4 on the next page.) With the expansion of American strike, intelligence and information assets, the JFC commander must be supported by deputy commanders and staffs that can employ the full compliment of air, ground, electronic information and logistical capabilities.

The deputy commander for maneuver inside the JFC directs the operations of the ground maneuver. As a major general, he brings an appreciation of the critical role that positional advantage plays in the calculus of warfare to the planning and execution of operations. Since attacks against U.S. forces will blur the distinction between sea and land combat, particularly in future battles for control of coastal regions, his role in the decision to commit ground forces is enormously important.

The IISR deputy commander will build, maintain and disseminate the common operating picture. This mission decrees that his responsibilities might range from launching battlefield satellites to tasking UAVs and Special Operations forces for reconnaissance missions. Thus, the integration of intelligence and information operations with reconnaissance and surveillance efforts under one deputy commander in the JFC is vital to the maintenance of a coherent operational picture of the battlespace.

Another major general or vice admiral (lower half) must command strike operations. His mission is to de-conflict and harmonize strike and maneuver operations in any fight, thus preventing fratricide. To date, the Army has resisted the creation of a

Figure 4.

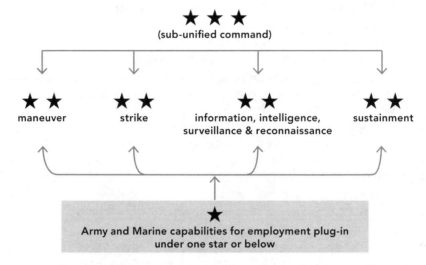

Command and control structures in the regional unified commands
must ensure that all Services act as a single unified force

uniform strike structure across the joint force designed to disrupt and shatter enemy ability to decide and act effectively and quickly. This is a mistake.

For a strategy of ground force maneuver to succeed, the means to employ strike assets are critical. The links from the deputy commander for strike to maneuver formations, as well as to the global strike complex, are pivotal.[20] With his links to strike coordination officers in every ground maneuver force, the deputy commander for strike can exploit capabilities residing in all strike and maneuver forces to suppress or defeat enemy air defenses, as well as enemy missile attacks.

Joint force commanders know they will have to command and control smaller force modules over greater distances in the future as already seen in Iraq and Afghanistan. For these reasons, a flag officer with the authority to direct sustainment operations across service lines is vital. Over time, the transition to progressively newer tactical forms in joint mobile dispersed warfare will only reinforce the need for greater independence in tactical formations and completely eliminate the concept of a rear area, except in the sense of a communications zone.[21]

The joint C2 structure described here will ensure that allied forces and services within an operational command would fight as a single unified force.[22] It would make sense to assign at least two or three JFCs in each regional unified command to supplant the single service operational structures. How many more should exist is a matter for decision by the national command authorities.

These changes in operational control should also involve commensurate reductions in unneeded Army and Marine Corps overhead. If done well, reducing and, where possible, consolidating the services' four star and three star institutional, administrative, logistical and training commands will return the personnel savings to Active component (AC) and Reserve component (RC) units with operational missions and also rationalize the distribution of tasks relating to the readiness and training of all maneuver forces, along with the development of weapons, equipment, force design and operational art.

Discarding the Industrial-Age acquisition paradigm

History demonstrates that cancelling a few billion dollar programs like the Future Combat System (FCS) and the Expeditionary Fighting Vehicle (EFV) will have minimal impact on the way the Army and the Marine Corps develop and field new equipment unless the structure, culture and thinking that drive current acquisition programs changes. It is far more important for the next administration to do what the Bush administration did not – move away from the industrial age Cold War production lines and dismantle the multi-decade acquisition system that defense contractors know and love.

From the beginning, FCS made no sense. The notion that FCS's software-dependent networked "system of systems" would eliminate the close fight in war by delivering on its promise of *perfect situational awareness* – a condition of superior knowledge of the enemy and his intentions, and of the friendly force[23] – was always unrealistic. Many of the FCS program's key components that are promoted as break-through capabilities are, in fact already, present on current battlefields. It is very hard to see what FCS will provide for $200 billion that the Army does not already have now.[24] Meanwhile, the cost of maintaining the Army's aging fleets of armored fighting vehicles developed in the 1970s for use in the 1980s and 1990s will soon reach $2 billion per year.[25]

Like the Army, the Marine Corps has worn out much of its equipment in Afghanistan and Iraq, and now wants large sums of money to pay for the force the Commandant says he needs.[26] However, the Marines are not addressing their shortfall in off-road mobility, armored protection and firepower discovered during the Marines' hard fighting in Iraq's Anbar province.[27] In a report to Congress, the Marine Corps inspector general asserted that the 30,000 Marines in Iraq needed twice as many heavy machine guns, more fully protected armored vehicles, and more communications equipment to operate in Anbar, an area the size of Utah.[28]

Instead, the Marines' are pressing their internally generated demand to conduct both missions – amphibious assault from the sea and warfighting operations on land. The Marine Corps leadership asked General Dynamics (GD) to develop the EFV, which was conceived as both a true amphibian that would operate with equal efficiency as a boat in the water and as an armored fighting vehicle (AFV) on land. It has been in development for over a decade. Unfortunately, whatever GD has done to increase the

EFV's land-combat capability has also detracted from its ship-to-shore, high-speed, over-the-horizon, attack mission. Originally, the Marine Corps wanted 1,014 EFVs, but the laws of physics combined with questions about the utility of re-enacting World War II amphibious assaults have reduced that number to roughly 400 at an estimated cost of $22 million each,[29] or nearly five times the cost of an M1A1 tank.[30]

If the Marines are going to be employed together with Army forces far from the sea as they are today in Afghanistan and Iraq, then, Marines should be equipped to do the job.[31] Dragging amphibious tractors designed to ferry Marines from ship to shore 300 miles inland is stupid.[32] In fact, it's worse than stupid because it puts the lives of Marines at unnecessary risk.[33]

In a perfect world, the Joint Capabilities Integration and Development System (JCIDS) as codified in the Chairman of the Joint Chiefs of Staff Instruction No. 3170.01F would help solve these problems, but it doesn't. JCIDS is just the latest in a line of requirements generations systems that are predominantly focused on "authorizing" procurement of material solutions; material solutions created inside the services' Cold War bureaucracies.

JCIDS is a year long process that starts a two-year budget cycle. At best, this represents a 36-month combined cycle before the defense community can field a solution to a requirement put in at the front end of the process (excluding urgent operational needs that shorten the process to about 6 to 18 months depending on the complexity of the solution/testing, etc.). The combatant commanders' (COCOM) planning horizon normally reaches out to 18 months, so the COCOM's advocacy of capabilities is disconnected from "long lead" procurement planning and execution. While the JCIDS process, Functional Capabilities Board Validation and JROC review and approval system promise greater warfighter influence, in practice the acquisition community and the technologists lead and dominate.

Part of the solution to this problem involves reform and a re-allocation of the power and the authority to new decision-makers with their roots in the warfighting community. But any solution also argues for a concomitant cultural change driven by a philosophy of acquisition that is very different from the thinking of the industrial age that plagues the big defense programs. When it comes to acquiring technology, the defense leadership must consider that a civilization didn't get this far by embracing every idea that came along. It got this far by accepting certain changes that were inevitable and certain others that were demonstrably beneficial, and by opposing, sometimes violently, changes that would have imperiled the species. With these points in mind, consider the following as the basis for a new philosophy of acquisition and modernization:

- Effectiveness in action is measured in terms of capabilities. New capabilities really emerge when soldiers employ new technology in a climate of innovation, and develop the concepts and organizations to exploit them.

- When it comes to rapid prototyping, always go for the most "bang for the buck." Buy the maximum amount of capability affordable at the time. The newest and greatest systems today will be outdated and bordering on obsolescence by the time the procurement process ends and fielding begins. Set the bar as high as possible, but stick with the concept of a *"good enough capability"* based on the best available technology.

- Given the pace of technological change, today's "gold-plated wonder weapons" are tomorrow's commercial off-the-shelf products. Invest in promising proto-types, but in small quantities before billions are invested, under conditions where the new technology can find its way into unintended uses, keeping in mind that technologies do not arrive without a price in cost, schedule and complexity – or that there are easy, quick fixes.

Opposition to rapid prototyping, however, remains strong. It stems from the established bureaucratic practice of controlling programs to reduce risk by organizing development around time-driven phases separated in time by approval points or milestones. In truth, this approach is a prescription for obsolescence years later when and if the promised gold-plated system arrives. And it is the antithesis of how businesses are run.

Applying business practices to the defense acquisition system means that account-ability must be assigned to uniformed and civilian leaders involved in acquisition for the maintenance of cost, schedule and delivery of a product that meets warfighter needs. The business world examines the efficient use of resources to sustain and grow market shares. The Department of Defense, including the Army and the Marine Corps must do the same.[34]

Conclusions

Armed Forces are more than military organizations. They are spiritual bodies vulnerable to the myth-making power of popular military history and the media. But myths do not trump the powerful technological, social and economic forces that shape history and these forces do not allow the nation's armies, navies and air forces to exist in a vacuum.[35] Either Americans adapt the old structures to new strategic conditions or we risk catastrophic defeat at the hands of a more agile opponent in the years ahead. It's also important to remember that as adaptation occurs, it is easier for the American military establishment to step down to fight a weak opponent than it is to step up and fight a strong one.

Change in leadership, structure and thinking will not be easy in the Army or the Marines. America's bureaucrats in uniform convey the impression of tolerating the civilian service secretaries who hold statutory legal authority over the services, but in reality, the generals and admirals treat them as liaison officers to Congress with the mission to secure from lawmakers whatever the service chiefs deem essential. The idea that a civilian appointee would exercise any real authority over the armed forces is actually repugnant to the service chiefs.[36] Even worse, despite the democratic demand for accountability from generals in wartime, in the absence of an existential threat to the United States and its military establishment, the demand has usually been frustrated by the generals as seen in Iraq and Afghanistan.

This is why change is not a mission for the generals and admirals who lead the defense bureaucracies. It's a mission for the civilians who are elected and appointed to command the nation's military establishments. Only resolute civilian leadership can break through the service-dominated decision-making processes and replace the old World War II/Cold War paradigm with a new paradigm that results in decisions that rationalize force design and acquisition.[37]

America needs a new operational military command structure to replace the joint staff and the JCS. Critical acquisition decisions must also be evaluated on a national level based on determined national needs by a unified general staff populated with competent officers who owe their allegiance to the national military system, not to the services. This system will have to be far more modern in outlook than the Prussian general staff system.

The national general staff system America needs must take control of officers' careers at the 0-5/lieutenant colonel/commander level and manage them to flag rank and beyond. Such a system must involve rigorous testing and evaluation to ensure the officer's grasp of technology, history, geography and culture, things of no consequence in the system of cronyism that currently dominates promotions. Military education must grow teeth, failing officers who do not perform, something that does not happen today. The system must also ignore service identity for flag rank selection inside an integrated, joint command structure making it harder for any one service to dominate large-scale operations and commands.

This kind of rational change will have an uphill climb against the generals' and the admirals' conventional wisdom. Senior military leaders who are easily threatened by new ideas frequently view new strategies, tactics and technologies that promise results and fewer casualties with suspicion and discomfort. Even after two years of bloody fighting in the trenches of World War I, Gen. Sir Douglas Haig, commander in chief of British Expeditionary Forces in France, thought the machine gun "a much over-rated weapon."[38] The truth is the nation's armed forces cannot reform themselves.

The real question is whether the next group of civilians who lead the Department of Defense will be unafraid to challenge the bureaucrats in uniform who lead the services? It is no understatement to suggest that the nation's security and prosperity depend on it.

ENDNOTES

1   Agence France-Presse, "U.S. Concerned About Spread of Insurgent Tactics from Iraq to North Africa," *Defense News*, June, 27 2005.

2   Thom Shanker, "Gates Says New Arms Must Play Role Now," *Colorado Springs Gazette*, May 14, 2008.

3   Thomas Friedman, "Who Will Tell the People?" *New York Times*, May, 4 2008.

4   Given the huge tooth to tail ratio of U.S. Army and Marine forces operating from fixed bases in Iraq, every additional soldier, Marine or U.S. paid mercenary that joins the "coalition" occupation force becomes a recruiting poster for the insurgents, a drain on the economy of the United States and the basis for a false, unsustainable economy in Iraq. See Rami G. Khouri, "America through Arab eyes," *International Herald Tribune*, April, 21 2008.

5   [i] Christopher J. Coyne, *After War. The Political Economy of Exporting Democracy* (Stanford, Calif.: Stanford University Press, 2008).

6   Ibid.

7   Suggested to the author by Steve Daskall, intelligence analyst.

8   Spencer Ackerman, "Obama's knowledge of Self," *The Washington Independent*, June 11, 2008. See Dr. Danzig's comments on mitigating the risks of biological attack.

9   Liz Rappaport and Justin Lahart, "Debt Reckoning: U.S. Receives a Margin Call," *Wall Street Journal,* March 15, 2008.

10 Tony Capaccio, "Pentagon Projects Weapons Spending To Rise 20% From 2009-2013," *Bloomberg News*, February 21, 2008.

11 General Sir John Hackett, *The Profession of Arms* (London: Sidgwick and Jackson, 1983).

12 William A. Owens, *Lifting the Fog of War* (New York: Farrar, Straus and Giroux, 2000).

13 Dr. David Johnson, *Arroyo Center project on Echelonment in Army organizations* (Santa Monica, Calif.: Rand Corporation, 2003).

14 Richard E. Simpkin, *Race to the Swift: Thoughts on Twenty-First Century Warfare* (London: Brassey's, 1985).

15 John Arquilla and David Ronfeldt, *In Athena's Camp: Preparing for Conflict in the Information Age* (Santa Monica, CA: RAND, 1997).

16 John R. Boyd, *Patterns of Conflict,* 1987, 1. (unpublished briefing available at http://www.d-n-i.net/boyd/patterns.ppt)

17 Tom Peters, *Liberation Management: Necessary Disorganization for the Nanosecond Nineties* (New York: Fawcett Columbine, 1992).

18 Robert Slater, *Jack Welch & The G.E. Way: Management Insights and Leadership Secrets of the Legendary CEO* (New York: McGraw-Hill, 1998), 18.

19 In *Iraqi Freedom*, Army brigades in 3ID and marine regiments in the 1st marine division had to be augmented to operate across the country in a non-contiguous environment. This resulted in brigade combat teams (BCTs) ranging from 5,000 to 7,000 men that contained the armed reconnaissance, sustainment, and combat power to operate independently. What they did not have that resided largely at division and corps were the joint C4ISR plugs and the armed reconnaissance. Most important, as they grew in size and complexity, the BCTs were really too challenging for a colonel with a staff of captains, and two majors to handle on an ad hoc basis.

20 Richard Hart Sinnreich, "Air-Ground Integration Requires More Than Patchwork," *Lawton Constitution*, October 6, 2002.

21 Alvin Bernstein and Martin C. Libicki, "High-Tech: The Future of War? A Debate," *Commentary*, January 1998.

22 Michael Deane, Ilana Kass, and Andrew Porth, "The Soviet Command Structure in Transformation," *Strategic Review* (Spring 1984): 64–65. Notice, however, that fronts (equivalent in size to American armies) were also fully joint commands. When the Soviet Union's 40th Army deployed to Afghanistan in 1979, it did so as part of a JTF structure that was fully joint. On the other hand, jointness stopped at the JTF level, which caused serious problems below.

23 Dependence on other programs like JTRS and TSAT presents additional problems. TSAT is crucial to FCS secure networking capabilities. If TSAT collapses, which looks like a distinct possibility, soldiers may have to rely on links that are harder to access on the move, more vulnerable to jamming and interceptions, and offer nowhere near as much bandwidth. See Alec Klein, "Weapons Upgrade Faces Big Hurdles: Problems With Wireless Technology May Threaten Army's Ambitious Plan," *Washington Post*, April 8, 2008.

24 Kris Osborn, "Battle Command' Summits. U.S. Army Brings Experts Together For IT Roadmap," *DefenseNews.com*, February 4, 2008.

25 Marina Malenic and Daniel Wasserbly, "Abercrombie skeptical of acceleration talk. FCS funds hang in balance as lawmakers focus on current readiness," *Inside the Army*, February 25, 2008.

26 Sydney J. Freedberg Jr., "Future Corps. The Marine Corps, like the Army, has worn out a lot of equipment in Afghanistan and Iraq, and is facing big bills to pay for the future force it says it needs." *National Journal*, May 10, 2008.

27 Ellen Knickmeyer, "Demise Of A Hard-Fighting Squad. Marines Who Survived Ambush Are Killed, Wounded in Blast," *Washington Post*, May 12, 2005.

28 Bryan Bender, "Marine Units Found To Lack Equipment, Corps estimates of needs in Iraq are called faulty," *Boston Globe*, June 21, 2005.

29 Given the dramatic changes in the technology of warfare since World War II, any contemporary American military attempt today to reenact *Operation Cobra*, the breakout from Normandy, or *Operation Iceberg*, the invasion of Okinawa, with an opponent that has access to a fraction of the modern technology that is available now would court disaster. Large concentrations of U.S. ground forces whether on land or at sea invite enemy attack with weapons of mass destruction (WMD) before the fighting even begins.

30 "Last Chance For The EFV," *Strategy Page*, June 11, 2008. EFV weighs nearly 36 tons, is 10.5 feet tall, 12 feet wide and just under 30 feet long. It's armed with one 30-mm automatic cannon (MK34 Bushmaster) and one 7.62-mm co-axial machine gun.

31 Alex Berenson, "Fighting the Old-Fashioned Way in Najaf," *The New York Times*, August 29, 2004.

32 Associated Press, "Study Faults Bureaucrats For Deaths Of Marines. Missteps slowed delivery of blast-resistant vehicles," *Arizona Republic*, February 16, 2008.

33 Michael Moss, "Safer Vehicles for Soldiers: A Tale of Delays and Glitches," *New York Times*, June 26, 2005.

34 Adm. William Owens, "The Business of Defense Does Matter" (to be published).

35 Alfred Vagts, *A History of Militarism: Civilian and Military* (New York: The Free Press, 1959).

36 Alfred Vagts, *A History of Militarism: Civilian and Military* (New York: The Free Press, 1959).

37 The Unified Command Plan (UCP), the Joint Strategic Capabilities Plan (JSCP), and the Forces for Memorandum are outputs of this process. The UCP and JSCP are produced biennially. The Forces for Memorandum is produced annually. The process implements the Chairman of the Joint Chiefs of Staff (CJCS) legal obligation for strategic planning. It is conducted by the joint staffs of the CJCS and the unified commands.

38 Alfred Vagts, *A History of Militarism: Civilian and Military* (New York: The Free Press, 1959).

CHAPTER 5

A TRAVELER'S PERSPECTIVE ON THIRD AND FOURTH GENERATION WARFARE

William S. Lind

The central problem facing the United States military is how to move from Second to Third Generation War, which is to say from French attrition warfare to German maneuver warfare, while simultaneously thinking through the challenge posed by Fourth Generation War (4GW).

Late last year, I had the opportunity to travel to two countries, Islandia and the Austro-Hungarian Empire, whose armed forces have made important progress on both of those tasks. The Islandian Marine Corps has adopted a highly innovative force structure, expressive of both the concepts and the culture of maneuver warfare that could serve as a model for the United States Marine Corps.

As is well known, Islandia is an independent nation located at the southern end of the Karain subcontinent (for a basic history of Islandia, see "Islandia" by Austin Tappan Wright [Holt, Rinehart and Winston, Inc., 1944]; for an update, see "The Islar" by Mark Saxton (New York, N.Y.: Signet Books, 1971]).[1] While Islandia's national security requirements differ substantially from those of the U.S. government, Islandia is the only country besides the United States to maintain a large Marine Corps.

Islandian Marine Corps Force Structure

The Islandian Marine Corps of 175,000 men is structured as 175 active-duty battalions of 1,000 men each. Each active-duty battalion has two mirror-image reserve battalions, both made up of veterans of the active battalion. On mobilization, it can triple in size in a matter of days, with cohesive, well-trained reserve units.

An unusual feature of the Islandian Marine Corps is that all Islandian Marines are at all times on the muster rolls of a battalion. This includes even the Commandant. The purpose, as Lord Dorn, the commandant of the Islandian Marine Corps, explains below, is transparency. At any time, it is easy to see where Marines are and what they are doing.

Each battalion keeps a muster roll, updated monthly, showing both total strength and the location of each marine, e.g., Cpl. Hythe Eck, a light machine gunner, 2nd fire team, 3rd squad, 3rd platoon, Company A. A Marine detached for school, staff assignment or senior command is still carried on the muster roll with his current location, e.g., commander, 2nd Marine Division. Officers above the rank of lieutenant colonel who are normally assigned away from the battalion are grouped on the muster roll as "supernumeraries."

In the Islandian Marine Corps' 175 active battalions, 100 are combat battalions, of which there are 48 light infantry battalions, 18 fire support battalions, six combat engineer battalions, six reconnaissance battalions and six light armor battalions. There are also 16 aviation battalions called "squadrons," again each of 1000 men. The strength of all Islandian units is defined by personnel count, not equipment count.

50 logistics battalions support these 100 combat battalions. By historical and world standards, this 1-to-2 ratio of logistics to combat battalions is high; a ratio of 1-3 is the norm. The reasons for this rather lavish support are laid out below by Lord Dorn.

Together, the 150 combat and logistics battalions comprise the Fighting Marine Forces (FMF). The remaining 25,000 men are in the 12 construction battalions, six medical battalions, three military police battalions, three penal battalions and one headquarters and support battalion. These units are called the National Support Forces (NSF) and are used not only to support FMF units but also in the case of national disasters such as storms, earthquakes and floods. Regular FMF units can be called on in such cases, but NSF units are optimized for disaster relief and other civic tasks.

Beyond this basic sketch of the Islandian Marine Corps' force structure, a few specific qualities should be noted. First, each active-duty battalion (the above figures are all active duty) has two reserve battalions, e.g., 33rd Infantry Battalion (Active) has attached 33rd A and 33rd B Reserve Battalions. An active-duty battalion "stands up" every four years, with new recruits enlisted for a 12-year term (four years active duty and eight years in the reserves). At the end of the four-year period, when it "stands down," all but a small active duty cadre of officers and staff noncommissioned officers go into the A reserve battalion; four years later, they go into the B reserve battalion as the active-duty battalion stands down again and releases most of its men into the A battalion. Because unit cohesion is maintained and men continue to do their active-duty jobs in the reserve battalions, the quality of the reserve battalions is high. With a few weeks training, they match or exceed the performance of the active-duty battalions.

In peacetime, the Islandian Marine Corps is organized into three divisions. This would appear to lead to overly large divisions by world standards, as each division has 16 infantry battalions, six fire support battalions, two combat engineer battalions, two reconnaissance battalions and two light armor battalions. However, the division headquarters, with the exception of one element, concerns itself only with the battalions that are deployed and thus facing possible combat. All training and other garrison activity is decentralized to the battalions, which essentially run themselves. The one divisional element left in the rear to assist them is the bulk of the division adjutant's office, whose job is to keep the paperwork burden off the troop units. Thus, the division commander has a manageable number of battalions to oversee under potential combat conditions. The aviation battalions are organized in three wings, separate from the divisions but under the command of the division commander.

On mobilization, the number of battalions expands three-fold. This again leads to what would appear to be overly large divisions. But mobilization also includes the activation of brigade headquarters, manned by reservists and retired Marines recalled to active duty. With four brigade headquarters per division, units are again of manageable size. The Islandians avoid permanent, active-duty brigades because of their strong aversion to the growth of staffs.

The active-duty Islandian officer corps above the rank of lieutenant colonel (battalion commander; the Islandians have no rank of major) is extremely small; their officer corps is shaped not like a pyramid but like a mesa with a small spike in the center. There are only six active generals: A commandant, assistant commandant, commandant of the War College and three division commanders. The air wings' commanders are colonels. They also serve simultaneously as assistant division commanders (colonel is the highest aviation rank). Active-duty colonels, who serve on division staffs and on the Marine Corps General Staff, number about 30. In contrast, the U.S. Marine Corps has 818 active- duty colonels and 80 generals.

All other colonel and general officer billets, such as those on joint staffs and in areas such as procurement and R&D, are filled with reserve or retired officers recalled to active duty on contract. The objective is to keep the active-duty officer corps focused exclusively on warfighting. Retired general officers are also recalled to active duty as brigade commanders on mobilization.

The Islandian Marine Corps Infantry Battalion

The basic unit of the Islandian Marine Corps is the infantry battalion.[2] All infantry battalions are light infantry, designed to be foot or bicycle mobile; they have no organic motor vehicles. Careful attention to the soldier's load means no man carries more than 50 pounds. As a result, sustained daily march rates of 40 kilometers are routinely attained. Where the terrain permits use of bicycles or mountain bikes, that rate can be tripled. Each bicycle has a trailer capable of holding 50 pounds.

Oddly, Islandian infantry tactics are built neither on the infantry platoon nor the squad but on the four-man fire team. The fire team is an independent unit, and fire teams are routinely employed separately. This reflects not only Islandian combat experience, which has demonstrated that no more than four men can act as a single unit on the modern battlefield, but also their belief that unit cohesion is strongest in the smallest possible unit. Corporals normally commands fire teams.

Three fire teams make up a squad, commanded by a sergeant, and three squads make up a platoon, which has the strength of one officer (lieutenant), four sergeants and 39 men (the fourth sergeant and three men, who serve as messengers, make up a small command team with the sergeant serving as second-in-command of the platoon).

Also unusually, none of these units have any standard weaponry. They are equipped on a case-by-case basis, depending on the environment in which they expect to fight. The company commander makes that decision. For example, when equipped for urban combat, it is possible that no member of the platoon carries a rifle; the individual weapon is a rocket-propelled grenade (RPG) or a shotgun. The number of light machine guns and light mortars is also varied according to the environment. All Marines are thoroughly trained on any weapon they may employ.

The Islandian infantry company is made up of three infantry platoons, a heavy-weapons platoon and a "company commander's unit" consisting of a three-man communications element, a small leadership team (first sergeant, weapons and equipment NCO and three "gallopers"), and a full infantry squad. The infantry squad is at the direct disposal of the company commander who can use it to reinforce his main effort, respond to emergencies and otherwise intervene directly in the fight. "Gallopers" are provided as messengers so that the unit can maintain radio silence and thus facilitate surprise.

The company heavy-weapons platoon – mortars, anti-tank weapons, heavy machine guns and other weaponry in whatever mix the situation warrants – has two unique features. First, it has no platoon commander. The platoon itself is regarded as a training unit, with its four squads employed independently in support of the infantry platoons. Second, the ratio of men to weapons is high. There are seven men for each mortar and five for each anti-tank weapon. The purpose is to keep the soldier's individual load below 50 pounds in the weapons platoon just as in the infantry platoons. Otherwise, the mobility of the company would suffer on the principle that the speed of a convoy is the speed of its slowest ship.

Four rifle companies and a "headquarters and supply" company make up a battalion. There is no heavy-weapons unit at the battalion level, reflecting the Islandian belief that modern combat is highly decentralized. The "headquarters and supply" company is large, which is consistent with the fact that the infantry battalion is responsible for its own supply under "ordinary" conditions (i.e., when it is not the *Schwerpunkt*, the unit with which the commander is attempting to attain decisive results). It also includes a full infantry platoon under the direct control of the battalion commander; as with the infantry squad commanded by the company commander, this unit gives the battalion commander an ability to intervene directly in crises or take immediate advantage of opportunities. The commander of the headquarters and supply company is also the supply officer for the battalion, who is in charge of its "ordinary" logistics. There is no battalion staff, other than the adjutant's office and four "gallopers," who in this case are lieutenants who have commanded platoons. Finally, there is a long-range communications platoon.

This organization gives the Islandian Marine infantry battalion two salient characteristics: almost everyone in the battalion is a "trigger-puller," and its "ordinary" support requirements are very small. The only maintenance requirement is for bicycles (when employed) and a few radios, since there are no internal combustion engines anywhere in the battalion. The only significant higher-level supply requirement is ammunition;

the battalion buys its own food other than "iron rations." When motorized transport is useful, it requisitions it on a "use it and leave it" basis.

The Islandian Marine Corps appears to have successfully bucked the trend visible in all other developed countries' militaries for trigger-pullers to get fewer while maintenance and supply requirements rise.

An Interview with the Commandant

The headquarters of the Islandian Marine Corps is a two-story, stone building located near the Doring Province docks in The City. The structure is unimpressive and could easily be mistaken for a warehouse. The second floor is a combined bar and library. Perhaps its most remarkable feature is that, while overseeing a military with 175,000 men, it houses only 19 active-duty Marine officers. One of those officers is the Marine Corps Commandant, Lord Dorn, who graciously granted me part of a morning for an interview.

My first question to Lord Dorn was, "What is your personal focus (*Schwerpunkt*) as Commandant?"

Lord Dorn: My focus is ensuring that the Islandian Marine Corps and the Fighting Marine Forces (FMF) are, to the greatest degree possible, identical.

ME: Is that difficult?

LORD DORN: It used to be, and it remains something that needs constant watching. All militaries, perhaps all organizations, must contend with a form of entropy that bleeds men away from the fighting forces into work that may have higher peacetime priority. At one point, not too many years ago, we found more than half our manpower was not in the FMF.

ME: How did you deal with that?

LORD DORN: By adopting the force structure you see now. Its purpose is transparency: at any given time, we can see exactly where every Marine is and what he is doing. The tools that permit that are two-fold: the battalion muster roll and the designation of each battalion as combat, logistics or national support.

Every Marine, including myself, is at all times on a battalion muster roll. That is true from the day he enters the Marine Corps until he retires. The muster roll also tells what he is doing – in school, manning a machine gun, cooking, whatever. The battalion adjutant keeps the muster roll, and it must be updated monthly. A copy is sent each month here, to this headquarters. If a battalion is allowing too many of its men to be drawn away from manning weapons, we see it immediately.

Similarly, we know what each battalion is supposed to be doing: fighting, supplying fighting battalions or supporting the nation as a whole, including but not limited to the Marine Corps. So for men to be drained away from the FMF, we either have to change the purpose of the battalion, which we do very seldom, or someone has to lie on his muster roll.

ME: Do people lie on their muster rolls?

LORD DORN: In the beginning, that sometimes happened. Surprise inspector general visits quickly put a stop to it.

ME: Is an Islandian Marine battalion in effect a regiment?

LORD DORN: Yes. An Islandian does not just enlist in the Marine Corps. He enlists in a battalion. He remains a member of that battalion until he leaves the service. Officers and NCOs from his battalion take him through boot camp; he goes into reserve with the other recruits of his battalion who leave after a four-year term of active service. He is with the same people, with few exceptions, through his entire service. This builds the strongest possible unit cohesion.

ME: How do you replace Marines who leave the service before their four years are up for health or disciplinary reasons?

LORD DORN: We don't. Over the four-year period between receiving new recruits, a battalion normally shrinks somewhat in size.

ME: Doesn't this reduce their readiness?

LORD DORN: No. We measure readiness by the result of force-on-force, free-play exercises, not statistically. The improvement of cohesion and training over time more than offsets the slow decline in numbers of men.

ME: How does this work in combat?

LORD DORN: If a unit is reduced in combat to a point where it is ineffective, it is withdrawn and reconstituted as if it had reached the end of the normal four-year cycle. But history shows that a combat-experienced battalion at half strength, or sometimes less, is as effective, or more effective, than a green battalion at full strength. If a battalion does fall to the point where it must be reconstituted, its A or B reserve battalion normally replaces it.

ME: How does your reserve system work?

LORD DORN: Very simply. At the end of four years, the Marines in a battalion who do not remain as cadre pass into the A reserve of the same battalion. Four years later, they pass into the B reserve battalion. Because the Marines are almost all doing the same jobs with the same people, the reserve units are as effective as the active-duty battalions, sometimes more so.

ME: How do you replace the people who remain as cadres?

LORD DORN: If someone leaves a battalion for any reason – to remain as cadre, to go to school or for any detached service – his immediate subordinate moves up and fills his place. This extends all the way down the chain. A Marine looks forward to doing his immediate superior's job even if the assignment is temporary.

ME: If I may shift the subject just a bit, why does the Islandian Marine Corps have such a high ratio of logistics battalions to combat battalions?

LORD DORN: This reflects our expeditionary nature, as well as our doctrine of maneuver warfare which you also call Third Generation War and which in origin is the Prussian-German way of war which culminated in *Blitzkrieg*. In a campaign, we do not want to hit a culminating point – to run out of gas, you might say – before we reach an operational decision.

ME: How does your supply system work?

LORD DORN: We think of all support – supplies, fire, medical and so on – in terms of "ordinary" and "extraordinary" support. This also reflects maneuver warfare doctrine. "Ordinary" support is what a unit needs when it is not the *Schwerpunkt,* "extraordinary" when it is the *Schwerpunkt*. Under ordinary conditions, a battalion supplies itself by going to the "store," a logistics battalion, and also of course by living off the land. Each battalion has a large headquarters and supply company, so it is well able to take care of itself.

If a unit is the *Schwerpunkt*, however, the support comes to it. This is true of fire support, air support, everything, including logistics support. It becomes the responsibility of the logistics battalions or battalions supporting the *Schwerpunkt* to make sure it is fully supplied.

ME: What do you mean when you say "fully supplied?"

LORD DORN: At all times, a battalion has a basic load, a "stash" of ammunition and other supplies. Under ordinary conditions, it is responsible for making sure that load is full. Under extraordinary conditions, keeping it full is the responsibility of the supporting logistics battalions.

ME: Does this not contradict the expectation that Islandian combat battalions live off the land, at least as far as food is concerned?

LORD DORN: No. Every battalion has a supply of iron rations – the equivalent of your "Meals Ready to Eat" (MREs) – as part of its basic load. In heavy combat or other demanding situations, it feeds off its iron rations. Otherwise, it cooks. Our experience is that what Marines prepare for themselves with the food they buy locally is far better than food supplied by a central military commissariat. Also, Marines who are buying food and drink locally often find information comes with it.

ME: How does your doctrine of maneuver warfare relate to the foot-mobile nature of your infantry?

LORD DORN: Unlike the foot infantry in many other modern militaries, ours is really foot mobile – it can move fast without vehicles. What is gained by vehicle mobility is often lost again in fueling and maintaining the vehicles. And we have vehicles ourselves, when the terrain allows – bicycles, which need no fuel and impose only a very small maintenance requirement.

ME: Aren't there some situations where motor vehicles would improve your mobility?

LORD DORN: Certainly. Where that is the case, we commandeer them, paying for their use, of course.

ME: And you have some armor.

LORD DORN: Yes, light armor, all wheeled. The purpose is operational mobility, not tactical invulnerability. The idea that an armored vehicle can be an impregnable rolling fort is not the way we think. Guerrillas have blown up plenty of M-1 and Merkava tanks.

ME: Plus 18 artillery battalions.

LORD DORN: Fire support, not artillery. Only three of those battalions are artillery, towed howitzers. The modern battlefield simply does not offer many targets for massed artillery.

ME: What is the rest of it?

LORD DORN: Rocket launchers – simple ones, like the Russian Grad, not like your Multiple Launch Rocket System (MLRS) – which are excellent suppression weapons. They are more terrifying than artillery, and in most cases what is needed is suppression, not pinpoint destruction. There are also mortars, small and large. It is not uncommon for a *Schwerpunkt* battalion to have a whole mortar battalion supporting it. We also have automatic cannon companies with weapons up to 40 mm to provide direct fire support to assaults. When a *Schwerpunkt* infantry battalion or brigade attacks, the fire support is massive, I assure you. But it is oriented toward the kinds of small, mobile targets the modern battlefield presents. A World War I artillery park is only useful for fighting World War I.

ME: What comprises your aviation?

LORD DORN: We have 16 composite aviation squadrons, with search-and-rescue helicopters, light STOL (short take-off and landing) transports, and ground support attack aircraft – what some U.S. Marines call "Jaeger Air." Our total aircraft inventory is 400 ground attack aircraft, 200 transports and 20 helicopters.

ME: Why so few helicopters?

LORD DORN: Two reasons. First, helicopters are extremely maintenance intensive. They need about 10 times as many maintenance hours per flight hour as fixed-wing aircraft. We don't want to put that much manpower into aviation maintenance. Second, they are extremely vulnerable to ground fire. They are big piñatas and everybody shoots at them. Why not? It's fun and it's easy.

ME: So you don't have a vertical envelopment option?

LORD DORN: No, and neither does anyone else. How often do you see someone actually try a vertical envelopment in combat? They know the losses would be prohibitive. When the U.S. Army's AH-64 Apaches attempted a mass assault early in the second Gulf war, they got creamed. Even in exercises, people may talk about a vertical envelopment option, but no one ever chooses it.

ME: What about moving troops and emergency consumables like ammunition around the battlefield?

LORD DORN: For that we have STOL transport aircraft, similar to the CASA Aviocar. They operate very nicely from roads and grass fields.

ME: Do you have any fighter aircraft?

LORD DORN: No, we don't. The Islandian Marine Corps tries to avoid duplicating capabilities available from other services. We let the Air Force boys be the white scarf in the windstream types. A Marine pilot makes ace by destroying five enemy tanks, not by shooting down five aircraft.

ME: So your attack aircraft are all for close air support?

LORD DORN: No. They can do close air support (CAS), of course, but that is not their main mission. Their main mission is preventing the enemy from moving on the roads by strafing his columns. That greatly delays the enemy in shifting operational reserves, which in turn contributes significantly to our winning at the operational level.

Our attack aviation also ranges ahead and above our *Schwerpunkt* in high densities. There, it performs multiple functions. It lets the ground commander see over the next hill, tells him when he has missed a road junction, discovers and attacks enemy ambushes, knocks out enemy artillery, disrupts enemy headquarters and so on. But if you are interested in our aviation, perhaps it would be useful for you to interview our Deputy Commandant (Supporting) for Aviation, Colonel Arn. Would you like me to ask him to meet with you after our conversation is finished?

ME: Certainly, that would be very kind of you both. But I am hesitant to interrupt his busy schedule on such short notice.

LORD DORN: Busy? What on earth makes you think he is busy?

ME: Well, everyone in our Marine Corps' headquarters is always terribly busy. Aren't you?

LORD DORN: Certainly not. If we were busy, we couldn't get anything done. Creativity requires leisure. A headquarters should be a place where creativity flourishes, creativity as to how to meet present challenges in new ways and to anticipate future challenges. A headquarters where people were busy would quickly become a closed system, a place concerned mainly with its own business. It would have no time for the world outside its own doors.

ME: That is a fair description of most American headquarters, I think. Anyway, I would very much appreciate a chance to interview Colonel Arn.

LORD DORN: Let me just send him a D-mail to let him know you are coming.

Lord Dorn wrote out a short note, then called to the black Lab I noticed snoozing by the fireplace. The dog came over wagging its tail, happy to be of service, and took the note carefully in its soft mouth. "Arn" ordered Lord Dorn, and the Lab loped off happily on its errand.

ME: You prefer D-mail to E-mail?

LORD DORN: Unlike electrons, even when intercepted, dogs don't talk, and we make our written messages undecipherable by virtue of code or unexplained context.

ME: Your small officer corps and absence of staffs obviously means your officers must be good decision-makers. How are they schooled?

LORD DORN: Officers go through two schools. All officers go through a basic school, and those who will rise above captain also attend our war college. Both schools focus on making decisions under stress in confusing situations. They are not staff colleges, but schools for commanders.

ME: By any standard, your staffs are extraordinarily small. Why is that so?

LORD DORN: Staffs quickly come to be agencies that work to make everything convenient for the staff. Their growth slows everything down, puts paperwork burdens on commanders and units, and centralizes decisions so that staffs have something to do.

ME: In America, the justification for vast staffs and large numbers of staff officers is the joint billets and the many jobs in the R&D and procurement areas. Obviously, you don't have those requirements.

LORD DORN: Unfortunately, we do. But we meet them differently. Reservists or retired Marines recalled to active duty on a contract basis fill all those positions. The system is called the Reserve/Retired Enhanced Manning Force, or RREMF. RREMFs enable us to keep the active-duty Marine Corps focused on warfighting. The RREMF officers serving on contract are not part of the "pipeline," if you will. They are there for just one purpose. The fact that they stay in one job for years is also helpful.

ME: Are retired Marines willing to do this in sufficient numbers?

LORD DORN: Yes. We have a saying in Islandia, "Once a Marine, Always a Marine." Our RREMFs are devoted to the Marine Corps, and they represent us better than active-duty Marines might. They know they can always return to collecting their retirement pay, and they are happy to comply with the law that forbids them forever from working for a defense company.

ME: So the RREMF system is really the secret of why you have so few active-duty officers above the rank of lieutenant colonel?

LORD DORN: Precisely.

ME: Why don't you have the rank of major?

LORD DORN: We did, until just a few years ago. We eliminated it because there are no commands for majors. Captains command companies and lieutenant colonels command battalions, so all that was left for majors was to push paper around. That drove many of our most promising commanders to leave the Marine Corps after company command, and it created a staff mentality among the majors. We realized that majors are in fact minor, so we just got rid of the rank.

We adopted one other reform at the same time. With the exception of a handful – and I mean handful – of staff positions, we decided that there would be no more officers than there were command billets. We did not want a situation where each commander had, in effect, a line of officers with the same rank standing outside his door panting for his job. Those officers just gummed up the works. They also pushed for short command tours, which are always deleterious.

ME: How long does an Islandian Marine unit commander hold his command billet?

LORD DORN: If he proves competent, five to seven years.

ME: How do you determine if he is competent?

LORD DORN: Every year, every Islandian Marine unit faces a free-play, force-on-force exercise against a similar unit. The results tell us what we need to know.

ME: The loser is relieved?

LORD DORN: Only if he shows clear incompetence. You can have two quite competent units and leaders go against each other and one is going to lose. But from the results of the exercise flow all promotions. For example, the winner gets fifty promotions to share within the battalion, loser gets five.

ME: In effect, you have created a market-driven outcome.

LORD DORN: Yes, exactly. Socialism in uniform doesn't work better than any other form of socialism.

ME: Your National Support Forces are something different from what we see in other militaries. Could you explain the thinking behind them?

LORD DORN: The Islandian Marine Corps is a servant of the nation and the people, not just the Defense Ministry. Like all nations, we have periodic disasters and emergencies. The Marine Corps always helped in such situations, but combat forces do not always have the optimal skills. And frankly, if they are involved in such affairs too often, it can take the edge off their combat skills. So we grouped the types of forces most useful in such cases and designated them National Support Forces. Of course, in wartime their first priority is serving our combat units.

ME: Would your NSF also be optimized for disaster relief, peacekeeping and nation-building in other countries?

LORD DORN: Yes, I suppose they would, although Islandia does not engage in such missions. Our foreign policy is what your ruling establishment would call "isolationist." We have no interest in other nations' internal affairs. We do not believe monarchy can be imposed on other countries by force.

ME: I noticed something curious about your NSF, in that they include your penal battalions. Why is that the case?

LORD DORN: Well, first, we have penal battalions because we don't think Marines should be able to get out of their enlistment by misbehaving. Misbehavior only gets them assignment to a penal battalion.

Traditionally, penal battalions are assigned the dirtiest and most dangerous missions, and in wartime, that is what ours get. But we found that it is in performance of precisely those missions that many of the men in a penal battalion redeemed themselves. They had, often for the first time in their lives, a chance to do something difficult, dangerous, and also important, something where they could make a real difference in other people's lives. That turned them around.

In peacetime, that kind of mission occurs most often in disaster relief. So we use our penal battalions in such cases. The work is often dangerous – pulling people out of flood waters, battling forest fires, working through burning towns shattered by an earthquake – and the combination of real danger and real achievement makes a difference in men's lives. I've seen it happen where one of our people who is one of our worst discipline problems is a different man after he spends a night saving a child from a flooded village.

ME: You've talked about most of the functional areas – logistics, administration, as well as operations with both air and ground forces. What about intelligence?

LORD DORN: Well, of course we prize it, but we go about it quite differently than some other countries.

ME: Why is that?

LORD DORN: My impression that altogether too much emphasis is placed on the gadgets and processes of acquiring intelligence and too little on the brainpower that makes sense of it. I've seen in other armies a veritable explosion of technicians, both in and out of uniform, who appear to hold sway over what is essentially a nontechnical problem. Of course, you need some technical tools to do intelligence, just as you do in anything else. But we aren't as obsessed by them as others are. We spend much less time and resources trying to get the latest and biggest "telescope" because no matter how wonderful it is, it still can't see everything. And even if it could, you would never find the one piece of information that explains everything else. No, the problem does not lie in getting information. While gathering information is certainly important, our challenges have always been in getting the most out of the information we get. I'd rather get less information and be able to derive more understanding out of it.

ME: How do you do that?

LORD DORN: We keep the technicians in their proper place. Less is more. Fundamentally, intelligence is a warfighting problem – "operations written in red ink," one of your people used to say. At battalion levels, the commander is his own intelligence officer. At the brigade and division levels, intelligence officers were last year's operations officers or battalion commanders. And our battalion commanders and operations officers are often last year's intelligence officers. The intelligence and operations officers are interchangeable; they can do each other's job. The advantage of having a separate intelligence officer is merely to have another head to think about the enemy – one who is doing that full time. The operations officer handles scouting and other information-gathering operations, not the intelligence officer. This frees him to analyze available information instead of monopolizing his time merely obtaining it.

ME: Aren't your intelligence officers much less technically proficient?

LORD DORN: It's a trade-off we don't mind making since our training regime is so realistic. With the experience our intelligence officers have as commanders and operations officers in force-on-force, free-play exercises, we find they grow a certain sixth sense about what an enemy is likely to do. This is more valuable to us than having an officer who knows various technical systems and processes but is unable to help his commander scope tactical risk. Of course, if an intelligence officer hasn't been a maneuver unit commander and operations officer and has no experience in force-on-force, free-play exercises, he would have nothing special to offer. It is only natural that such officers would gravitate to something technical, a niche they can claim for their own. We see this phenomenon in other functional areas too, not just intelligence – you can find it in administration, logistics, communications – even in operations where someone is too preoccupied with a particular weapons system or air platform.

ME: Lord Dorn, I'd like to thank you for your time. This interview sheds light on some very different ways of organizing a modern marine corps. Perhaps our own U.S. Marine Corps could learn something from it.

LORD DORN: Perhaps they could.

....

Following my interview with the Islandian Marine Corps Commandant, his Labrador led me to the office of the Islandian Marine DC(S) Air, Colonel Arn. I entered his small office to find him in a flight suit, feet up on his desk, reading Rommel's "Infanterie Greift An!" The walls of his office were well-decorated with paintings and posters of infantry in combat. No aircraft models were in evidence.

ME: Thank you for seeing me on such short notice, Colonel Arn.

COL. ARN: No problem. Have a seat. Want a beer?

ME: Thank you; that would be welcome. A bit of alcohol stimulates the brain.
    I see flight suits are acceptable in the Islandian HQMC. I assume that's your squadron patch on your shoulder?

COL. ARN: No. Like all Islandian aviators, I wear the patch of the infantry battalion that is twinned with my squadron.

ME: What do you mean twinned?

COL. ARN: As DC(S) Air, my *Schwerpunkt* is making sure every Islandian Marine aviator always thinks of himself as an infantryman, not a flier. One way we do that is by twinning, in which every Islandian air squadron is closely linked in a multitude of ways with a specific infantry battalion. The squadron and the battalion are physically located together. They share the same clubs. They informally exchange personnel all the time. For example, it is common for a pilot to command an infantry platoon or company in an exercise, or for an infantry officer or NCO to go up in an aircraft as the observer. In our attack aircraft, by the way, the commander is the observer, not the pilot.

ME: Like the Germans in World War I.

COL. ARN: *Jawohl.*

ME: Do your twinned aviation and ground units train together?

COL. ARN: All the time. The squadrons are on the battalion training and exercise plans; they are on the battalion schedules every day. An Islandian Marine infantryman would find it odd indeed if, when he went to the field, his twin aviation unit did not have some aircraft over his head the whole time.

ME: Does this carry through into combat?

COL. ARN: In part. Like all support, air support in the Islandian Marine Corps works on the ordinary/extraordinary principle. The bulk of the aviation always acts in support of the *Schwerpunkt*. But when some is left over, we try to use it to support the battalions with which it is twinned.

ME: You have far more infantry and light-armor battalions than you have aviation squadrons. How do you twin the leftover infantry units?

COL. ARN: We don't. Every squadron has a twin battalion, but not every battalion has a twin squadron. The problem is to get the aviators to think like infantrymen, not the other way around. Once the mindset is created, it carries over for any infantry or light armor the air is supporting.

ME: The United States Marine Corps tries to get the same effect by sending its future pilots through The Basic School.

COL. ARN: I know your Marine Corps places a lot of credence in its Basic School. But frankly, the air-ground relationship both starts and ends there. True, your pilots go back to be FACs [forward air controllers]. But they never command ground units, as our best aviators do. By the time one of our aviators is serving as a wing commander and assistant division commander, he will have commanded an infantry or light-armor platoon, company and battalion. His command tours will have been shorter than those of his infantry counterparts, but he will have done it, not just seen it.

In the Islandian Marine Corps, any fire team or squad leader, platoon, company or battalion commander can be an FAC. We put the "actuals" in charge, not technical specialists. Frankly, we think your FACs, as part of a large, centralized control system, would become impediments in a fluid battle. They would be responding to a set process, not the situation.

ME: What is more important in Jaeger Air, the aircrew or the aircraft?

COL. ARN: The pilot and the observer are much more important than the platform. Both must have a deep sense of what the ground guys are most concerned with. Their understanding must reach the point where they can take charge and direct the battle from the air. Not every pilot or observer can reach this point. It takes years of experience and a certain talent as well. Those who don't have it, who cannot conceptualize the ground situation in their mind, end up flying the transports and helos.

We're currently trying an experiment in this respect. All our squadrons are composite squadrons in terms of aircraft type, but we have a new experimental squadron that also includes 40 light armored vehicles (LAVs). Normally, they will be commanded from the air. We want to see how this works in terms of increasing operational tempo. The early results are promising. The LAV company commander told me that in the one exercise we've done to date, he was able to move twice as fast with greater security because he had a much clearer sense of what was going on beyond his range of vision.[3]

ME: How successful do you think you have been in creating aviators who really think of themselves as infantrymen?

COL. ARN: Our fliers are not candy asses, bombing orphanages from 20,000 feet at 550 knots so they don't get shot down. They think of themselves not as knights on white horses but as street fighters. They get down and dirty, down low and slow so they can see what is going on. We do like to save the aircrew, but the airplane itself is expendable.

ME: I take it your aircraft do not cost upwards of $30 million apiece?

COL. ARN: Of course not. Any piece of equipment that is too expensive to lose is also too expensive to use.

ME: Would that rule out the new American Joint Strike Fighter?

COL. ARN: The JSF is a flying piano.

ME: Could you tell me something about your aircraft types?

COL. ARN: The helos and the transports are standard, but our attack aircraft is somewhat different from what you will find elsewhere. Its closest cousin would be your A-10. Ours is prop-driven, but the design philosophy is the same. It is cheap, rugged, built around powerful cannon for strafing, and highly survivable. Its design reflects the most important fact of life in the ground support business, namely that the problem is not hitting targets but finding and identifying them. That can only be done at low altitudes and slow speeds. You are going to take hits. Our attack aircraft are designed to take them. I've seen them come back with hundreds of bullet holes, one wing, one prop and no canopy. But the crew was alive.

ME: Why don't you have any fighter aircraft?

COL. ARN: Because we don't want any fighter pilots.

ME: Do you have an air refueling capability?

COL. ARN: Yes, the transports can convert to refuelers.

ME: Lord Dorn told me you don't do much close air support.

COL. ARN: CAS is an emergency procedure. Our Jaeger pilots only perform this mission if the infantry are in real trouble. The infantry only requests CAS in such emergency situations. They know the importance of having the pilots ranging forward of them, finding gaps and keeping them open, pulling the infantry and light armor through. All know that when CAS is requested, someone has failed.

ME: It is obvious that you know a fair amount about U.S. Marine Corps aviation. How would you sum up the difference between them and yourself?

COL. ARN: Our pilots can look out of their cockpits and not only see but make sense of what is going on below them, on the ground. They decide how to use their aircraft to influence, perhaps determine the outcome of the ground battle. They operate off the same map as the ground commander and have the same intent, mission and *Schwerpunkt*.

ME: They have no centralized system of control?

COL. ARN: No, of course not. The ground situation changes too rapidly for that. Any type of centralized control quickly reduces pilots to mere technicians, and if that happens, all your aircraft can do is bomb orphanages.

ME: And your casualty rate operating this way is?

COL. ARN: High enough so that the infantry see an occasional dead aviator. It's good for their morale to understand that others share their extreme danger.

....

Does the Islandian Marine Corps offer a possible model for the United States Marine Corps? Those who believe that U.S. Marines actually depend on their vast, multilayered headquarters structure would certainly say no, but one who has observed the U.S. Marine Corps over time might reply that real life is lived at the battalion level. All the Islandians have done is take that fact and make it official. In so doing, they have achieved some goals that might not be irrelevant to the American situation. They have obtained a large number of combat units from their total manpower. They have assured that, within those combat units, most Marines are trigger-pullers. They have made their Marine Corps and the FMF almost the same thing. They have given their Commandant simple, effective tools he can use to see where his Marines are and what they are doing. In sum, they have adopted a force structure consistent with maneuver warfare doctrine, a doctrine the U.S. Marine Corps also espouses.

The Islandian leg of my tour offered lessons in how to organize for both Third and, by implication, Fourth Generation War. The latter requires lots of light infantry, which the Islandian model provides.

But the greatest challenge facing states that find themselves fighting Fourth Generation wars is intellectual. No one has thought through how to do it. Resurrecting old counterinsurgency doctrine – as the U.S. Army has recently done – is a step forward from simply using firepower to destroy targets, but at best it marks a way station. Fourth Generation War's multiplicity of parties, fighting for many different kinds of goals, creates an environment that is qualitatively different from insurgency and counterinsurgency waged within the state framework. Mao was a brilliant guerrilla leader, but he was not fighting Fourth Generation Wars.

Fortunately, someone is working to meet this intellectual challenge. I returned from Islandia via Vienna, the capital of the Austro-Hungarian Empire. There I discovered that the Imperial and Royal (K.u.K.) Marine Corps is issuing a series of field manuals on Fourth Generation War, the first such publications produced by any armed service. To date, the series includes FMFM-1A, "Fourth Generation Warfare," which is the foundational doctrinal work; a manual on light (Jaeger) infantry in Fourth Generation War, a second volume of which is forthcoming; a short book of 4GW tactical decision games, with a second book in preparation; and FMFM1-3A, a manual on policing 4GW. All of these works are available at the Defense and the National Interest Web site at http://www.d-n-i.net/dni/category/strategy-and-force-employment/4gw-theory/.

One appendix to the FMFM-1A is so valuable that a summary is reproduced below:

The Canon

There are seven books which, read in the order given, will take the reader from the First Generation through the Second, the Third and on into the Fourth. We call them "the canon."

The first book in the canon is C.E. White, "The Enlightened Soldier."[4] This book explains why you are reading all the other books.

The next book is Robert Doughty, "The Seeds of Disaster."[5] This is the definitive history of the development of Second Generation Warfare in the French army during and after World War I.

The third book, Bruce Gudmundsson's "Stormtroop Tactics,"[6] is a story about how to change an army.

Book four is Martin Samuels's "Command or Control."[7] Its value is the clear distinctions it draws between the Second and Third Generations, distinctions the reader will find useful when looking at the U.S. armed forces today.

The fifth book in the canon is again by Robert Doughty, the head of the history department at West Point and the best American historian of the modern French army, "The Breaking Point."[8] This is the story of the battle of Sedan in 1940, a brilliant example of operational art.

The sixth book in the canon is Martin van Creveld's "Fighting Power."[9] This book is important because it illustrates why you cannot combine Third Generation, maneuver warfare doctrine with a Second Generation, inward-focused, process-ridden, centralized institution.

The seventh and final book in the canon is Martin van Creveld's, "The Transformation of War."[10] Easily the most important book on war written in the last quarter-century, it lays out the basis of Fourth Generation War, the state's loss of its monopoly on war and on social organization.

ENDNOTES

1 The books are real.

2 The Islandian infantry battalion is remarkably similar to the light infantry battalion proposed by German General Franz Uhle-Wettler. See, Franz Uhle-Wettler, *Gefechtsfeld Mitteleuropa, Gefahr der Übertechnisierung von Streitkräften* (München: Bernard & Graefe, 1980).

3 The report of Captain Glen Cunningham, U.S. Marine Corps, Commander of the LAV company supported by Jaeger Air in exercise Hunter Warrior. The report is an internal Marine Corps document and is not publicly available.

4 Charles Edward White, *The Enlightened Soldier: Scharnhorst and the Militärische Gesellschaft in Berlin, 1801-1805* (Praeger Publishers, 1988).

5 Robert A. Doughty, *The Seeds of Disaster: The Development of French Army Doctrine, 1919 -1939,* (Archon Books, 1986).

6 Bruce Gudmundsson, *Stormtroop Tactics: Innovation in the German Army, 1914-1918* (Praeger Paperback, 1995).

7 Martin Samuels, *Command or Control?: Command, Training and Tactics in the British and German Armies, 1888-1918* (Routledge, 1996).

8 Robert A. Doughty, *The Breaking Point: Sedan and the Fall of France, 1940* (Archon, 1990).

9 Martin Van Creveld, *Fighting Power: German and U.S. Army Performance, 1939-1945* (Greenwood Press, 1982).

10 Martin Van Creveld, *The Transformation of War: The Most Radical Reinterpretation of Armed Conflict Since Clausewitz* (Free Press, 1991).

CHAPTER 6

THE NAVY

William S. Lind

To understand what military reform means for the Navy, it is necessary to proceed from two facts. The first is that America's geography, with two long seacoasts, requires us to be a maritime power. That geographic requirement is reinforced by an economic requirement. Our economy, including our energy supply, depends on large volumes of seaborne imports and exports. Put together, these two requirements generate a third: the United States Navy must be able to dominate the Atlantic and Pacific Oceans and control portions of other seas (such as the Strait of Hormuz, through which much of our imported oil passes) against any opponent.

Reforming the Navy cannot and does not mean weakening American naval power. Reformers know that when the United States tried a policy of abandoning the high seas in favor of coastal defense under President Thomas Jefferson, it was an abject failure. The Jefferson administration sold off many of the U.S. Navy's frigates, refused to build ships of the line, and created instead flotillas of gunboats for harbor defense. When war came in 1812, the gunboats proved useless, American commerce was swept from the seas (causing an economic depression in New England that almost led to secession) and the United States was invaded at several points by seaborne British forces. Only the fact that we had retained our few large frigates enabled us to emerge from that war without complete humiliation.

The second reality from which reform of the Navy must proceed is that unlike the U.S. Army and Air Force, the U.S. Navy today is not designed for a Cold War confrontation with the Soviet Union. That sounds like better news than it is. The U.S. Navy is not designed to fight the Soviet navy because it never was. The Soviets recognized that the submarine is the modern capital ship, and throughout the Cold War the Soviet navy outnumbered the U.S. Navy in submarines by a ratio of about 3-1.

Rather, the U.S. Navy was, and is, structured to fight the imperial Japanese Navy. That navy's main strength was its aircraft carriers, and aircraft-carrier task forces or "battle groups" remained the focus of the U.S. Navy throughout the Cold War and into the present. From the Soviet navy's perspective, American aircraft carriers were little more than targets for submarine attack. When Adm. Hyman Rickover, a fierce proponent of building nuclear-powered carriers, was asked in a Senate hearing how long those carriers would survive in a war with the Soviet Union, he replied, "About two days."

When the last trumpet sounds and the Japanese carriers sunk at Midway – *Akagi* and *Kaga*, *Soryu* and *Hiryu* – rise from their watery graves, the U.S. Navy will be ready and waiting. While military reformers may appreciate historical *tableaux vivant* as entertainment, we usually do not consider them the main function of the fleet. Some modest reforms would seem to be in order. To see what those reforms might be, we will consider the U.S. Navy's personnel, guiding concepts, and materiel, which is to say ships and aircraft. This reflects reformers' belief, often reiterated by Col. John Boyd, that for winning wars people are most important, ideas come second and hardware is only third.

People

The principal personnel problem of the U.S. Navy is that its officer corps is dominated by technicians. This is in large part the legacy of Admiral Rickover, who ensured that the nuclear power community was made up entirely of engineers and that engineering was the main focus of the Navy's officer education, especially at the Naval Academy. All skippers of U.S. Navy submarines, our capital ships, must be nuclear engineers. This is in strong contrast to Britain's Royal Navy, whose submarine commanders have nuclear engineers working for them where they belong, in the engine room. The other influential community in the U.S. Navy's officer corps, the aviators, are also primarily technicians, people whose main skill is flying high-performance aircraft.

The reason this is problematical is that the technical-engineering way of thinking and the military-tactical-strategic way of thinking are opposites. War is not an engineering problem. The opponent is men, not machines, and as Colonel Boyd said, they use their minds. If they are clever, their minds lead them away from a direct trial of strength, which may be roughly calculable, to asymmetric strategies and tactics, which put a premium on indirectness, imagination, creativity and surprise. Most engineers, which is to say most U.S. Navy officers, cannot deal well with challenges of a type they do not expect and that do not lend themselves to quantitative calculation. While those officers usually do a superb job of navigating and operating their ships under peacetime conditions, fighting them effectively may require qualities few engineers possess.

The domination of the U.S. Navy by engineers reinforces the service's Second (or perhaps First) Generation War institutional culture. Like the other U.S. armed forces, the Navy's culture is inward-focused, risk-averse and centralized, preferring obedience to initiative and relying on top-down control rather than self-discipline. Ironically, the opposite of this culture, the outward-focused, decentralized, initiative-oriented culture of the Third Generation, began at sea in the Royal Navy of the second half of the 18th century, long before the German army developed it for land warfare. Third Generation institutional culture is every bit as beneficial to navies as to armies, as the Royal Navy's record in the French Revolutionary and Napoleonic wars demonstrated. And it is instructive that during the 19th Century, a centralizing technology

– signaling – would play the primary role in destroying that outward-focused Third Generation culture in the Royal Navy.[1]

Reforming the U.S. Navy's personnel requires, above all else, adopting the institutional culture of the Third Generation. The late 18th century Royal Navy can serve as a useful prototype. We want that navy's iron men in today's iron ships. Attaining that goal means we must put the engineers back in the engine rooms (and the aviators back in their cockpits) and have tacticians and strategists, not technicians, commanding our ships and fleets.

This should begin with a wholesale reform of the Naval Academy. Not only is Annapolis now overwhelmingly an engineering school, it is also oppressed by a stultifying atmosphere of political correctness, itself largely a product of adding women to the Brigade of Midshipmen and then trying to forbid what happens naturally among young men and young women. It is hard to imagine a worse atmosphere for creating the officers of strong character, those always looking for opportunities to take initiative, that a Third Generation institutional culture requires. Reform requires separating the women from the men, perhaps educating them somewhere else; revamping the curriculum to replace the focus on engineering with a focus on warfare; and introducing opportunities for the midshipmen to make military decisions. (Paintball at sea in the Academy's dinghies would be a good start.)

One additional personnel reform is urgently required. At present, any time a U.S. Navy ship touches ground, the commander is relieved. This leaves Navy ship captains terrified and timid when operating in coastal waters. There should be no penalty for running a ship aground as a consequence of handling her in a bold manner tactically.

Ideas

In the realm of ideas, the principal reform to the U.S. Navy should be reorienting the service away from blue-water warfare and toward controlling green and brown water, i.e., coastal and inland waters, places where the United States is fighting Fourth Generation, non-state opponents.

This reorientation does not contradict what we said at the outset, namely that the Navy must retain its ability to control the seas. Rather, it reflects the fact that neither now nor in the foreseeable future do we face a potentially hostile navy that can contest control of either the Atlantic or the Pacific. The only two navies that come close are those of Russia and China. Both are roughly our equal in number of capital ships, i.e. submarines, although only 25 of the Russian navy's 46 attack submarines are nuclear powered, and only five of China's. The Russian submarine force may also be our approximate peer qualitatively. The Chinese submarine fleet is far inferior qualitatively to our own, both in personnel and in materiel.

Overwhelming any comparison of fleets is the fact that war with either Russia or

China would represent a catastrophic failure of American strategy. Such wars would be disastrous for all parties, regardless of their outcomes. In a world where the most important strategic reality is a non-Marxist "withering away of the state," the United States needs both Russia and China to be strong, successful states. They need the United States to be the same. Defeat of any of the three global powers by another would likely yield a new, vast, stateless region, which is to say a great victory for the forces of the Fourth Generation. No American armed service should be designed for wars our most vital interest dictates we not fight.

Beyond Russia and China, it is impossible to identify any potentially hostile navy that can do more than contest control of its local waters with the U.S. Navy. This brings us back to where we began, with the need to reorient the Navy toward coastal (green) and inland (brown) waters. While it is possible that we may face the opposition of local navies in coastal waters, cases where we do so will again almost always represent a failure of strategy. With smaller states as with the Great Powers, defeat will tend to lead to disintegration of the state itself and the creation of another stateless region. The futility (and cost) of our efforts to date to recreate the state we destroyed by invading Iraq should warn us of the folly of such conflicts.

Rather, our presence in coastal and inland waters far from home should most often result from a Fourth Generation conflict, a situation where a state has vanished (in fact, if not in name) and non-state forces that threaten vital American interests are dominant. In such situations, the ability of the U.S. Navy to control coastal and inland waters, as part of an effort either to restore a state or to limit the spread of stateless disorder, can be immensely valuable.

The reason this is so is simple: when a state breaks down, it takes land transportation with it. The railroads cease to run. The roads are fragmented by checkpoints manned by local militias and bandits. Only water transport remains to permit life beyond the most local, subsistence level. Whoever controls the routes of water transport, both coastal and inland, controls a great deal. He can facilitate the use of those routes by his friends and prevent their use by his enemies. In time, the advantages accruing to those who can transport their goods and people will help to make them dominant over those who cannot. It is through such indirect actions that America can best work to restore order and defeat hostile 4GW forces in stateless regions.

The ideas that guide the U.S. Navy need to evolve substantially before it can think in these terms. At present, its thinking remains the prisoner of Alfred Thayer Mahan, who believed that navies should concern themselves solely with winning decisive battles between fleets of capital ships. The Navy needs to release Mahan to history, where he belongs, and turn to a more sophisticated theorist, Sir Julian Corbett. Corbett's understanding of how maritime powers could use their navies in limited wars for purposes reaching beyond control of the sea translates well into a Fourth Generation world.[2]

At the same time, the U.S. Navy must come to understand that war in coastal and inland waters is qualitatively different from naval warfare in blue water. The inland and coastal waters regime is far more complex than the blue water environment, thanks to the multitude of civilian ships, boats and aircraft. The Navy had an unfortunate but typical encounter with that complexity when the Aegis cruiser U.S.S. Vincennes shot down an Iranian airliner over the Persian Gulf that it had mistaken for an attacker. Afterward, a designer of the Aegis system wrote a letter to the U.S. Naval Institute Proceedings in which he said, "Of course, it was never designed to deal with ambiguity." Ambiguity is a constant in coastal and inland waters.

For any of this intellectual progress to take place, the Navy must first begin to think. It has been a long time since it thought about anything beyond budgets and hardware (here, again, we see the dominance of technicians at work). The renaissance of thinking about land warfare that began in the U.S. Marine Corps and, to a lesser extent, in the U.S. Army in the 1970s had no naval counterpart. The Navy's aircraft carrier battle groups have cruised on mindlessly for more than half a century, waiting for those Japanese carriers to turn up. They are still cruising today, into, if not beyond, irrelevance.

Hardware

While people and ideas are more important than hardware in navies, just as they are in armies, hardware is a more powerful tool for shaping navies (and air forces) than armies. If you give an army tanks, it can use them in radically different ways depending on whether it is a Second or Third Generation army. In contrast, if you give a navy submarines instead of aircraft carriers, you shape the institution in ways it cannot avoid. The German navy of World War II, whose main strength was in submarines, could not fight the kind of naval war the Imperial Japanese Navy fought in the Pacific with its aircraft carriers.

Reformers can shape the U.S. Navy in ways that lead it away from Mahan and toward Corbett, which in a 21st century context means toward 4GW in coastal and inland waters, by altering its mix of ships and aircraft. To see what those alterations might be, let us open the pages of *Jane's Fighting Ships* and see what we have to work with.

Submarines

Submarines are today's and tomorrow's capital ships, the ships that most directly determine control of blue water. Only a fleet of submarines can drive both enemy surface ships and enemy submarines from the high seas, clearing the way for our own surface forces to cross the oceans with impunity. That is what is called control of the sea, and the ability to establish it has been the hallmark of capital ships since the age of sail. The submarine indisputably ended the aircraft carrier's brief reign as the capital ship with the advent of nuclear-powered submarines in the 1950s, and arguably with the appearance of the German type XXI high-performance conventional submarines of 1945. The U.S. Navy now has 53 nuclear-powered attack subs, with six building; 14 Ohio-class ballistic missile submarines, which are part of our strategic nuclear forces; and curiously, four Ohio-class boats converted into support ships for Navy SEALS, thus creating the world's first and only 18,750 ton coastal submarines. If ever actually employed in coastal waters, they would seem to be another "Whiskey on the rocks" incident waiting to happen.[3]

The U.S. Navy's fully justified need to remain the dominant navy in both the Atlantic and the Pacific means we must continue to maintain a force of about 50 nuclear-powered attack submarines. Whether those submarines need to be as large (7800 tons) and expensive ($3.1 billion) as the current Virginia class is another question. Admiral Rickover's legacy includes a stodgy approach to submarine design. Reformers would want to investigate alternatives, including approaches taken by other countries that have yielded smaller nuclear attack submarines. We would also build some number of small, conventionally-powered submarines optimized for shallow coastal waters. In subs as in fighter aircraft, large size is a disadvantage in combat, as it makes detection easier.

Aircraft Carriers

During the Cold War, military reformers sought to move away from the large nuclear-powered aircraft carriers the Navy prefers to smaller carriers that could be acquired in larger numbers. The objective was to disperse our naval airpower in the face of the Soviet submarine threat. That issue is now moot. Regional opponents may be able to sink one American carrier, but they cannot threaten the whole carrier force the way the Soviet navy did.

The U.S. Navy currently possesses 11 large aircraft carriers, with one building. Whether 12 carriers are too many or too few is a question that is unanswerable in prospect. It depends on scenarios, which vary widely and are all arbitrary. Twelve carriers is as good an arbitrary number as any. Reformers' objections to the U.S. Navy's carrier force now relate less to number and size of ships than to their air wings and escorts. Other than some support and anti-submarine aircraft, the air wings on Navy carriers are now made up entirely of F-18 fighter-bombers. As a fighter, the F-18 is satisfactory. However, as an attack aircraft, like all "fast movers," it is close to useless in Fourth Generation Wars and not much better for supporting friendly ground forces in wars against regional powers. That means the carrier's air wing is useful primarily for defending the carrier, which turns each of the Navy's $20-plus billion carrier battle groups into sailing tautologies. Their main mission is to exist.

From the perspective of military reform, the aircraft carrier's utility is that it is a big empty box that can carry lots of things – not just F-18s, and not just aircraft – to almost any point in the world. Reformers therefore seek two reforms of the carrier force: first, to decouple the carriers from any standard air wing, and second, to acquire some carrier-capable aircraft that can intervene effectively in the ground war, whether Third or Fourth Generation.

An example of the first reform came in the 1990s, during one of the endless series of crises in Haiti. An aircraft carrier was dispatched to Haiti without its usual air wing. Instead, it carried hundreds of Army troops and helicopters, of both attack and troop-transport types. So outfitted, it was very useful. Reformers would make that one rare example the norm. Carriers would have no standard air wing. They would become general purpose carriers, not aircraft carriers. They might carry troops (Army or Marine Corps), combat or transport fixed-wing aircraft, helicopters, relief supplies, containerized logistics – whatever a particular crisis or conflict required.

At the same time, the Navy would acquire a new type of attack aircraft, similar to the Air Force's A-10 in design philosophy, as part of a new "Jaeger air" capability. The Navy and the Marine Corps did a series of Jaeger-air experiments in the 1990s. The aircrews of fixed-wing aircraft cooperated directly with highly mobile ground forces in Light Armored Vehicles, bypassing the remote headquarters that reduce pilots to mere technicians following mechanical orders. The results suggested that Jaeger air could improve the effectiveness of both air and mobile ground units substantially beyond current levels. In Jaeger air, attack aircraft must fly low and slow so pilots can see and understand the ground situation. (This also requires educating pilots in ground tactics.) High-performance aircraft, such as the F-18, cannot do this, and if they tried, they would easily be shot down by ground fire. Their armament is also inappropriate for close-air support, as they lack a gun to effectively attack heavily armored vehicles such as tanks. No aircraft currently in or scheduled for the American inventory in the future, other than the A-10, is suitable for this mission.

Jaeger air plus decoupling the carriers from their standard air wings would give the U.S. Navy a stronger power projection capability, one that could influence the outcome of a ground battle or war. Its current claimed power projection capability, based on F-18s and Tomahawk cruise missiles, is usable, with a few exceptions, only against fixed targets. Most enemies quickly figure out what fixed targets we are likely to hit and make sure they are empty when we hit them. All the expense represented by current carrier battle groups ends up raining blows on air.

There is a third element to the carrier battle group: the cruisers and destroyers that escort the carriers. These are separable from the carrier itself, so we will consider them below.

Surface Warships

Surface warships comprise cruisers, destroyers and frigates. Since frigates, of which fewer than 30 ships of the Perry class remain in active service, are being phased out with no replacements, we will focus on cruisers and destroyers. Unlike submarines and aircraft carriers, which remain useful ships, cruisers and destroyers are obsolescent as warship types. In their main role, carrier escort, they add little to the carrier's own defenses, represented by its aircraft. They carry one or two anti-submarine helicopters each, useful aircraft, but provided in small numbers at high expense.

All current and building U.S. Navy cruisers and destroyers – 22 Ticonderoga-class cruisers, 52 Arleigh Burke class destroyers with 10 building, two "stealth" Zumwalt-class destroyers building (at a cost of $4.2 billion – perhaps even more – for one destroyer!) and a new class of cruisers planned – carry as their main armament the Aegis air defense system. Aegis was designed to protect carrier battle groups in the North Atlantic from massed raids by Soviet Backfire bombers during the Cold War. As the U.S.S. Vincennes demonstrated, it has little utility in coastal waters, where air traffic is likely to be heavy with civilian aircraft. Its capability against low-flying aircraft and anti-ship missiles is also in doubt, as many tests have demonstrated – tests that the Navy has refused to disclose. Aegis is a classic legacy system, running on endlessly at great expense long after the mission for which it was designed disappeared.

Reformers would mothball or transfer to the Naval Reserve all or almost all Aegis ships, and build no more. Nor would they build "stealth" warships, which can easily be detected by old fashioned long-wave radars (which can also pick up stealth aircraft). A few Aegis ships might be kept in active service for anti-ballistic missile duties if a program to give Aegis that capability proves successful. Despite several much-ballyhooed "tests," the actual capability of an Aegis ship for missile defense has yet to be tested in anything resembling a real-world scenario, where warning times can be short, the ship's position is usually less than optimal, and a chance storm may be tossing the ship around, to name just a few common difficulties.

The best escort for a carrier is another carrier, with an air wing task-organized to defend against the particular threats anticipated in the mission. Landing Heli-copter Attack (LHA) and Landing Helicopter Dock (LHD) ships, which are classed as amphibious ships but are actually small aircraft carriers, could function usefully as escort carriers. Should other escorts be required, they would best be provided by converting merchant ships, giving them modularized weapons, sensors and aircraft maintenance facilities. One converted merchantman could provide several times as many anti-submarine helicopters as a cruiser or destroyer at far less cost.

Amphibious Ships

Amphibious forces will be highly useful in Fourth Generation conflicts, because they can remain based at sea even during operations ashore. That helps us keep down the size of our "footprint" in a country where the obvious presence of U.S. troops is likely to alienate the local population. More broadly, it is no accident that a majority of Sir Julian Corbett's historical studies were devoted to amphibious warfare. Amphibious warfare usually works to the advantage of maritime powers, just as participation in continental wars usually works to their disadvantage.

The U.S. Navy is well-provided with large amphibious ships. Reformers would look to modifying merchant ship designs to provide large amphibious ships in the future, rather than building more overly expensive specialized designs. Virtually all the capabilities found in current amphibious ships are duplicated in ships in merchant service. The Royal Navy has used modified merchant ships successfully as amphibious ships, including in the Falklands war. What the Navy now lacks are small amphibious ships, such as the Landing Ship, Tank (LST), that are suited to coastal waters. This leads us to the principal weakness of the current U.S. fleet, which reformers want to address with a substantial building program.

Ships for Coastal and Inland Waters

Reflecting its Mahanian blue-water orientation, the U.S Navy today has few small warships suitable for warfare in coastal and inland waters. The Littoral Combat Ship (LCS) program, which recently attempted to build some, has foundered. Both competing designs exploded in cost so badly that second ships in the initial order were cancelled. The cost for either design of what should be a small, simple warship has escalated to half-a-billion dollars. It now appears the program, intended to produce 55 LCSs, will be fortunate to build the three additional ships it is now seeking with a new bidding process. Needless to say, neither of the first two LCSs has yet been subjected to any real testing. Beyond the LCSs, the Navy today has only eight Coastal Patrol ships, 20 Mark V class SEAL insertion and extraction boats and 20 riverine Special Operations craft. The Navy does assure us that the Virginia-class nuclear attack submarines, which are 377 feet long and displace 7800 tons, are "optimized for coastal operations," which is something of a bad joke.

What would reformers do to expand the Navy's capability in coastal and inland waters? First, they would build some appropriate watercraft (most "ships" are too big for green and brown water). Types would vary, but in general all would make extensive use of standard civilian design practice in order to avoid another cost debacle like the LCS. Many would be modifications of standard civilian types (which can conveniently provide "stealth" in crowded coastal and inland waters by giving Navy craft the same general "signatures" as civilian craft). Their vital spaces would be armored against the types of weapons they would face, e.g., up to heavy machine guns and RPG-7s. They would be well armed themselves, with machine guns, light automatic cannon, recoilless rifles and in some cases mortars to hit land targets. Some coastal and most river craft would be designed to carry Marines, both as boarding parties and for minor amphibious landings. Riverine warfare in particular is amphibious in nature.

Second, these new craft would be formed into deployable "packages" or flotillas that would include the support capabilities they need, such as maintenance shops, fuel and ammunition resupply and barracks (many of the craft being too small to have crews live aboard permanently). In the case of coastal craft, these support capabilities would be based on a "mother ship" that would deploy as the flotilla's home base. Support facilities for flotillas for inland waters would be designed for basing ashore or afloat. Flotillas could deploy quickly to take control of a troubled region's coastal and inland waters as the Navy's contribution to dealing with either a Fourth Generation conflict or a state-on-state regional conflict. Flotillas designed for inland waters should be air-deployable, as some of those waters may not have navigable outlets to the sea. Marines would be inherent to both types of flotillas.

How many flotillas do we need? As is usually the case (despite pretense otherwise), numbers can only be arbitrary until situations unfold. A reasonable place to start might be with six coastal flotillas, each capable of controlling a small country's coastal waters, and three flotillas for inland waters. Some or all of these flotillas might be manned by naval reservists. The wide variety of skills (and common sense) reservists bring from civilian life often makes them more capable in Fourth Generation conflicts than active service personnel.

Conclusion

The military reform Navy outlined here maintains America's naval dominance of the Atlantic and Pacific oceans, plus selected other seas when needed. America would retain a force of capital ships equal or superior to any other in the world. This would not be done in anticipation of any particular conflict, but as a reflection of our geographic and economic realities.

At the same time, the military reform Navy would enhance our capability to project naval power in ways that are relevant to where war is going in the 21st century. Our aircraft carriers would become more useful as we decouple them from standardized air wings that can do little beyond defend the carrier and bomb civilians ashore, as happened routinely in Iraq and Afghanistan. Big, empty boxes that can quickly carry lots of different kinds of things, including Jaeger air, almost anyplace in the world are worth their high cost. The Navy's new flotillas for coastal and inland waters would provide a highly relevant capability that at present is almost completely lacking. The ability to take control of a country's or region's coastal and inland waters is real naval power projection.

How much will it all cost? We would rather avoid the usual Washington practice of pulling numbers out of thin air and leave that question open. The fact that we will retire the cruisers and destroyers to the naval museums where they belong and build no more means it will cost less than the current Navy budget. We can buy a lot of flotilla craft for the price of a single Zumwalt-class destroyer.

ENDNOTES

1   Andrew Gordon, *The Rules of the Game* (Annapolis, Md.: Naval Institute Press, 1996).

2   Julian S. Corbett, *Some Principles of Maritime Strategy* (London: Longmans, Green & Co., 1911; new edition by Annapolis, Md.: Naval Institute Press, 1988).

3   Late in the Cold War, a Soviet "Whiskey"-class submarine that was spying on the Swedish navy at Karlskrona ran on the rocks and stranded where it was quite visible, well inside Swedish waters. Both the Soviet navy and the Soviet government were badly embarrassed.

CHAPTER 7

REVERSING THE DECAY
OF AMERICAN AIR POWER

Col. Robert Dilger and Pierre M. Sprey (U.S. Air Force, ret.)

U.S. Air Force resource allocations and tactical/strategic decisions from the 1930s to today have been heavily dominated by the theories expressed in Giulio Douhet's 1921 book, "The Command of the Air." Douhet's premise was that strategic bombardment of an enemy's heartland can win wars independently of ground forces. The unchanging dominance of that strategic bombardment paradigm has caused the Air Force to discount effective, sometimes war-winning, forms of air power and to spend vast sums on air power technologies that are ineffective and often counterproductive. Further, this focus on bombardment technologies has created the huge cost, maintenance and logistics burdens of the present steadily aging and shrinking fleet of U.S. Air Force aircraft.

The aircraft in Table 1 (on page 130) comprise the Air Force's major combat and support aircraft inventory. All but two of the 15 aircraft listed began their development 30 or more years ago and will remain in the active inventory for a long time to come. (Two – the B-2 and the F-22 – are "younger" at 20 plus years.) At the extreme, the B-52, a 1944 requirement concept which began development in 1952, is scheduled to remain in inventory until 2030 – almost a full century. The age and enormous burden of this inventory will only deteriorate further under present Air Force plans.[1]

In the late 1960s and early 1970s, the U.S. Air Force received an unasked for bonanza of three warfighting aircraft. It despised all three: a 40,000-pound F-15 (the Air Force wanted a very different 80,000-pound aircraft); the smaller, lighter F-16 (considered a Mattel toy by most in the Air Force leadership); and the greatest heresy of all, the A-10 dedicated to the mission of close support for troops in combat, a mission the Air Force wanted to forget. A group of individuals of various backgrounds, known as the "Fighter Mafia,"[3] fought a long and harsh battle to place all three aircraft into the Air Force inventory – and won. Of the Air Force's 2,581 warfighting aircraft listed in Table 1, 2,390 (or 93 percent) are the very same designs the Air Force originally did all in its power to scuttle.

Air Combat and Funding Lessons of History (1918-2008)

The most reliable gauge of any air force's underlying beliefs is its funding decisions for key combatants, in this case the relative funding for bombers versus fighters, that is for strategic bombardment versus air-to-air and close support.

Table 1. Major U.S. Air Force Active and Reserve Component Aircraft in 2008[3]

U.S. Air Force Active/Reserve Aircraft	First Year of Development	Quantity	Direct Combat Aircraft	Support Aircraft
A-10	1967	249	249	-
OA-10	1967	108	-	108
AC-130	1966	21	21	-
B-1	1965	64	64	-
B-2	1980	20	20	-
B-52	1952	94	94	-
C-5	1964	111	-	111
C-17	1981	165	-	165
C-130	1951	514	-	514
F-15	1968	714	714	-
F-16	1969	1,319	1,319	-
F-22	1986	100	100	-
E-3	1971	32	-	31
KC-135	1955	532	-	532
KC-10	1977	59	-	59
Total		**4,102**	**2,581**	**1,521**

Shortly after World War I, the U.S. Army Air Corps,[4] as well as the British Royal Air Force (RAF) and the German Luftwaffe, became captivated by General Douhet's theory of air power: strategic bombardment could win a war by itself by attacking the enemy's heartland.

At the close of World War I, our Army Air Corps possessed approximately 12,000 pursuit fighters. By 1930, it let this fleet became a worn out and dated force of 400 obsolescent biplane pursuit aircraft – a mere 3 percent of its former greatness. No other U.S. military arm was cut so severely. On the other hand, by 1941 the Army Air Force had developed an inconceivable 71 separate bombers.[5] Throughout this period, bomber funding dominated the air power budgets. Typically, while four to six fighters would equal the cost of one bomber, the force ratios actually procured were heavily biased in favor of bombers.[6] Because of the almost exclusive budgetary emphasis on bombers by the U.S. Army Air Force, the Royal Air Force and the Luftwaffe, the three great air superiority fighters of the World War II western combatants (the U.S. Army Air Force P-51 Mustang, the RAF Spitfire, and the Luftwaffe ME-109) were all developed by private ventures quite independently of their respective nations' air force leadership.

The German Luftwaffe: Stuka Versus Bomber Analysis
Beginnings of the Stuka

Although it is rarely discussed by historians, from the '30s on the Luftwaffe was dominated by bomber generals and bomber spending. In the early stages of World War II, they undertook major strategic bombardment campaigns against Britain and Russia. As late as the Battle of the Bulge in the winter of 1944, they were still focused on major bombardment efforts against the rear areas of the Allies. From the German perspective, this focus had disastrous results.

At the most senior Luftwaffe levels, the only prominent advocate of a fighter-based approach to air power was Col. Gen. Ernst Udet, a close personal friend of Field Marshall Hermann Goering, the Supreme Commander of the Luftwaffe. Almost alone in the early 1930s, Udet supported the development and production of the Ju-87 "Stuka" dive bomber. The Luftwaffe Air Staff tolerated the Stuka but limited its procurement to a tiny percentage of aircraft procurement funding. The Luftwaffe decided to cancel Stuka production in 1943, shortly after Udet's death and well before the war's end.

Implications of German air power in the Spanish Civil War (1936-1938)

Field Marshall Wolfram von Richthofen, the head of the German Condor Legion fighting in Spain, realized that multi-engine, horizontal (i.e. level bombing) bombers were a poor fit for the conflict. Against considerable opposition and without official sanction, he went on to develop the techniques and tactics of close support based on the Stuka and other fighters.[7]

Despite impressive combat results achieved by von Richthofen, not much changed at the Luftwaffe air staff. Luftwaffe crew authorizations in 1938 tell the story: only 300 Stuka air crews were authorized, compared to 1,409 crews for multi-engine bombers.[8] The Luftwaffe bomber paradigm was clearly apparent in the 5-to-1 bomber advantage. This imbalance also resulted in an even larger training burden imbalance of 600 Stuka crew members (at two per aircraft) versus over 7,000 bomber crew members (five per aircraft). Ratios of similar magnitudes held all the way to the end of 1943; at that point, the production of most bombers and all Stukas was canceled.

However, far more importantly, the bombers' funding was 25 times greater than the Stukas' – given that one bomber equaled the cost of five Stukas. This advantage provided the bomber a funding advantage of 96 percent bombers to 4 percent Stukas.[9] It is also notable that the Germans produced 114,000 aircraft of all types. Despite the failure of the German strategic campaigns (discussed below), this total included 25,000 bombers but only 4,900 Stukas.[10] Had the investment made in multi-engine bombers been transferred to Stukas, 125,000 Ju-87s would have resulted.

Holland, Belgium and France, 1940

Despite the swift and overwhelming defeat of Dutch and Belgian resistance by the Germans, the Luftwaffe took relatively heavy bomber losses in the two day campaign: 67 bombers and 16 Stukas were lost.[11]

In France, the Germans easily crossed the Meuse River, innovatively using the Stukas in continuous close support over the German army spearhead. In a panic, the RAF sent their conventional bombers (they had no Stuka equivalent, nor would they develop one) to destroy the German pontoon bridges. On a single day, May 15, 1940, the RAF lost 56 percent of the horizontal bombers sent to destroy these bridges.[12] And, they failed to eliminate the bridges. (Later in the war, on the eastern front, Stukas easily destroyed many pontoon bridges constructed by the Soviets.) Nonetheless, neither side's air leaders acknowledged the effectiveness of the Stuka and the failure of the conventional bomber for such missions.

During the British-French evacuation from the port city of Dunkirk, the Luftwaffe's strategic bombers were tasked to destroy the Allied forces. They also failed.[13] The British extracted 338,000 soldiers. RAF fighter aircraft attacked the German bombers attacking the Dunkirk area. Apparent losses were great on both sides. The loss data was presented in a simple sentence by one historian: "...from May 26 through June 3, the RAF lost 177 aircraft destroyed or damaged; the Germans lost 240."[14] This quote demonstrates how combat data can be warped to support a favored position. Seemingly, the Luftwaffe lost 36 percent more aircraft than the RAF. With a moment's thought the bias can be plainly seen: the statement equates destroyed or damaged RAF aircraft with destroyed German aircraft. An "apples to apples" comparison of just destroyed aircraft would mean approximately 60 RAF fighter losses – plus 117 damaged to equal the 177 "destroyed or damaged" in the quote. (The RAF on average suffered two damaged fighters for each loss.) The comparison of aircraft destroyed should be more like 60 RAF losses compared to 240 Luftwaffe losses, or a four to one defeat for the Luftwaffe.

However, a second, larger bias is still present. The RAF lost exclusively inexpensive fighters, while the Luftwaffe lost mostly expensive bombers. This fact is unreported even though it is crucial to understanding the combat realities. The investment cost for each Luftwaffe bomber was about 4 to 5 times greater than for each RAF fighter. A better comparison can be made based on estimated costs; Table 2 shows the results.

Table 2. Dunkirk Aircraft Losses – Investment Cost Comparisons

Air Force	Losses	Cost Ratio
RAF	60 exclusively fighters	60 fighters
Luftwaffe	240 mostly bombers	960 aircraft cost equivalents (where each bomber = 4 fighters)

Ignoring relative casualties is the final distortion. RAF single-seat fighter casualties occurred at a rate of about 0.5 crew members per aircraft lost. The Luftwaffe bomber casualty rate is unknown. However, later in the war, the U.S. Army Air Force/RAF bomber casualties were generally about 80 to 85 percent of the crew in each bomber loss. Thus, the British lost approximately 30 pilots with their loss of 60 fighters, while the Germans may have lost about 960 crew members in the loss of up to 240 bombers. The Luftwaffe was potentially losing crew members at a rate 32 times greater than the RAF in the Dunkirk scenario, and the Luftwaffe was loosing expensive bombers at a 400 percent greater rate than the RAF was losing fighters. In cost terms, the Luftwaffe losses were 1,600 percent greater, and their crew casualties were 3,200 percent greater. All of this was almost certainly distorted, obscured or missing in the combat data presented by the air staffs to their senior leadership. As we shall see, this practice did not end with Dunkirk or even World War II.

In addition, historians of the Dunkirk battle seldom mention that British shipping took a fearful beating. Britain lost 6 destroyers, and 23 other warships were damaged.[16] In addition, 230 lesser ships and boats were lost. This Luftwaffe success was accomplished mostly by Stukas. Author Peter C. Smith states categorically, "Dive bombers ... were proved to be the quintessential weapon for destroying ships. ...By contrast ... no major warship was ever sunk. ...[by multi-engine, high altitude bombers]."[17] The Luftwaffe leadership was completely silent on this great disparity. As so often happens, the Air Staff allowed the bombers to amass most of the combat credit earned by Stukas. It must be understood that Field Marshall Goering surely approved of this deception. If Goering had actually gathered, analyzed, and presented bomb damage assessment data by aircraft type, his bomber program advocacy to Hitler would have floundered.

The Battle of Britain

The Battle of Britain began with a huge imbalance of forces: 2,600 Luftwaffe aircraft versus 741 RAF fighters. Less than 300 of the RAF fighters were Spitfires. Only these were a good match against 800 German ME-109s. See Table 3.

Table 3. Aircraft Committed to the Battle of Britain[15]

	RAF	Luftwaffe
Bombers	Not applicable	1.134
Fighters	741 (279 Spitfires)	1,109 (809 ME-109s)
Stukas	Not Available	316
Total	741	2,559

Phase I of the battle began on July 1, 1940. The Luftwaffe was tasked to close the English Channel to shipping and to clear British destroyer flotillas from their anti-invasion bases. Rather rapidly, the Stukas sank one out of every three British ships using the Channel. Within a few weeks, on July 27, the British gave up using the Channel. Ship losses were too great.[18] It was the Stuka's victory, but once again, the Luftwaffe bombers acquired the lion's share of this success through tailored air staff reporting.[19]

In Phase II of the battle, the Luftwaffe planners predicted their strategic bombers would achieve air superiority in four days of bombing the RAF fighter bases. The bombers failed. They did not achieve air superiority in four days, nor in four months.[20] During the three months of July through September 1940, the Luftwaffe lost 621 bombers (45 percent of initial strength) and 88 Stukas (21 percent of initial strength).[21] The Stukas were pulled from the air battle three weeks before the end of September but shortly returned again in October. Correcting for the three week hiatus would result in an estimated 29 percent Stuka loss compared to a 45-percent bomber loss rate. As a percent of initial strength, the bombers' losses were 150 percent greater than the Stukas'. However, the Stukas generally flew sorties each day at about three times the bomber rate. Thus, on a per sortie basis, the bomber loss rates were five times the rate of the Stukas.

Fortunately for the Allies, the Luftwaffe ignored its own data. Bomber production numbers remained five times that of the Stuka and about 25 times that of the Stuka in funding. The Luftwaffe had a winner in their inexpensive Stukas but put almost all their air-to-ground funding into the expensive but ineffective multi-engine bomber.

As a direct result of the Luftwaffe's crushing bomber daytime losses, the Germans switched to night attack in October 1940. As is well known, this effort failed in its objectives to reduce British production and to lower civilian morale. In fact, "direct attacks on British industrial targets and population centers only spurred British desires to repay in kind."[22] Worker morale and British war production increased rapidly. The strategic objective of Goering's Battle of Britain bombing campaign was defeated. Operation Sea Lion, the German cross-Channel invasion, had to be put on indefinite hold. Despite huge bomber losses and lack of military gain, neither the Luftwaffe – nor the RAF – altered their unbalanced, massive commitment to bomber production.

Gen. Adolf Galland, commander of German day fighters succinctly summarized how the resources wasted on bombers harmed the German war effort:

"In the beginning of 1940 the monthly production figure for the ME-109 was approximately 125 ... the peak was reached with a monthly production of 2,500...in autumn 1944. [During and after a year and a half of massive bombardment of German manufacturing plants.] At the end of 1944, we had a fighter production about 20 times larger than it had been when the Luftwaffe entered the Battle of Britain. Had the fighter production reached in 1944 been reached in 1940, or even 1941, the Luftwaffe would never have lost air supremacy and the tide of the war would have taken an entirely different course. Neither technical reasons nor shortages of raw material prevented it. ...It was the fundamental ideology of the German leadership with regard to aerial warfare according to Douhet [that] this was to be done by annihilating the enemy on the ground by surprise attack [with bombers]. ...Fighters were only to be tolerated as a necessary evil, a concession to the unpopular act of defense."[23]

Bomber and Stuka use in Russia

Operation Barbarossa, the German invasion of Russia, began on June 22, 1941. A part of the early Soviet retaliation was the use of large multi-engine bombers on June 30, following the paradigm of the Western air forces. German Me-109s shot down 179 of these, among the 3,808 Soviet aircraft destroyed in this very early phase of the war.[24] Unlike the Allies, the Soviets rapidly altered their paradigm of bomber employment (see below).

As early as July 1941, a fuel shortage was limiting Luftwaffe missions. Despite this, the Luftwaffe used great quantities of fuel to launch a strategic bombardment campaign against Moscow. On July 22, 1941, 238 bombers conducted their first Moscow night attack. Thereafter, the Luftwaffe sent 76 ever-smaller bomber raids against Moscow. The raids accomplished nothing except to consume huge quantities of scarce fuel.[25] The Moscow campaign was the fourth Luftwaffe bomber campaign that ended in failure following on the heels of Spain, Dunkirk and the Battle of Britain. Nonetheless, the high Luftwaffe bomber procurement priority remained unchanged.

The German armies made lightning advances across the wide 2,200 mile Russian front. On average only 300 Stukas were available to cover the entire front. Obviously, they could not properly service the enormous "turkey-shoot" opportunities the Soviets presented in their wild retreat. Despite great carnage, a substantial portion of the huge Soviet armies escaped. By the middle of December, the German armies reached the tram lines of Moscow before Arctic weather and a Soviet counterattack stopped them. A reduction as small as 10 percent in Luftwaffe bomber funding would have allowed the procurement of 15,000 Stukas, while only reducing bombers to 22,500 from 25,000. Given the effectiveness of Stukas against tactical battlefield targets (discussed below), the high priority provided to their ineffective bombers and the near-complete rejection of the Stuka cost the Germans the possibility of success on the eastern front.

Luftwaffe bomber losses in 1941 came to 1,798 aircraft, from a beginning number of 1,339 (a 134 percent loss, which includes replacement aircraft). Stuka losses were 366 from a beginning base number of 456 (an 80 percent loss).[26] Bomber losses five times those of the Stuka amounted to 25 times larger losses in cost. On a per sortie basis (assuming three Stuka sorties per day, compared to one for bombers), bomber loss rates were about 500 percent greater. By every measure, the Stuka had a significantly smaller loss rate than the bomber. Nonetheless, the Luftwaffe air staff continued the myth of Stuka vulnerability and left the aircraft production priorities unchanged.

On September 21-24, 1941, several Stuka missions were sent against the Soviet Baltic fleet operating in the Finnish Sea near Leningrad. Lt. Hans Rudel, of *Stuka Pilot* fame, damaged the Soviet battleship *Marat* on his first sortie. In an ensuing mission Rudel sank a cruiser. A few days later, he dropped a delayed fuse 2,000 pound bomb that detonated an ammunition magazine in the *Marat*. It broke in half and sank while in port.[27] The cost of all 4,900 Stukas produced over a 10-year period was about $25 million – approximately the same cost as the battleship. The entire 10-year Stuka production run was justified on a single sortie. Other Stukas hit the *Marat's* sister battleship, the *Oktobrescaig Revolutia* 10 times, inflicting great damage; they also sank seven other ships and damaged eight.[28]

Contrast that performance to the RAF bomber performance over a one-year period on nearly identical missions. Two German battlecruisers, the *Gneisenau* and *Scharnhorst*, plus a cruiser, *Prinz Eugen*, had been forced into Brest harbor just a short distance across the Channel from England. Over the next year, the British sent 299 heavy bomber attack missions against the German ships – approximately 8,000 sorties. They lost 43 aircraft, all bombers and 247 airmen.[29] On Feb. 11, 1942, a year after the ships had entered the port, they made a successful dash through the English Channel to Norway. The British sent continuous waves of multi-engine bombers to stop their escape. They lost another 60 aircraft, again mostly bombers, and an estimated 345 airmen. The Luftwaffe employed 150 ME-109s to provide cover over the escaping ships. They lost 17 fighters and only 11 airmen.[30]

Both the Luftwaffe and the RAF had complete reports on the Stuka and RAF bombers' results against battleships. Neither altered their advocacy of multi-engine bombers over single engine dive-bombing.

Despite its successes in other missions, the primary utility of the Stuka was its timely and effective close support of the German army. It was a key component of the blitzkrieg operations that were brilliantly successful in the German conquest of Poland, Denmark, Holland, Belgium and France. In the first year of the Russian campaign, Stuka close support was devastating even though only about 300 Stukas were operating across a 2,200-mile front. No total of Russian tanks destroyed by those 300 Stukas is available but they must have accounted for many thousands. Rudel alone had confirmed kills of 518 tanks; the next highest Stuka pilot had approximately 300 tank kills.[31]

In 1943, the Luftwaffe bomber generals canceled Stuka production. The last Stuka was produced in July 1944.[32] To replace it, the Germans had already developed the Hs-129B, a well conceived follow-on. It had two widely spaced engines, an armored cockpit and, most importantly, a 30-mm internal cannon that carried enough rounds for 18-tank killing attacks compared to only six for the Stuka. Due to low priority, it was equipped with an unreliable French surplus engine and then canceled before mass production. Once again, the bomber advocates prevailed.

Neither the British nor the United States saw value in a Stuka equivalent. Unlike the western forces, the Soviets paid attention to their initial bombing failures and abandoned their huge ineffective bomber force. Instead, they developed the highly robust Shturmovik IL-2 close-support fighter and produced an astonishing 36,000 of them. With this huge close-support fleet the Shturmovik became a major player in Russian successes.

Luftwaffe air defense and revenge weapons

The British had won "The Battle of Britain" using 700 to 800 fighters, but they immediately rejected their population's experience with strategic bombing ineffectiveness. Instead, they embraced the same losing strategic bombardment policy as the Luftwaffe by launching a new, huge night bombing offensive against German cities. The Luftwaffe, in mirror-image fashion, rejected the idea of boosting fighter production to defeat the city-busting bombers, despite having just experienced the defeat of their own bombers at the hands of the RAF fighters.

Hitler and Goering were so focused on bombing and revenge that they would not entertain diverting funds to defensive fighters. Instead, Germany's primary air defense weapon was heavy flak artillery. These were relatively ineffective. Given the large round size, the rate of fire was only 1 round per 30 seconds. The timed-fused rounds were none too accurate and expensive. By 1944, 1.25 million men manned about 12,000 heavy guns. They were a great burden on German military resources and they provided, at best, a rather leaky defense.[33] There were also a limited number of German night fighters; these extracted a huge toll from the British attackers.

The V-1 was a relatively low cost, air-breathing missile. It delivered a 2,000-pound warhead with miss distances of several miles, a 75-percent failure rate and a nearly 90-percent shoot-down rate by RAF fighters. The V-1 accomplished little. The V-2 rocket had an equally poor accuracy and failure rate. It was a notably complex and very expensive liquid-fueled rocket; 6,000 were produced although only 3,000 were successfully launched. It was the most expensive weapon produced by the Germans. (The 6,000 V-2s equaled the cost of 48,000 tanks.) Given its high failure rate and poor accuracy, its military utility was negligible, and yet it was one of the most fabled "weapons" of World War II, touted by defense analysts for decades.

The U.S. Strategic Bomber Survey, discussed below, estimated that the V-2 cost Germany's aircraft production capacity the equivalent of 24,000 fighters. Assume that instead of the V-2, the Germans procured 24,000 additional Stukas. Like the V-2, the Stuka could also carry a 2,000-pound bomb and could deliver up to 50 sorties for each Stuka. Thus, the 24,000 Stukas could deliver up to 1.2 million 2,000-pound bombs with accuracy vastly superior to the V-2. It was amazing that the Germans had the technological expertise to develop the complex V-2 but were unable to appreciate the V-2's minuscule effectiveness.

Luftwaffe conclusions

In the Battle of Britain, German bombers attacked British airfields but achieved little with heavy losses. Even less effective were the following fall's night incendiary offensives against London, Essex, Canterbury and other cities. Not only were German losses high, but the British population became so outraged that war volunteers and war production soared. In contrast, the tiny force of 300 or so operational close-support Stukas achieved real successes in support of the Blitzkrieg armies slashing their way into France and Russia.

German historian Cajus Bekker summarized the Allies' successes and failures against the Luftwaffe as follows:

> "From 1944 on, the possession of long range fighters [P-51 Mustangs] ...enabled the Americans to win air control over Germany. ...British Bomber Command's endeavor to decide the issue of the war by carpet bombing of the German cities was unsuccessful. ...[German] war production ... reach[ed] its highest ever output at the peak of the bombardment. ...Victory for the Allies was much more [due] to the overwhelming superiority of their tactical forces during and after the invasion. ...In other words it was attacks on military targets, not those on the civilian population. ...that decided the issue. That lesson should never be forgotten."[34]

RAF Bomber Command

Sir Arthur "Bomber" Harris was the commander of the RAF Bomber Command. He was a true believer in the Douhet bombardment theory. Professor Williamson Murray described his philosophy: "Harris possessed an unshakable belief that, with the necessary resources, his command could win the war by itself. ...[He] became a convert to an "area" [city busting] bombing strategy."[35]

Bomber Command's forces consisted of only between 400 to 500 bombers in 1942. The RAF's attempted bomber buildup barely progressed because of continuing heavy losses, which totaled 1,404 four-engine heavy bombers for 1942.[36] To lose almost three times the initial bomber force in a single year was horrendous. The bombers caused great civilian damage to Ruhr cities but had little effect on German military production, which accelerated throughout the year.

To fight the "Battle of Berlin" between August 1943 and March 1944, Harris was convinced that his bombers alone could kill enough civilians to cause the German state to capitulate. The RAF Bomber Command lost its entire bomber fleet every three months. Losses for January 1943 to March 1944 came to 5,881 bombers.[37] To have lost almost 6,000 bombers with 30,000 associated aircrew casualties in 15 months was a bloody massacre. The RAF Bomber Command had decisively lost their war against the German night fighters.

Fortunately, for the RAF bomber crews, Operation Overlord, the D-Day invasion, took priority after March 30, 1944, despite Sir Harris' strong objections to any diversion of force from city-busting. Bomber losses dropped instantly. Professor Murray wrapped it up well, noting that "...the Battle of Berlin was a mistake – one in which Harris came close to wrecking his command ... and as [Air Vice Marshal] Bennett noted, the battle, 'had been the worst thing that could have happened to the RAF Bomber Command'."[38]

The British "strategic" city-bombing campaigns of 1942-1945 were just as ineffective as the Luftwaffe's bombardment of English cities. In four years of bombing German cities, RAF bomber command suffered over 70,000 aircrew casualties while German military production soared. British strategic bombardment achieved none of its objectives, and it came at a crippling cost.

The U.S. Army Air Force: World War II
Preliminary operations

Unfortunately for the Allies, Gen. Erwin Rommel, the infamous "Desert Fox," had been creating havoc in North Africa since 1941. In response, American troops were sent there in large numbers. Their first significant battle against the Germans was at Kasserine Pass, in February 1943. It was one of the worst U.S. Army defeats in its history. While the U.S. Army Air Force outnumbered the Luftwaffe in North Africa by a 3-1 ratio, it was unable to provide the Army any useful help. General of the Air Force Henry H. "Hap" Arnold, a Douhet advocate, summarized his faction's view of the issue; "Torch [the code name for Allied invasion of Northwest Africa] offered about as poor an air deal as could have been dreamed up. Practically every one of our principles for the use of air power ... had to be violated." He further explained to Gen. Carl Andrew "Tooey" Spaatz the basic problem as he saw it, "The development of the war is just about the worst case scenario as far as our air plans are concerned."[39]

In actual fact, North Africa armored warfare was an ideal setting for air power. American air power was presented with an enticing tactical target turkey shoot. German armor was out in the open and on the move, perfectly delineated against a barren desert background. Only the fanatical belief in strategic bombardment blinded the Army Air Force generals to this obvious close-support opportunity.

Despite the terrible performance of U.S. air power, Rommel's army surrendered on May 10, 1943. His army was not so much defeated as it ran out of armor, fuel and ammo. The origins of this achievement can be traced back to 21 RAF Swordfish torpedo biplanes that successfully destroyed four Italian battleships protecting the Axis' Mediterranean sea lanes. It was the beginning of an intensive Allied naval interdiction campaign that strangled Rommel's army.

In 1943, the Americans needed to conquer the small Italian island of Pantelleria and the nearby Pelagian atoll to provide air fields near Sicily to support an invasion there. They were held by dispirited Italian units. Gen. Hap Arnold ordered the Army Air Force to "Bomb the Hell out of them."[40] Over 1,100 aircraft flew 7,000 sorties dropping 12,400,000 pounds of ordnance on these two tiny outcroppings of land. Twice the Italians refused Gen. Dwight Eisenhower's surrender offer despite the bombing. He had hoped to avoid an invasion. Finally, he sent a 600-ship force into their harbor. The Italians surrendered to the invasion force.

Despite this, the strategic bombardment leaders were ecstatic, claiming the lion's share of the victory. Tooey Spaatz declared the old debate about bombardment dead, "The application of air available to us can reduce to the point of surrender any first class nation now in existence."[41] Nonetheless, less than 5 percent of the bombs came within 300 feet of their target. Almost all of the Italian big guns survived. Their hangars dug into the side of the hills were unscathed. Very few Italian casualties resulted. In other words, bombing accomplished little of military value.[42] The air staff – in this case the American one – studiously avoided the data and its implications.[43]

U.S. European fighter operations

On June 27, 1943, an Allied landing force of 1,200 ships was en route to an invasion of Sicily. There were 1,500 German aircraft within striking distance. American and British fighters were tasked to provide air cover. Despite repeated Luftwaffe mass attacks, not a single ship was lost. On that day the Anglo-American fighters had won the air battle for the Mediterranean. This was the last Luftwaffe mass attack in the theater.

The European war was fought by the United States primarily with three fighters, the P-38, P47 and the P-51. All three were developed after the World War II build-up started in late 1937. The P-38 and the P-47 failed as high-altitude dogfighters. Eventually the P-38 was withdrawn from Europe as a fighter, while it did continue in other roles. The P-47 was pulled from the bomber-escort role and then employed on close support and interdiction ground-attack missions. It failed as a high altitude, long-range dogfighter but became pre-eminent in the close support and interdiction ground-attack missions.

The P-51 was initially developed as a private venture independent of the Army Air Force's development bureaucracy. They favored the larger, less maneuverable and more expensive P-47 and P-38. After the P-51 was mated with the Rolls-Royce Merlin engine, license-built in the United States (a modification strongly opposed by the Army Air Force leadership), it became perhaps the best fighter aircraft in any World War II theater. Over 15,000 P-51s were ultimately procured, most of them with the Merlin engine. Interestingly, it was also the smallest and least expensive U.S. fighter – yet it had the longest range: 600 miles, compared to only 375 miles for the larger P-47.[44]

The U.S. bomber generals' assumptions proved particularly wrong about their oft-repeated claim that heavily armored bombers would always get through. Once unescorted daylight raids entered the German heartland in 1943, the U.S. Army Air Force bomber losses grew exponentially. The loss rate average for 1943 was an untenable 6 percent per sortie.[45] After crippling losses of 30 percent at Schweinfurt and at Regensburg, the Army Air Force was forced to cease almost all strategic bombardment operations in August 1943. They only resumed in force in early 1944 when the long-range P-51 escort fighters belatedly became available.

The P-51 changed the equation. The bombers acted as a sacrificial goat that attracted the Luftwaffe day fighters. The escort P-51s engaged the Luftwaffe fighters and with their numerical advantage, a superb performing aircraft, and pilots with far more training hours, they prevailed. It was P-51s that won air superiority over Germany just shortly before D-Day, which was the critical precursor necessary for a successful D-Day invasion.

In fact, the U.S. fighters had so decimated the Luftwaffe that it could only launch a pathetic 200 sorties against the exposed D-Day landing force at Normandy on June 6, 1944. Utterly dominant, Allied aircraft flew 15,000 sorties that day.[46] Of course, not all Allied sorties were effective. Over a thousand heavy bombers with thousands of tons of bombs blasted the Omaha landing site, but most missed their target area by as much as 3 miles. Maj. Gen. Charles Gerhardt, the division commander, in disgust stated, "Very few of the bombs fell on the beach or the fortifications commanding it ... the failure cost heavily in men and material."[47]

Maj. Gen. Elwood Richard "Pete" Quesada, the Army Air Force's pioneer in air-ground cooperation, performed magnificently with his 1,500 tactical fighters, primarily P-47s, against the tenacious German defenses in the Normandy area. His P-47s roamed the French road and rail network feeding into the area from dawn to dusk, wreaking tremendous damage and delays on the 23 German divisions trying to reach the Normandy beach head to overwhelm the invaders. The German divisions' planned three-day travel time took as long as six weeks – and those that finally made it arrived badly mauled by the P-47s.

Without the P-47s under Quesada's leadership, the Normandy invasion could have been a rout of monumental proportions. It was Quesada and his 1,500 fighters that pulled our chestnuts out of a potentially very hot fire. It was the effectiveness of the U.S. fighter bombers performing close-in tactical interdiction missions against the German reinforcing divisions that prevented a potential defeat of our forces on the Normandy beaches. The American ground commander Lt. Gen. Omar Bradley stated, "The fighter-bomber operations against road traffic played a major part in the success of the invasion," – perhaps the biggest understatement of the entire war.[48]

Multi-engine strategic and tactical bombing

Half of America's total World War II budget went to U.S. air power and, of that half, 65 percent went to multi-engine bombers. A major study to quantify the effectiveness of this huge investment was initiated in October 1944 at the direction of President Roosevelt. The United States Strategic Bombing Survey (USSBS) was to consist of a small group of civilian experts. The Army quickly dominated the Survey team with 850 military participants versus 300 civilians.

The Survey's summary report contains a wealth of information. Embedded deep in it were a few sentences that succinctly summarized the results of the U.S. Army Air Force/RAF strategic bombardment campaigns:

> "...City attacks by the RAF prior to August 1944 did not substantially affect the course of German war production. German war production as a whole continued to increase. ...while production received a moderate setback after a raid, it recovered substantially within a relatively few weeks. [Though unstated, the U.S. daylight raids had the same outcome.] In late 1944, there were so many forces making for the collapse of production ... that it is not possible separately to assess the effects of these later area raids on war production. There is no doubt, however, that they were significant."[49]

What is missing in the above summary is the fact that only 35 percent of bomber missions after March 1944 were strategic, that is, against cities, war production and other strategic targets, as opposed to against ground forces. Secondly, the Survey's experts did, in fact, document the effects of bombing on specific target systems such as railroads, bridges, oil production and munitions production.

The following data are extracted from the USSBS summary report:

- 5.4 billion lbs. of ordnance were dropped.
- 1,440,000 bomber sorties were flown.
- 60,000 U.S. and 40,000 RAF bombers were manufactured.
- On average, each bomber manufactured produced 15 sorties.
- 60,000 U.S. fighters were manufactured.
- 2,680,000 Allied fighter sorties were flown.
- On average, per aircraft manufactured, fighters produced three times as many sorties as bombers.
- 1,300,000 men were in the U.S. air combat commands.
- 79,200 American airmen were casualties: 73,000 in bombers and 5,600 in fighters.
- Total Allied casualties for airmen were 158,500.
- 18,000 U.S. planes were lost: 12,400 U.S. bombers and 5,600 U.S. fighters.
- 22,000 British planes were lost for a total of 40,000 Allied planes lost.

We also know from other sources that the U.S. bombers suffered average losses of 4.5 percent per sortie throughout the war, more than four times the rate of fighters.[50] The human cost of bomber losses was far greater: total casualties were 13 times greater in bombers than fighters. A fighter loss resulted in a single aircrew member casualty; the much larger number of bomber losses resulted in 6 to 10 crew members lost per aircraft lost.

These costs must be measured against the bombers' achievements. The USSBS examined nine separate campaigns against specific target systems. The eight campaigns against ball bearing, aircraft, steel, armored vehicle, electrical power, truck production and submarine pens were all judged failures that had little effect in advancing victory. The ninth, fuel production, was assessed a success, though some experts attributed the dire German fuel shortages of late 1944 to the Russian capture of the Ploesti oil fields in August 1944. All the bombers that flew the eight failed strategic bombardment campaigns could have remained home without effect on the war's outcome – except to reduce U.S. casualties by at least 50,000 airmen.

The multi-engine bombers had somewhat better success against tactical targets. As noted earlier, in March 1944, both RAF and U.S. bombers were pulled off most of their strategic raids and tasked to battlefield interdiction missions to prepare for the D-Day invasion. This occurred over the strongest objections of both the RAF and U.S. Army Air Force senior leadership. From this period forward until the war's end, 65 percent of the bomber missions were not strategic but tactical interdiction. Bomber losses dropped from an average of 6 percent during 1943 to about 1.5 percent by D-Day and thereafter.[51] Not only did the bomber loss rate drop by 75 percent but, more importantly, their mission success rate took a turn for the better.

From this perspective, one can find some success on the part of the heavy bombers. First, by luring the Luftwaffe into the skies to be shot down by Allied escort fighters, the bombers enabled the defeat of the German fighter force; second, bomber attacks on road and rail networks contributed to hampering German reinforcement of a number of battles, though tactical attacks by fighter types very probably had a much more direct effect.

In conclusion, the RAF and U.S. Army Air Force bomber commands fared rather poorly in their strategic bombardment campaigns. Eight of nine of the strategic bombardment campaigns were failures, contributing little to Allied victory. With the switch to interdiction missions, the bomber loss rate rapidly dropped, and they started achieving some observable military effects.[52]

Post-World War II fighter draw down, bomber largess

When the war ended, almost all the fighters were sent to "boneyards," with a small contingent sent to the reserves. The fighter production rate had been 2,000 fighters per month at the war's end. A short three years later the Air Force was producing 11 F-86 fighters per month.

In 1945, the Army Air Force planned and approved a force that would consist of 112 heavy bomber groups (about 10,000 bombers) and 95 light bomber/fighter groups.[53] The bomber planners believed that a bomber carrying atomic bombs was the equivalent of 1,000 World War II B-17s; the absurdity of an approved force structure the equivalent of 10 million B-17s is astonishing.

In 1947, the U.S. Air Force reduced these numbers to 75 heavy bomber groups and 25 light bomber/fighter groups, a bomber force the equivalent of "just" eight million B-17s. Note also that they grouped the light bombers (i.e. two-engine bombers) with the fighters, thereby burying the tremendous cut in fighters. Assuming an even split of light bombers and fighters in those units, the approved force had 88 percent bombers and only 12 percent fighters.[54] In terms of dollars, this amounted to 96 percent for bombers versus 4 percent for fighters.

The worst was yet to come. In 1948, the Tactical Air Command (i.e. fighters) under the war's most successful air power leader and close support innovator, General Quesada, was downgraded to a planning-only command, stripped of its fighters. It was the last ignominy for Quesada. Convinced that continuing as TAC Commander would make him a "conspirator in an ugly mistake," he resigned his command and retired – a huge loss for the country, as the U.S. Air Force's failures in Korea would soon prove.[55]

Korean War

North Korea invaded South Korea in June 1950. Elements of the U.S. 24th Infantry Division showed up in early July, and the Air Force sent a few obsolete fighters and 90 B-29 bombers. There was no close support capability of any kind to help those few beleaguered Army battalions as they were being mauled and pushed to the southern tip of Korea. Instead, the Air Force strategic planners came up with a preposterous plan to fire bomb five North Korean cities. Still mesmerized by Douhet's dream, they were convinced that the North Koreans would quickly capitulate.[56] The commander of the United Nations' forces, Gen. Douglas MacArthur vetoed the plan, but only temporarily.

The B-29 strategic bomber crews were, unsurprisingly, a horrible fit in a limited conventional war. They had the wrong equipment, the wrong training and the wrong motivation. Out of an eventual force of 150 B-29s they lost 107 while accomplishing virtually nothing. The entire fleet of B-29s flew less than 1,000 sorties in *three* years, averaging about one ineffective sortie per day. Their loss rate was more than 10 percent per sortie.[57]

If the Air Force had not expunged most of their fighter aircraft and fighter experts, they could have rounded up at least 700 P-47s that would have been a real combat close support capability and the cost equivalent of the 90 B-29s that were originally sent, and a lot of American lives would have been saved.

The Far East Command Operations Research Office reviewed the actual close support delivered. It reported that all the U.S. Air Force assets available flew just 13 of what were termed "close support" sorties per day. The ordnance was delivered not in direct support of the troops but an average three miles forward, a distance that made the strikes all but useless to the supported troops.[58]

Providing 13 useless close air support (CAS) sorties per day constituted virtually criminal neglect that our army grunts paid for in blood. It should have been a national scandal, but wasn't. Over the previous four years, the Air Force had dismantled the in-being capability to deliver 3,000 highly accurate and effective CAS/interdiction sorties per day, fundamental to winning the war in Western Europe. By the summer of 1950, that superb combat potential had been wantonly scattered to the wind, and the American infantryman in Korea was on his own.

On Aug. 4, 1950, the B-29s were released by the U.N. Command from their ineffective interdiction/CAS missions. The Air Force immediately implemented their original Douhet strategy: the bombers eventually bombed and then firebombed five major North Korean cities and some lesser cities. As in World War II, the enemy's military production was unaffected as was his military action in the field. There was great privation among the North Korean civilian populace, but not a sign of capitulation.

If the 900,000 Chinese that intervened the following winter had run up against United Nations forces supported by 700 P-47s, it would have been a far more difficult war for the Chinese. The rout of the U.N. forces in the north could have been prevented, and American infantry casualties would have been far lower.[59]

Once released from CAS duty, the Air Force's bombers also conducted deep interdiction missions, particularly on the Yalu River bridges and rail lines. The effects were minimal, as exemplified by the following account: "For 44 days, beginning January, 26th, 77 B-29s plus 125 B-26s dropped a total of nearly 4,000 500lb bombs on the objective [railroad transportation lines]. They achieved only 33 hits and succeeded in blocking the railway and road for just one week."[60]

A new Air Force campaign, presented in May 1952, was more of the same strategic bombardment of North Korean cities, with electric power plants added in. Both Bomber Command and Air Force Fighter Command were queried as to the estimated length of time for a campaign to shut down 50 percent of the electricity production capacity. Bomber Command said it needed nine to 29 days for the effort; the 5th Fighter Command said it needed just two to three days. In four days, not 50 percent, but 90 percent of the electric power was shut down by the fighters.[61]

Subsequent to the city-bombing, both fighters and bombers were tasked with the newly named "air pressure" campaign, another rerun of the discredited idea that strategic bombardment can win by itself. Gen. Charles Banfill, chief of intelligence, pointed out that the principal source of military supplies and most important strategic targets were outside Korea and the North Koreans had already moved their smaller industries to the far northeast outside the range of the fighter-bombers and of SHORAN, the radio navigation system for bombers. He concluded, "We are somewhat in the position of trying to starve a beggar by raiding his pantry when we know that he gets his meals from his rich relatives up the street."[62]

In January through July 1951, the North Koreans set out to gain air superiority. The Soviet Union supplied 500 of its latest MiG-15 fighters. These MiGs could outperform all U.N. aircraft but the American F-86, with which it had performance parity. At that point, there were just 90 F-86s in the theater. The North Koreans' plan was simple: (1) from their Manchurian sanctuary they would establish air superiority over a small area extending south; (2) they would build dispersal airfields in this area and extend air superiority further south; (3) the MiGs would use these fields in further extending their reach south. In successive steps, they would leapfrog to the southern tip of Korea, having attained air superiority.

The North Korean plan failed. Even 500 MiGs could not defeat 90 F-86s. Over time, they built up to 1,300 MiGs, which could not defeat the 200 F-86s they then faced.[63] The communists finally supplied the latest MiG-15Fs with Soviet pilots. Nothing changed. In total, the U.S. Air Force lost 78 F-86s versus 960 MiG losses.[64] The exchange ratio was about 12-1, even though the MiGs had a numerical superiority of 6-to-1.

The B-29/B-26 bombers had been an extremely poor fit for the Korean War. As in Europe, they had little effect on war production; they certainly did not cause capitulation. In Korea, the bomber close air support efforts had no discernable results. In the three years of war the B-29s only flew 994 sorties, losing 107 aircraft for an intolerable 10-percent loss rate. In contrast, the Air Force had overall losses of 1,466 aircraft on 721,000 sorties – a per sortie loss rate of 0.2 percent.[65]

Waging the Post-Korea Peace

Despite the bombers' poor showing throughout the Korean War, the funding floodgates were once again opened for lots of new bombers, as shown in Table 4 on the next page.

Bombers dominated 65 percent of the Air Force funding obtained under the huge budget windfall that occurred with the onset of the Korean War. The same budget windfall also launched fourteen jet "fighters" into development in the 1950s. However, most of these were, in reality, single-seat nuclear strike bombers or all weather/night interceptors, with seriously compromised performance as air-to-air fighters, but they fit nicely under the strategic bombardment paradigm. No close support aircraft were developed.

The Korean War "fighter" resurgence was short-lived. A few years after the end of the war, the fighters suited for the traditional tactical roles were once again sent to the bone yard or the reserves. Only the Air Defense Command's all-weather interceptors and the Tactical Air Command's F-100s or F-105s, equipped for nuclear strike, remained active.

Table 4. Bomber Development: Korea to Start of Vietnam War

Aircraft	Start	Quantity Produced	Comments
B-47*	1948	1,700	First all-jet strategic bomber
B-52*	1950	744	Carried 12 times the load of the B-17
B-57*	1950	403	Twin-engine tactical subsonic bomber; built under license from Britain
B-58*	1951	115	Mach 2 medium-range nuclear bomber
B-66*	1953	294	Twin-engine subsonic bomber; based on a U.S. Navy design
B-70	1955	2	1 million pound Mach 3 bomber; most expensive development ever attempted by the United States up to that point
F-111	1961	500	Tactical nuclear and conventional bomber; 1,000-plus planned
FB-111	1965	76	Medium-range strategic bomber; 210 planned

*All started, developed or built under Korean War budgets.

In 1961, Robert McNamara, President Kennedy's secretary of defense, took over the U.S. Air Force's tactical nuclear bomber development, the F-111. He promoted it as a tri-service, multirole fighter supposedly capable of air-to-air, close support and conventional interdiction bombing for the Air Force, Navy and Marine Corps. However, in design it remained a nuclear bomber and grew to 80,000 pounds. It proved to have no capability in the tactical role except night bombardment. It was deployed to Vietnam in this role, quickly failed, and was withdrawn.

Vietnam War

The Vietnam War was the third consecutive conflict that began with a terrible shortage of fighter aircraft. Much to its chagrin, the Air Force was forced by Defense Secretary McNamara to procure from Navy production lines large numbers of F-4s as fighter-bombers and A-7s as light bombers. As unlikely as it may seem, the U.S. Air Force had no active fighter production lines in the 1960s – though it was actively procuring F-111s and FB-111s and developing the absurdly expensive million-pound Mach 3 B-70 bomber. The Air Force fought the entire air war in North Vietnam with aging F-105 nuclear bombers plus Navy F-4s and A-7s.

The war in the north was mainly fought around the cities of Hanoi and Haiphong. Targeting was pure strategic bombardment by heavy bomb-laden fighters married to air-refueling tankers. Due to the inadequate range of F-105s and F-4s, the new employment equation became 1 fighter plus 1 tanker equals 1 strategic bomber. Interestingly, the payloads were similar to those of the World War II B-17s.

Our strategic bombardment campaign in North Vietnam was unsuccessful. Once again, the Douhet objectives were not achieved. Moreover, a total of 1,737 combat aircraft losses were recorded, including about 900 F-100s, F-105s and F-4s from the Air Force, not counting the substantial Navy losses. Combat experience had again shown that the strategic-bombing mission is short on effectiveness and costly in both treasure and blood.

A very different air war was fought in South Vietnam. There the regular Air Force flew interdiction against enemy logistics and base camps, plus some close support of friendlies, using mostly jet aircraft. The jets were often ineffective due to the difficulty of finding and hitting small tactical targets at high speed. On the other hand, the Special Air Warfare forces, flying many sorties per day with small numbers of 1944-designed A-1 propeller attack aircraft, were highly effective in night and day close support of Special Forces camps. The A-1 was slow, maneuverable, highly survivable and had extraordinary loiter endurance which was essential for continuous support of forces in contact with the enemy.

The B-52s flew missions only in the south for almost the entire war, bombing suspected Viet Cong base camps in the jungle. However, in 1972 they were sent north for a short while. They immediately lost 15 aircraft while flying 724 sorties, a loss rate seven times higher than the F-105s and F-4s.[66] Their combat return was indiscernible.

Waging the post-Vietnam peace

Unlike the post-World War II and post-Korean eras, there was little apparent fighter drawdown after Vietnam. The reason is simple. Most of the U.S. Air Force's Vietnam-era "fighters" were already strategic bombers, or pseudo-strategic bombers supported by 600 air-refueling tanker aircraft.

The small fleet of F-100s and F-105s that started in Vietnam had already been replaced by a large fleet of big, heavy F-4s configured for bombing. Soon after the war, these started being replaced by F-15A/C fighters, as well as by the bombing-only F-15E. The Air Force also procured, albeit reluctantly, a larger number of the smaller but longer-range F-16s. The F-16 was designed originally as a superbly maneuverable dogfighter, but it was immediately reconfigured by the Air Force into a heavier "multirole" (in other words, mostly bombing) aircraft.

The "stealthy" F-117 light bomber started entering the fleet in 1983.[67] While the Air Force strongly supported it, it proved disappointing. It was sluggish and only had a two-bomb payload. In its 13-year development and production run, only 54 operational aircraft were procured, the sure mark of an inefficient, ultra-expensive program.

The most unexpected post-Vietnam development was the A-10, the only single purpose, close-support aircraft ever built by the Air Force. This precedent-shattering program was largely initiated and shaped by the so-called "Fighter Mafia." Though opposed by almost every Air Force general, the A-10 reached production in 1976 after a unique, live-firing, "fly-off" prototype competition. The Air Force leadership eagerly cut off production in 1984 after a very short eight-year run of 715 aircraft. The A-10 program cost was minor: all 715 A-10s cost less than three B-2 bombers.

At the same time, in the decade after Vietnam the incredibly expensive B-1B, and then the even more hugely expensive B-2 bomber aircraft, entered development and production. Eventually, 100 of the 200 planned B-1Bs and 21 of the planned 132 B-2s were built. Despite the tiny numbers produced, huge bomber budgets were being spent in the late 1970s through the 1980s leading up to the first Gulf war.

Gulf War I, 1991

On Aug. 2, 1990, the Iraqi army invaded its oil-rich neighbor, putting 43 divisions inside Kuwait. After a six-month buildup of U.S and coalition forces, on Jan. 17, 1991, the U.S. Air Force launched the strategic-bombing campaign it had advocated, the "softening-up" prelude supposedly indispensable for the ground attack. Against weak and ill-trained air opposition,[68] the 39 days of bombing knocked out electric power and civilian communications, but had little real effect on Iraqi military activities, Iraqi radar surface-to-air missile (SAM) sites or military communications.

The campaign opened with massive attacks against SAMs, command centers and major communications in and around the capital city, Baghdad. In the first hour, seven B-52s also fired 35 Air-Launched Cruise Missiles (ALCMs) against targets in and around Baghdad.[69]

The mainstays of the Air Force campaign were the F-111, F-15E, F-16, A-10 and the B-52 – all aircraft developed 20 to 40 years earlier. The one new participant was the F-117. However, with just 42 F-117s available in the entire theater, at 0.7 sorties per day, they generated less than 1,300 sorties (3 percent) of the 44,000 flown by all aircraft types. The F-117s made only about 2,000 laser bomb attacks during the entire war.[70] In terms of bombs delivered, they were a minor player in the war. Nevertheless, the F-117 was broadly touted by the Air Force for its ability to "knock-the-door-down," i.e., to enter Baghdad unseen, to destroy the SAM network and to allow non-stealth aircraft to operate safely. All three elements of these assertions failed.

On the first night, 167 non-stealth "Wild Weasel" jamming and other aircraft also engaged the SAMs without a loss. The "stealth" F-117s were only able to launch 15 precision strikes against air defenses on the first two nights.[71] This was a few drops in the torrent of thousands of bombs and missiles launched those first two nights. The meager F-117 attack could hardly scratch the 59 SAM batteries present, a network of many hundreds of point targets. The CIA assessed that of the 15 SAM batteries reported as attacked by the F-117s, 13 continued to operate, as did most of the radar control centers that the F-117s were sent to knock out. As for ensuring the safety of other aircraft, Baghdad radar SAMs shot down two F-16s on day three; apparently the door was not knocked down after all. Radar SAMs continued to make kills throughout the war with 20 percent of their kills made in the last week of the war.

B-52s and F-16s conducted a maximum campaign against elite Republican Guard Divisions located along the Iraqi-Kuwaiti border. From the first day of the air war onward, a flight of three B-52s bombed the deployed, dug-in Republican Guard positions about every three hours. Also, roughly 300 high-altitude F-16s sorties were flown daily against the Republican Guard.[72] Historically, high-altitude bombing against a dug-in, static army is seldom productive – and so it was in this case. Ground forces can only be successfully attacked from the air when: a) they are moving and thus necessarily exposed; and b) the attacking aircraft can fly (and survive) low and slow enough to discern targets.

The official, almost certainly optimistic, U.S. Air Force estimate of the actual combat attrition suffered by the Republican Guard at the end of the 39-day bombing campaign showed that four divisions had an attrition rate between 15 and 45 percent, and two suffered little to no attrition at all.[73] Similarly, an unclassified CIA report found a notable lack of significant effect on the Guard divisions.

The survival of the Republican Guard was very probably the greatest shortcoming of the war. The predictably ineffective high-altitude, high-speed air attacks on the Guard permitted important elements to escape intact to Basra at the end of the war – and to subsequently suppress a major Shi'ite rebellion against Saddam Hussein's Sunni regime. Other Guard units remained unaffected in the Baghdad area. The intact, and still loyal, Republican Guard ensured Saddam's survival after the war, just when his regime was critically vulnerable to collapse.

In the war's second week, Saddam sent significant elements of his army across the Kuwaiti-Saudi border toward the Saudi city of Khafji. These Iraqi army units had to come out of hiding in order to move, thus setting up a U.S. turkey shoot opportunity. Fortunately, two A-10s plus an AC-130 gunship were immediately available. In short order, they destroyed 58 targets in a 71-vehicle convoy. This would have required about 20 effective attack passes per each A-10. Unlike all Air Force "F" designated aircraft, they actually had the 20 attack passes worth of cannon ammunition (and other weapons) on board. The two A-10s put it all to good use. This was typical of the many A-10 missions flown over the Khafji incursion in the next two days. According to Saddam, this was to be the "Mother of all Battles." Instead, the Iraqi force was decimated en route and the remnants were destroyed in Khafji. The Iraqi army never again maneuvered any of its divisions, save during their final retreat.[74]

The strategic bombardment campaign in the Baghdad area ended abruptly after three weeks. An attack by two F-117s against the Al Firdus command bunker went awry. Unknown to our intelligence, the Iraqis were using it as a civilian bomb shelter. CNN and other international television displayed the appalling results of our mistake to the world: almost 300 women and children were killed. This ended the bombardment of Baghdad. But there was another, less publicized lesson. Iraqi military activities were unaffected when the strategic bombing of Baghdad ended. Militarily, the cessation appeared to be a nonevent – just as in North Vietnam.

After the Khafji incursion, the war saw many further examples of the need for multipass lethality in close support and tactical interdiction. For example, two A-10 pilots, Capt. Mark Salmonson and Lt. John Marks, were credited by ground observation with killing 23 tanks in a single encounter using the 30-mm cannon.[75] On Feb. 27, 1991, the Iraqi rocket force assembled 20 Scud mobile missile launchers with the plan to swamp the Israeli Patriot SAM missile defense against Scuds. An Air Force forward air controller with a Special Operations Force (SOF) observer team deep inside Iraq spotted the SCUD launchers en route to their launch site. Two A-10s were called in. Using their cannon, they destroyed all 20 Scuds and their mobile launchers, as verified by the ground observer team.[76]

Right after the war, the Air Force and other analysts praised the F-117 for its zero-loss performance while at the same time damning the A-10 for its losses. Some pertinent facts were omitted. Night was a much safer combat environment than day, and the F-117 flew only at night. Two squadrons of A-10s flew at least as many night sorties as the F-117. Their losses were the same as the F-117's: zero. F-111Fs also flew at night and also had no losses.

The A-10s and the F-117s flew in both the first Gulf war and the next war in Kosovo in 1999. The day-flying A-10s suffered a total of four losses in both wars.[77] The night-flying F-117s suffered two casualties, both to radar missiles in Kosovo.[78] The important point is the number of sorties flown and the overall survival rate. (See Table 5.)

Table 5. Combined Losses First Gulf War and Kosovo

Aircraft	Approximate Total Sorties Flown Both Wars	Losses	Loss Rate/ Sortie
F-117	2,600	2	1/1,300 sorties
A-10	12,400	4	1/3,100 sorties

The A-10 had a per sortie loss rate less than half that of the F-117 in the combined campaigns. It will never be heard from official U.S. Air Force channels that the A-10s were twice as survivable as the F-117s by this more meaningful measure, but in fact, they were.

In many thousands of daytime missions, the A-10 suffered three losses to infrared (IR, heat seeking), man-portable missiles. The aircraft brought the pilot home after three other IR missile strikes – two of them were repaired and quickly put back in the battle. The third was not economical to repair. The A-10s also survived multiple anti-aircraft artillery (AAA) hits, were repaired, and promptly sent back to the air battle.

Because the "Fighter Mafia" imposed survivability requirements of unprecedented stringency on the initial A-10 design, analysts projected that it would survive most combat hits at least long enough to bring the pilot back to friendly territory. In Gulf war combat, 83 percent of A-10s that were hit made it to a safe landing, even better than the early projections. Moreover, of all combat aircraft in the war, the A-10 had the highest sortie rate as well as the highest in-commission rate, 95.7 percent.

Lt. Gen. Charles Horner, the air commander in the first Gulf war, said, "I take back all the bad things I've said about the A-10s. I love them. They're saving our asses."[79]

Waging the post-Gulf War peace: changing the tune, punishing the victors

With the war over, the U.S. Air Force strategic bombardment paradigm and the need to defend bomber budgets returned to the fore. The Air Force revived the 20-year-old canard used by the generals opposing the A-10 citing that the A-10 is vulnerable to hits because its speed is limited. That despite the extraordinary daytime survivability the A-10 had just demonstrated in combat, not to mention its actual tactical target kills, far higher than any other fighter or bomber in the war. The post-war official Air Force view was that the F-16s, F-15s, F-117s, B-1s, B-2s and B-52s "will posses the capability to conduct close air support and will be able to do so in the most demanding threat environment which the A-10 cannot survive."[80] "One reason we're keeping the A-10 is for the niche environments – very, very low-threat environments where you're doing counter-insurgency operations."[81] That is Lt. Gen. David Deptula speaking. At the time, he was in charge of planning for the Air Force's highest combat aircraft headquarters, the Air Combat Command. Every phrase contradicts the empirical combat data.

By the end of the first Gulf war, the Air Force had almost achieved its strategic bombardment dream. Its entire warfighting force was already strategic bombers or pseudo-strategic bombers. The exceptions were the A-10 and the F-15A/C. Accordingly, a major unfilled need for more complete fighter drawdown was to purify the force by sending all the A-10s to the bone yard. Outside pressures and saner heads prevailed, partially: "only" half the A-10s were sent to the bone yard. In the meantime, the Air Force leadership was preoccupied with finding procurement funding to cover still-continuing cost overruns for the B-1B and B-2 bomber programs while cranking up the hyperinflating F-22 program, the world's first fighter to top one third of a billion dollars.

Kosovo Air war

Led by the United States, eight NATO nations' air forces planned a quick, two-day strike against Yugoslavia in order to bomb the Milosevic government into submission, the classic Douhet strategy. Seventy-eight days and 36,000 sorties later, Milosevic settled for terms that were the equivalent of those he had offered before the bombing and that the U.S. government had already rejected.

During the war, U.S. Air Force Lt. Gen. Michael Short, who commanded the NATO air effort, restricted his pilots to altitudes above 15,000 feet to hopefully eliminate any possibility of losses. Unfortunately, this exacerbated an already difficult problem. It proved to be all but impossible to find camouflaged military targets in hiding at an altitude of three miles with or without sensors. So, despite 24 million pounds of ordnance dropped, the Serbs' military losses were extremely minor.[82]

The NATO air forces made a major effort. They launched 36,000 sorties, fired 743 HARM anti-radar missiles, and dropped 24 million pounds of munitions of which 6,728 were precision-guided. Their claimed bomb damage seemed sizable. However, after the war, the Serbian government reported shockingly lower damage levels than NATO had claimed. Only three of 80 radar missile batteries were actually destroyed. NATO had claimed 5,000 to 10,000 military casualties; Belgrade reported 387. Belgrade also reported 1,400 civilian casualties, an astonishingly low number for 36,000 sorties of bombing effort, much of it against urban targets.[83]

During the course of the war, Yugoslavians fired 845 radar SAMs. As in other wars, they were all but ineffective. They accounted for only three kills – an F-16 and two stealth F-117s. The SAM ineffectiveness rate was 99.7 percent.

Given a 78-day bombing campaign, the results were minimal. This illustrates, yet again, how tactical air effectiveness depends crucially on integration with a simultaneous ground campaign, that is, combined arms. A friendly ground force is essential to move the enemy army out of hiding into the open. Air attacks against an enemy army that is never forced to maneuver are certain to show negligible military results. This is especially true when attacks are conducted from 10,000 or 15,000 feet, even with "precision" munitions. Who is available to penetrate the camouflage to find a target? Who is available to sort decoys from real targets? Who is available to distinguish wedding parties from terrorists?

Afghanistan

In the Afghanistan war in 2001, American forces were primarily small units of Special Operations Forces (as small as four U.S. soldiers) that teamed up with fighters of the indigenous Afghan "Northern Alliance." These forces were supported by American close-air support in a multitude of minor engagements, most of them highly successful with few U.S. casualties.

The following typical encounter illustrates the great effectiveness of a small four-man Special Operations unit supported by A-10s. The thread is abbreviated and excerpted from a published account by the Army News Service:[84]

A four man American special ops team leading a force of 26 Afghan National Army (ANA) troops was ambushed several times by 800 enemy Taliban fighters. The 7 vehicle convoy led by Staff Sgt. Jamie Osmon was ambushed for the first time at a valley edge. Fortunately, the convoy was able to extricate itself from this ambush. Sgt. Osmon "... knew they were going to hit us again, it was just a matter of where." Just 3 kilometers later it happened. They were in deep trouble. At that point they noticed the ANA troops were missing. "We headed back south to the other ambush point." The first close support aircraft, a B-1B bomber, flew overhead. "It didn't seem to have much effect," Osmon said. [No matter how badly the B-1B pilot wished to help, a single B-1B bomber at high altitude flying close support is still an oxymoron.]

The special ops team got back to the original ambush site and discovered that the other team was still pinned down. Osmon asked about A-10 close air support.

On the Baghram flight line, Tonto and Lobo [call signs of the two A-10s] had just taken off and refueled en route. Once the A-10s were close to the ambush site, Tonto explained, "We were told they didn't have radio capability ... We flew over the canyon to put eyes on the situation." Private Schloss, "We could hear the A-10s come in... It was like it was Christmas – the happiest moment of my life."

Captain Tonto pointed out that, "It took us a little time to determine exactly where the friendly forces were, as well as where they were taking fire from. ... Once we identified the enemies, we marked their positions and opened up with 720 rounds of 30-mm high-explosive incendiary ammunition."

Sgt. Osmon, "When the Vulcans [the A-10's 30-mm cannons] opened up, the enemy fire ceased. It was great." [Note that up to this point the A-10s did not have radio contact. The entire encounter was accomplished by eyeball.] The Army team finally made radio contact with the pilots.

"The A-10s came around for a second gun pass," Tonto said, prompting Sergeant Osmon to quip: "Grip-21, this is Maverick. This may be a bit quick, but I think I love you."

The convoy discovered the whereabouts of the missing ANA members. "One of the ANA members came up to the group in a lull in the fighting – he told us they had been captured by the enemy forces...The enemy said they would release the rest of the ANA team and let us go if we called off the aerial close air support." The enemy dispersed and the reconstituted convoy limped home on two bad tires.

The normal three hour trip took six hours, covered by the A-10s the entire trip.

There are a few lessons to be learned from this incident:

- Though few, if any, Air Force documents praised the A-10s, the Army grunts love the Warthogs, and Army periodicals had much praise for the A-10s.

- The close-support effort provided by the B-1B bomber was useless.

- The 30-man force would have been "goners" without the A-10s.

- When the small force recognized their peril, the first question they asked was, "Where are the A-10s?"

- The air battle began without radio contact. Nevertheless, the A-10 pilots had the low- speed maneuverability and survivability necessary to sort out the ground battle disposition.

- Even in terrain that offers cover, the 30-mm cannon is devastatingly effective against enemy combatants.

- Note the enemy's offer to release captives as a bribe to shut off the A-10's attack.

- Thirty men backed-up by two A-10s can prevail against an enemy force of 800 men. No high-speed, high-altitude jet could have achieved this.

Second Gulf War

The U.S. Air Force planners complained that the plans for the air portion of the second Gulf war were too timid. They advised that a 40-day air campaign (shades of the first Gulf war) would topple the regime without a ground invasion: the old Douhet dream again. They later offered to settle for 10 days. Their campaign was advertised as "shock and awe," a newly minted synonym for strategic bombardment. Well over 10,000 precision weapons were to be delivered on the first two days of the war. The Air Force actually dropped only 1,500 precision bombs on the first two days, just 15 percent of their advertised plan.

U.S. intelligence felt sure they knew the bunker where Saddam Hussein was located. It was decided to assassinate Saddam from the air by bombing the bunker, thus starting the war one day early. The Navy fired 34 high-cost Tomahawk missiles at the underground bunker. Two F-117s dropped four 2,000-pound, precision-guided bombs. The Air Force and Navy both failed.

Gen. Tommy Franks, in charge of the war, ignored the Air Force "shock and awe" advice, perhaps based on the results of the first Gulf war's 39-day bombing campaign. He simultaneously launched the air and the ground battle without a precursor air campaign. Saddam's regime toppled in just 21 days. American casualties were almost insignificant. Nonetheless, strategic bombardment missions had been performed from day one with few noticeable effects.

Helicopters

For the first Gulf war, the Army had sent 1,644 helicopters of 11 different types to the theater, including 274 AH-64 attack helicopters. Except for some highly publicized attacks early in the air campaign, these remained mostly on the sidelines for the first 39 days of the war. This was presumably an acknowledgement of their low survivability against AAA and IR SAMS. The AH-64s launched 2,764 Hellfire anti-armor missiles. The 132 A-10s, at half the fleet size and at much lower procurement and operating costs, fired 5,000 Maverick missiles, dropped 40,000 bombs of various types, and made thousands of gun-strafing passes.

In the second Gulf war from March 19, 2003 to July 4, 2007, 103 helicopters were combat and operational losses, including 32 AH-64/AH-1 attack helicopters. During this same four year period of the war, there were 18 fixed-wing aircraft combat and operational losses, including two CAS aircraft (one A-10 and one Marine Corps AV-8B). 214 people were killed in the helicopter losses; 18 were lost in the fixed-wing losses.

Attack helicopters simply do not compare successfully to an effective CAS aircraft, such as the A-10, in terms of either effectiveness or survivability.

Historical wrap up

In sum, the combat record of strategic bombing shows very small military returns, very high aircrew casualties, and enormous cost burdens in terms of money and lost opportunities for building more effective forces.

In contrast, the combat record of dedicated close-air support and of air-to-air dogfighters shows them to be real contributors to winning wars with unexpectedly low casualties and costs. The question now is: "What to do?"

Reversing the U.S. Air Force's Shrinking Forces and Growing Ineffectiveness

Since World War II, the U.S. Air Force has, in each succeeding war, provided less aircraft and has had less effect on the outcome of the war while steadily increasing the costs of doing so. The causes of these unfortunate trends are many. Principal among them are:

- A dogged Air Force adherence to the strategic bombardment paradigm, impervious to any correction from combat experience, and

- Development incentives and an acquisition process that guarantees ever-escalating unit cost and technical complexity without regard to the effect on either combat effectiveness or force size.

Below, we outline our approach to reversing the seemingly inexorable trend of shrinking U.S. Air Force numbers and effectiveness.

Air Force procurement planning has traditionally been based on a wish list for favored aircraft types with unrealistically high production quantities and notoriously low procurement cost estimates. As discussed in Chapters 10 and 11 at greater length, these wish list plans become hopelessly expensive and unachievable within any conceivable overall defense budget. This wish-list behavior and the inevitable shortfalls in meeting it serve as a way of putting pressure on the secretary of defense, the president and Congress in the annual negotiations that lead to the real-world budget that is finally approved. Table 6 below shows the Air Force's current – unattainable – wish list with the procurement quantities that are most likely to be actually attained if we simply continue down the business-as-usual path.

Table 6. Air Force Wish-List Acquisition versus Business as Usual

Apparent Current Air Force Wish List	Approximate Estimated Costs
Total force of 383 F-22 (Adds 200 aircraft at $200 million each[85]	$105 billion
1,750 F-35 As at $180 million each[86] (650 Marine/Navy aircraft not included)	$315 billion
100 Global Strike Bombers at up to $5 billion each	$500 billion
400 Air Refueling Tankers at $280 million each	$112 billion
400 New Airlift Aircraft at $250 million each	$100 billion
Total Aircraft on wish list: 3,033	
Cost Total	**$1,132 billion**

What Business as Usual Will Produce	Approximate Estimated Cost
183 F-22 at $355 million each (sunk or already under contract)	$65 billion
500 Air Force F-35 As at $200+ million each	$100 billion
0 Globe Strike Bombers	$0
200 Air Refueling Tankers	$56 billion
100 New Airlift Aircraft	$25 billion
Total U.S. Air Force Aircraft: 983	
Cost Total	**$246 billion**

The present Air Force aircraft wish-list program, costing over $1 trillion, is shown in the upper part of Table 6 on the preceding page. It costs about four times the actual budgets likely to be available for the next 20 years, exemplified by the lower part of Table 6.[87] While the table's contents will appear very controversial to some; it is simply an extrapolation of past history and current behavior. Skeptical readers will find an explanation and documentation of that history and behavior in Chapters 10 and 11 of this anthology. In spite of the massive budgets and purchases envisioned, a result of only about 1,000 aircraft is far more likely. This is an insignificant production rate of 50 aircraft per year, but it mostly exceeds what the Air Force has bought each year for the past decade. In other words, it will take the Air Force another 40 to 80 years to replace its current legacy fleet. When this finally occurs, the Air Force will just have a different legacy fleet of even older aircraft. Nothing will have changed except that cost escalation will probably squeeze the final total force down from 4,000 aging aircraft toward 2,000.

Clearly, the nation needs a new and fundamentally different approach to aircraft procurement.

Ground rules for increasing combat capability

The business-as-usual policy dooms us to an Air Force of decreasing effectiveness, uselessly small force size, and such inflexibility that it can only be employed for strategic bombardment, against only mostly incompetent enemies. Here we propose a very different approach to an Air Force that can flexibly serve the real, and highly diverse, defense needs of the nation. This approach is based on the following common ground rules, each a complete departure from present U.S. Air Force planning assumptions:

- Based on realistic, auditable cost estimates validated by objective and independent analyses, stay within the roughly $250 billion the Air Force is likely to be allowed to spend on aircraft procurement over the next 20 years or so.

- Ensure that the following missions can be performed effectively in real-world combat as a matter of the highest urgency:

    1. close air support of American troops anywhere, whether in counterinsurgency missions or in sophisticated armored warfare;

    2. battlefield airlift to American troops in remote areas, and

    3. air-to-air superiority (dogfighting) against any air force, modern or aging, large or small;

4. battlefield interdiction, particularly in adverse terrain and against primitive, highly camouflaged supply lines.

• Develop and procure only aircraft and weapons of the utmost austerity, stripped down to only the capabilities directly required by actual combat experience. "Nice-to-have" features and capabilities for hypothesized future combat lead directly to shrinking force size and degraded effectiveness in real combat.

Table 7 is an example of applying these effectiveness-based procurement ground rules.

Note that this effectiveness-based procurement outline provides nearly 10,000 aircraft over 20 years without exceeding current annual aircraft procurement budgets. The plan does include 183 F-22s for the simple reason that they have already been acquired at no further acquisition cost after 2010; it includes 200 F-35s, redesignated as A-35s, simply to fill commitments to allies who remain interested in it and to serve as battlefield interdiction aircraft in some limited-stress missions, albeit less effectively and at higher operating cost. The F-22 and the A/F-35 commitments were made years

Table 7. Effectiveness-Based Aircraft Procurement Outline

Mission	Aircraft Design	Number to be Procured	Approximate Total Cost
Close Air Support and Battlefield Interdiction	Close Air Support Fighters at no more than $15 million each	4,000	$60 billion
Close Air Support	Forward Air Control (FAC) Aircraft at ~$1 million each	2,500	$3 billion
Airlift	New Air Refueling Tankers	100	$28 billion
Airlift	Dirt Strip Airlifters at $30 million each	1000	$30 billion
Air-to-air combat	F-22s already purchased at $350 million each	183	already sunk; no actual additional procurement cost.
Air-to-air combat	New Air Superiority Fighter at no more than $40 million each	1,100	$44 billion
Battlefield Interdiction	F-35. Redesignate as A-35; acquired mostly to meet commitments to allies at $250 million each	200	$50 billion
Totals		**9,983**	**$251 billion** (does not include sunk F-22 costs)

ago by Air Force leaders driven by strategic bombardment single mindedness and cost-maximizing incentives. Unfortunately, we will have to live with the expensive fallout of those flawed decisions for additional decades.

Description of aircraft envisioned

Some might believe the cost estimates for the new aircraft listed in the chart above are unrealistically low. In fact, they are conservative. The five new aircraft in the table above are designs tailored by combat experience using the ground rules described above. They will provide the expanded force structure with a remarkable real-world increase in combat potential – and they will begin to chip away at the seemingly intractable problem of our ever-aging and shrinking fleet. Indeed, some of the Air Force's current business-as-usual leaders may be perplexed with the idea of managing such a greatly enlarged, combat-oriented fleet. Such perplexity on their part should be interpreted as a sure sign that they are not the right people to lead such a combat-oriented Air Force.

The close support fighter

This is a significantly smaller, more maneuverable and even more survivable improvement on the A-10. It is based on two, off-the-shelf, 9,000-pound class commercial/military turbofan engines. The aircraft would mount a much more compact, lighter and quicker-accelerating cannon system that fires the same highly lethal, combat-proven 30-mm round at the same muzzle velocity as the A-10. The weight savings of just using the smaller gun should be around 7,500 pounds. With a much smaller aircraft size also permitted by the more compact gun, and with other weight savings, the Close Support Fighter is projected to have an empty weight of less than 14,000 pounds compared to the A-10's 25,000 pounds. With 10,000 pounds internal fuel this aircraft will have range and loiter well beyond the A-10. Combat takeoff weight will be less than 25,000 pounds. At the mid-point of its combat mission, it would have a near 1:1 thrust to weight ratio. The sustained G, acceleration, quick re-attack time, and rate-of-climb will be world class for a close support aircraft. Survivability will be even better than the A-10, due to higher maneuverability, smaller size and new improvements in control-system hardness and fire suppression. The unit cost of $15 million is based on the actual production price of the A-10, inflated to today's dollars plus 30 percent. In other words, we are using as a model the price of an airplane that is 50 percent larger than the Close Support Fighter and have added another 30 percent to the cost just for conservatism.

FAC aircraft

The forward air controller (FAC), both air- and ground-based, is the crucial link in delivering close support, but one that is *always* neglected in peacetime. The FAC coordinates air attacks with the supported ground units, ensuring that no friendlies get hit. Effective FAC aircraft are traditionally light observation aircraft. They need good visibility, the ability to land on dirt roads and pastures right next to supported units, long loiter time, survivable controls and fuel, and the ability to fly low and slow enough to find pinpoint, camouflaged targets like machine-gun nests, artillery/ rocket emplacements, and teams laying mines. There are several light single-engine turbo-prop aircraft in production that meet all these needs. The candidates currently cost about $1 million each.

Dirt strip airlifter

This Army forward-area support transport, a modern analog of the superbly useful C-123 that the Air Force retired during the Vietnam War, is an upgraded version of existing two-engine cargo planes in the 50,000- to 60,000-pound weight class that carry 12,000- to 15,000-pound payloads. Upgrades are focused on unpaved/ rough- field landings and takeoff capabilities to better serve Army units far from paved runways. The cost of $30 million is based on current quotes for the C-27J now being acquired.

Air-refueling tanker

The Air Force is contemplating a follow-on air-refueling tanker. This is a continuation of those efforts but, with so much less emphasis on the strategic bombing paradigm, substantially fewer of these aircraft will be needed. Chapter 8 of this anthology discusses other alternatives, both for this and for other airlift aircraft.

Air-to-air fighter

This fighter is 30 percent smaller than the F-16 with vastly better acceleration and turning performance. It will be, by a large margin, the hottest performing and most maneuverable fighter in the world – both subsonically and supersonically. Size is 18,500 pounds gross weight with a current in-production engine of 32,500 pounds thrust, or more. It will be able to accelerate to supersonic speeds going straight up *without using afterburner.* Electronics will be cutting edge, all-passive with 360-degree infrared and radar warning gear. Weapons will be the most advanced and effective (as demonstrated by realistic, live-fire testing) current IR air-to-air missile, a passive radar-homing air-to-air missile for attacking any stealth/non-stealth fighter radar in the world;[88] and a new, more lethal, higher velocity 20-mm cannon based on an in-production round. The small size and the 100 percent passive electronics and weapons approach will maximize surprise relative to the always-larger stealth fighters or any radar-using fighter in the world. (Surprise is the number one factor in achieving aerial victories.) Unit cost is estimated at $40 million, about 20 percent below the cost of the currently overloaded, radar and avionics-laden F-16 now in very low-rate production. We assess the cost estimate as conservative because this new fighter is 30 percent smaller than the current model of the F-16, the avionics suite is three times smaller and half the complexity of the radar-/radar missile-based F-16, and the annual production rate would be a large multiple of the current F-16 rate.

Final Thoughts

The simple aircraft procurement outline presented here can release us from the air power morass that the U.S. Air Force and our country have been experiencing for decades. If we fail to make the kind of changes outlined, we will continue to face a vanishing close-support capability, a rapidly diminishing air-to-air force increasingly unable to control the skies over our ground and naval forces, and a continuing failure to support ground forces and special operations with the emergency remote-area airlift they always need. Every military objective then becomes inordinately more difficult or even impossible. We will have no air power options other than bombing the enemy's heartland, albeit less and less every year.

The Air Force is awash in money (approximately $150 billion each year), more than it had, on average, during the Cold War. Despite this, it is being forced to cut the buy of every major program and to stretch schedules in order to pay for cost overruns and technical failures. So few airplanes are being produced that the average age of the tactical force has increased from 15 to 20 years in just the last seven years. Either age for a fighter inventory is intolerable.

A frightening example is the B-2 bomber program, right at the heart of the strategic bombardment mindset. The Air Force planned for 132 B-2s. It doubled the funding and bought 21. When the B-2s finally went to war in the Kosovo air war, the entire $44 billion fleet was able to support, on average, only one sortie per day. The B-2 proved completely irrelevant.

In contrast, the A-10 program developed and procured 715 aircraft of unprecedented close- support capability at the equivalent cost of three B-2s. Even though the Air Force leadership sent only 132 of the several hundred A-10s available in 1991 to the first Gulf war (and only under duress from the secretary of defense), this handful of aircraft generated over 200 sorties per day and may well have destroyed more tactical targets by themselves than all the remaining combat aircraft combined. As soon as the war ended, the Air Force's reward to the A-10s for their superb results was to get rid of as many as possible by sending increased numbers to the National Guard and to the Air Force's "bone yard" at Davis-Montham Air Force Base.

If we continue to rely on Air Force procurement wish lists and 90-year-old strategic bombardment theories, there will be more and more fiscal and military failures like the B-2 and the F-35. If new leadership in the Congress and the executive branch can find the courage and the open-mindedness to examine the combat history and the combat results of the last 70 years, they will find a simple solution to the air power morass written there loud and clear.

ENDNOTES

1   For an additional discussion of larger budgets buying a shrinking, aging inventory, see Chapter 11.

2   To learn more about this group, see Robert Coram, *Boyd: The Fighter Pilot Who Changed the Art of War* (Boston: Little, Brown, 2002).

3   Find these data at http://en.wikipedia.org/wiki/List_of_active_United_States_military_aircraft. However, it is notable that various sources differ, sometimes significantly, in their count of Air Force active-duty and reserve- component aircraft. In response to inquiries, we were informed that the Air Force, even its historical offices, does not have a publicly available, apples to apples, consistent count of its aircraft over time.

4   U.S. air forces went by various names up to the creation of the U.S. Air Force in 1947; U.S. Army Air Corps, U.S. Army Air Force, and other titles were used.

5   These data were collected by author Dilger at the National Museum of the U.S. Air Force, Bomber Archive.

6   As an example, the U.S. B-17 bomber cost $278,000 while the P-40 cost $46,000, a 6-1 ratio. (National Museum of the U.S. Air Force archives).

7   Williamson Murray, *Luftwaffe, 1933-1945: Strategu for Defeat*, (Westport: Brassey's, 1996), 40.

8   Murray, *Luftwaffe*, p. 18.

9   For further discussion of these ratios, see Murray, *Luftwaffe*, p. 18.

10 Cajus Bekker, *The Luftwaffe War Diaries: The German Air Force In World War II* (New York: Ballantine Books, 1966), 539.

11 Murray, *Luftwaffe*, p. 40.

12 Murray, *Luftwaffe*, p. 41.

13 It is worth noting that some of the Luftwaffe's multi-engine bombers were equipped to conduct dive bombing. However, such variants of the Do-17 were quite small in number and frequently tasked to horizontal bombing, and such variants of the Ju-88 were found not to have the structural strength to perform high-angle dive bombing. See Wikipedia.com entries on these Luftwaffe bomber aircraft.

14 Murray, *Luftwaffe*, p. 42.

15 Murray, *Luftwaffe*, p. 50.

16 Peter C. Smith, *Ju-87 Stuka, Volume One: Luftwaffe Ju-87 Dive-Bomber Units, 1939-1941 (Luftwaffe Colors)* (Classic Publications, 2007), 41.

17 Smith, *Stuka*, p. 27.

18 Smith, *Stuka*, p. 49.

19 In another success attributable to attack aircraft other than high-altitude, horizontal bombers, against ships, in 1941, Italy had dominated the Mediterranean with four battleships. In a daring mission, the British sent 21 Swordfish torpedo aircraft to attack them at very low level. These were simple, single-engine, old and tired biplanes with a cruise speed of 88 MPH. Nonetheless, they successfully sank all four battleships on a single day in November 1940. (Luftwaffe, Murray, p. 76) This altered the balance of power in the Mediterranean in the Royal Navy's favor.

20 Murray, *Luftwaffe*, p. 49.

21 Murray, *Luftwaffe*, p. 57.

22 Murray, *Luftwaffe*, p. 59.

23 Adolf Galland, *The First and the Last* (Buccaneer Books, 1990), 12.

24 Murray, *Luftwaffe*, p. 85.

25 Bekker, *The Luftwaffe War Diaries*, p. 322.

26 Murray, *Lufewaffe*, p. 95.

27 Hans-Ulrich Rudel, *Stuka Pilot* (New York: Bantam Books, 1979), 34.

28 Peter Smith, *Luftwaffe 9: Stukas Over Steppe (Luftwaffe at War Series, No 9)* (Greenhill Books, 1999), 24.

29 Galland, *The First and the Last*, p. 90.

30 Galland, *The First and the Last*, p. 116.

31 Rudel, *Stuka Pilot*, p. 128.

32 Smith, *Luftwaffe 9: Stukas Over Steppe (Luftwaffe at War Series, No. 9)*, p. 16.

33 Murray, *Luftwaffe*, p. 161.

34 Bekker, *The Luftwaffe War Diaries*, p. 539.

35 Murray, *Luftwaffe*, p.127.

36 Murray, *Luftwaffe*, p. 161. The types lost included 228 Sterling, 249 Halifax and 202 Lancaster bombers. Another 2,724 were damaged in 1942.

37 Murray, *Luftwaffe*, p. 210.

38 Murray, *Luftwaffe*, p. 211.

39 Thomas Alexander Hughes, *Overlord: General Pete Quesada and the Triumph of Tactical Air Power in World War II* (Free Press, 2002), 86.

40 Hughes, *Overlord*, p. 94.

41 Hughes, *Overlord*, p. 97.

42 Hughes, *Overlord*, p. 97.

43 It is also notable that on June 27, 1943, an Allied landing force of 1,200 ships was en route to an invasion of Sicily. There were 1,500 German aircraft within striking distance. American and British fighters were tasked to provide air cover. Despite repeated Luftwaffe mass attacks, not a single ship was lost. On that day the Anglo-American fighters had won the air battle for the Mediterranean. This was the last Luftwaffe mass attack in the theater.

44 Murray, *Luftwaffe*, p. 167.

45 Murray, *Luftwaffe*, Appendix 4, p. 319.

46 Hughes, *Overlord*, p. 4.

47 Hughes, *Overlord*, p. 5.

48 Hughes, *Overlord*, p. 12.

49 United States Strategic Bombing Survey, Summary Report, September 1945.

50 Murray, *Luftwaffe*, p. 319.

51 Murray, *Luftwaffe*, p. 319.

52 Time and space prevents an analysis of the strategic bombing campaign against Japan. However, it should be noted that the driving factor in America's strangling the Japanese war machine on the home islands was the U.S. Navy's brilliantly successful submarine campaign. In addition, while firebomb and nuclear raids on Japanese cities did indeed kill hundreds of thousands of civilians and cause horrible damage, it is also notable that some historians and political analysts of the time question whether the nuclear raids were indeed the single factor that caused the Japanese to surrender when they did. See, for example, Robert A. Pape's *Bombing to Win: Air Power and Coercion in War* (Ithaca: Cornell University Press, 1991).

53 Hughes, *Overlord*, p. 311.

54 Hughes, *Overlord*, p. 311.

55 Hughes, *Overlord*, p. 312.

56 Conrad C. Crane, *American Air Power Strategy in Korea 1950-1953* (University of Kansas Press, 2000), 31-32.

57 Crane, *American Air Power in Korea*, p. 61.

58 Crane, *American Air Power in Korea*, p. 62.

59 Robert Jackson, *Air War over Korea* (New York: Scribner's, 1973), 136.

60 Jackson, *Air War over Korea*, p. 136.

61 Jackson, *Air War over Korea*, p. 118.

62 Crane, *American Air Power in Korea*, p. 128.

63 The 200 F-86s were more than defended the entire U.S. military. When the U.S. Air Force decides to get rid of their fighters, they do a thorough job.

64 Jackson, *Air War over Korea*, p. 172.

65 Richard Hallion, *Storm over Iraq: Air Power and the Gulf War* (Washington: Smithsonian, 1997), 354.

66 Hallion, *Storm over Iraq*, p. 65.

67 Their maximum takeoff weights in the bomber mode varied from 42,500 pounds for the F-16, 52,500 for the F-117 and 80,000 pounds for the F15E. For comparison, the average World War II B-17 heavy bomber at maximum takeoff weight came in at about 50,000 pounds.

68 After 33 losses, the Iraqi air force remained grounded until multiple aircraft fled to Iran. The 39-day air war was followed by a four-day ground engagement.

69 The air war required a huge air-refueling effort. A gallon of fuel air-delivered cost 20 times as much as a ground-delivered gallon. The requirement for airborne tankers adds enormously to mission expense and mission complexity.

70 Hallion, *Storm over Iraq*, p. 251.

71 Williamson Murray, *Air War in the Persian Gulf*, p. 141-142.

72 Murray, *Air War*, p. 242.

73 Murray, *Air War*, p. 263.

74 Hallion, *Storm over Iraq*, p. 223.

75 Murray, *Air War*, p. 286.

76 Hallion, *Storm over Iraq*, p. 184.

77 This tally does not include the loss of OA-10 FAC aircraft in the first Gulf war. Because these aircraft fly a significantly different mission profile from the A-10 attack aircraft, they are not counted here. Even if they were included, the points that follow would be the same, just with different details in the numbers.

78 The Air Force asserts that only one F-117 was shot down in the Kosovo air war. In fact, a second was also destroyed; it was severely damaged and managed to return to base, never to fly again.

79 William L. Smallwood," *Warthog: Flying the A-10 in the Gulf War* (New York: Brassey's, 1993), 96.

80 Email from Maj. Gen. David Deptula, HQ ACC/XP, to Robert Odonohue, sent on June 4, 2003 at 5:20 p.m.; forwarded to the authors by sources inside the Pentagon.

81 Elaine Grossman, "Air Leaders: A-10 Upgrades May Be Cut But Retirement Not Accelerated," *Inside the Pentagon*, June 5, 2003.

82 Andrew J. Bacevich and Eliot A. Cohen, *War over Kosovo* (New York: Columbia University Press, 2002), 14.

83 Bacevich and Cohen, *Kosovo*, p. 26.

84 Master Sgt. Andrew Gates, "A-10s Rescue Ambushed OEF Ground Forces," Army News Service, August 18, 2004.

85 Current flyaway cost is just above $180 million per aircraft. The cost cited here is based on internal memoranda circulated by the former secretary of the Air Force in advocating the additional aircraft.

86 The current total program unit cost of the F-35 is $180 million, each; given the early stage of the current program, that cost is likely to climb dramatically. This unit cost, even as a so-called "flyaway" cost is a very likely understatement.

87 The right-hand column cost of $251 billion over 20 years or so is consistent with the current U.S. Air Force yearly aircraft procurement of about $12 billion and is also consistent with internal OSD estimates published by the media. For example, see "Cutback On F-35 In 2008 Rejected," by Tony Capaccio, *Fort Worth Star-Telegram*, January 4, 2007. That article stated, "The Pentagon estimates that it will spend about $231 billion over the next 20 years buying aircraft."

88 Not just the F-22 and F-35 but apparently all U.S. combat aircraft of the future will include both stealth and radar. The radar of the F-22 and the F-35 incorporates spread spectrum techniques. These spread the electronic energy of the radar's pulses over a very wide band of frequencies to confound the enemy's ability to detect or intercept the signal. The energy is intended to appear as low level, undecipherable white noise on a standard passive receiver, or "fuzzbuster." Over 30 years ago, Dr. Thomas Amlie commented on this radar technology. At the time, Dr. Amlie was head of the Navy's China Lake test and development facility and a world-class expert on radar. His point was that such a radar would be of great expense and size and would emit a signal that was 1 million to 10 million times greater than real-world background noise. It would be relatively simple to develop a passive receiver or fuzzbuster device to detect these radar spread spectrum emissions at least four times further away than the radar's own maximum range. Dr. Amlie wrote that trying to hide the radar's immense signal would be similar to trying to camouflage an elephant in the living room by painting its toenails red. The only thing that has changed since his statement is that lots of cell phone and wireless computer devices now use spread spectrum techniques, so it is vastly easier to build a spread spectrum passive receiver today. For further discussion, see James Stevenson, *The Pentagon Paradox* (Annapolis, Md.: U.S. Naval Institute Press, 1993), 367.

CHAPTER 8

AIR MOBILITY FOR A NEW ADMINISTRATION

James P. Stevenson

Special thanks to Thomas Christie whose technical expertise and critiques were extremely valuable in making this chapter possible.

To implement U.S. National Military Strategy (NMS), the United States relies heavily on moving personnel, equipment and supplies by air. Transport Command (US-TRANSCOM) operationally oversees transportation, sustainment and distribution of personnel, equipment and supplies whether it be air, sea or land. USTRANSCOM consists of three components: 1) U.S. Air Force's Air Mobility Command (AMC); 2) U.S. Navy's Military Sealift Command (MSC); 3) U.S. Army's Surface Deployment and Distribution Command (SDDC). Special Operations Air or Specialized Airpower consists of airpower provided by Air Force Special Operations Command (AFSOC) as part of Special Operations Command (SOCOM).[1] AMC is one of the Air Force's 10 Major Commands (MAJCOMs). AMC's responsibilities include air refueling, special missions, airlift and aeromedical evacuation for all U.S. troops.

Airlift is segmented into tactical and strategic airlift. Tactical airlift is the airlift in a particular area or theater of operation – it has much shorter distances than strategic airlift, and usually involves smaller and less expensive aircraft. Strategic airlift moves between continents or across theaters. It usually involves larger and more expensive aircraft. In-flight air refueling extends the range of all air assets.

Important examples of air mobility include the Berlin Airlift (1948-49), the Yom Kippur war (1973), operations Desert Shield and Desert Storm (1990-1991), and Operation Enduring Freedom (OEF) in Afghanistan (2001). In June of 1948, as the Soviets blocked land routes to Berlin, the airlift became center stage and literally kept approximately two million Berliners from starvation. At the geopolitical level, the Berlin Airlift maintained the strategic status quo and averted war.[2] In the subsequent examples, in-flight air refueling was essential, with specialized airpower vital in the final two examples. Air mobility is not just important in the traditional "hard power" and "soft power" instances, but is increasingly important in "smart power" – using both hard and soft power in an integrated way.[3] One example of "smart power" is Building Partnership Capacity (BPC). BPC is defined as "Targeted efforts to improve the collected capabilities and performance of the Department of Defense and its partners."[4] In practical terms, this means we train and empower other countries to do similar military operations (e.g., tactical airlift). BPC requires that the United States buys the same or similar equipment that it wants its allies to acquire. Fundamentally, this should allow us to leverage our current forces for greater effect, and/or potentially reduce our force structure because the capability exists elsewhere.

What Are the Issues?

The United States has the best air mobility capability in the world. No other military or combination of other nations' capabilities can equal its power. This comes at a significant cost. Even with record-level defense spending, plans for air mobility are unrealistic without significant increases in the defense budgets or a drastic shift of Air Force funding. In a nutshell, there is a significant Plans-Reality disconnect.[5] The following are but some of the critical questions for the next administration concerning air mobility plans and programs:

- How much and what kind of strategic airlift, air refueling, tactical airlift and special operations ("ops") air capabilities do we need in the coming decades?

- Do we continue aerial refueling, airlift and special ops air dominance based on the current military service and DOD plans?

- Do we increase, decrease or maintain current capability?

- Do we implement innovative initiatives to substantially lower costs?

- Do we trade some capability in these areas for other areas?

- Do we develop hybrids of the above recommendations?

Strategic Air Refueling

The importance of the air refueling (AR) mission has grown in the post-Cold War period; it has evolved from a former emphasis on strategic bombers to a new emphasis on deploying and operating tactical and special operations forces (SOF), both shore-based and ship-based, in distant regions. The tanker "air-bridge" concept provides mobility to get forces to the theater, and then tankers in theater act as force multipliers, making assets more capable by enhancing their range and persistence. Air refueling is a critically important consideration for the next administration in its deliberations about future defense acquisition programs, even more so as the result of the Boeing tanker scandal. How and what the next administration does to resolve the root causes of the original scandal, and the subsequent sustained protest upheld by the U.S. Government Accountability Office (GAO), is central to any real procurement and acquisition reform.[6]

The vast majority of the aerial refueling tankers will reside in the U.S. Air Force and, by fiscal year 2009 (FY 09), will consist of approximately 420 Eisenhower-era KC-135s and 59 KC-10s, for a total of just under 500 strategic tankers. It is important to note that a strategic tanker refers to the aircraft itself as being strategic (usually larger and longer range like strategic airlift), not what it refuels. The next tanker, the KC-X[7], will have the capability and flexibility to be both tanker (refuel with a boom for Air Force aircraft and "hose and drogue" for Navy aircraft on each mission) and airlifter, similar to the KC-10.[8] The Navy uses F-18s to air refuel other carrier aircraft and turns to contracts, such as with Omega Air, for niche air-refueling capabilities. However, the vast majority of the U.S. Navy's wartime air-refueling requirements are provided by the U.S. Air Force. On the other hand, the U.S. Marine Corps uses about 75 KC-130s (several variants) for air refueling (fixed wing, helicopters and CV-22s) and ground refueling. Since fiscal year 2000, the Marine Corps has been buying KC-130Js, permitting them to retire all the older KC-130 models with an eventual goal of approximately 80 KC-130Js. In addition to these capabilities, air refueling for special operations by the multi-mission MC-130/HC-130 aircraft (sometimes referred to as tactical air refueler) is particularly important in today's environment.[9]

Strategic Airlift

Strategic airlift carries passengers, materiel and weapons long distances between continents or theaters (intertheater). By fiscal year 2009, the United States will have approximately 300 strategic airlifters consisting of 190 C-17s, 59 C-5As and 52 C-5B/C/Ms. The C-17 has been one of the U.S. Air Force's "crown jewels" since the mid-1990s. Its effectiveness has been touted by the Air Force, but it has come with high acquisition and operating costs. The C-17 is arguably versatile, serving as both a strategic and tactical airlifter but not as efficient as a pure strategic airlifter (e.g., C-5B or C-141B). At the tactical level, the C-17 is costly to operate and it exposes a $300 million aircraft when it flies into a combat zone.

Procurement of C-5s in the 1970s resulted in one of DOD's biggest acquisition scandals. Recently, the U.S. Air Force went through cost reporting proceedings, based on the Nunn-McCurdy legislation, with the C-5 Re-engineering and Replacement Program (RERP), because of excessive cost growth resulting in an approximately 50 percent increase in unit costs.[10] As a result, in January 2008, the Office of Secretary of Defense (OSD) decided to limit RERP to only about 50 C-5B/C aircraft (these are the C-5s that were bought in the 1980s) but to continue the modernization of all C-5 avionics.[11]

Another critically important segment of strategic airlift is the Civil Reserve Air Fleet (CRAF). The CRAF supports DOD airlift requirements in emergencies with commercial airlines pledging aircraft for various segments of the strategic lift mission.[12] Currently, the CRAF is capable of meeting approximately 40 percent of the wartime cargo airlift requirements, about 50 percent of the aeromedical evacuation requirements and approximately 90 percent of the passenger transport requirements.[13]

Among the strategic airlift questions for the next administration will be:

- What is the right mix and capacity of strategic airlift?

- Do we continue the C-17 production line past fiscal year 2009? If so, for how long and how many?

- If not, what do we do with C-5As that appear to have a limited service life?

- What do we do about the high cost of C-5 RERP?

- What do we do about the other high costs associated with modifying both old and new strategic airlifters?

- What are some innovative and more cost-effective courses of action?

- Do we focus more on sealift versus airlift?

- Can we leverage more capability out of CRAF?

- Should we count a portion of the new tankers as part of airlift?

Tactical Airlift

Tactical airlift consists of airlift used primarily within the theater. The venerable legacy C-130Hs and other models, of which there are approximately 275, have been the mainstay of the force. The latest U.S. Air Force plans call for the retirement of all the C-130Es by around 2014. Since the mid-1990s, the U.S. Air Force has been purchasing the latest version of the C-130 – the C-130J, with current plans going from about 80 C-130Js to about 120 C-130Js – almost all of them the C-130J-30s. With new engines and avionics, this is clearly an upgrade over the C-130Hs, but at more than twice the real cost for only about 25-percent improvement in capability and performance.[14] Despite no major scandals, the C-130J program has had a very rocky road. As of just a few years ago, DOT&E submitted a scathing report on C-130J performance and acquisition problems to the Secretary of Defense and Congress.[15]

Since 2004, the U.S. Air Force and U.S. Army have been working on the Joint Cargo Aircraft (JCA). In 2006, the C-27J Spartan was selected as the JCA. The C-27J is about half the size of a C-130J, carries about half the load, costs half of a C-130J (flyaway), and costs less to operate than the C-130J-30.[16] Tactical airlift has been extremely important in Operation Iraqi Freedom (OIF) because of the need to reduce truck convoys; the long distances in the OIF theater requires more airlift for time-critical supplies and passenger movements for effective counterinsurgency operations. The effective use of specialized tactical and strategic aeromedical evacuation has led to numerous lives saved in Operation Iraqi Freedom (OIF) and Operation Enduring Freedom (OEF).[17] In OEF, although a much smaller scale operation, Afghanistan's geography, combined with the lack of an effective transportation infrastructure, makes tactical airlift critical.

The big tactical airlift questions for the next administration will be:

- What is the right mix and capacity of tactical airlift?

- Does the U.S. Air Force continue to buy the MC-130J? If so, how many?

- Does the U.S. Army and Air Force continue with the Joint Cargo Aircraft (JCA or C-27Js)? If so, how many?

- Can a mix of JCAs (or C-27Js) with MC-130Js be effective?

- What are some cost effective innovations in tactical airlift?

- What should replace C-130Hs?

Special Operations Air

Special Operations Air consists of a potpourri of aircraft. It has several models of MH-60s and MH-47s, AH-6 and MH-6 helicopters, and 15 Air Force Special Operations Command MH-53 helicopters that are currently being phased out. The U.S. Air Force is currently acquiring 50 CV-22s, bringing new capabilities very different from the MH-53s. One of the largest groups of aircraft – the MC-130s – work as air refuelers and carry out a number of other roles for special operations forces.

One of the critical mainstays of the Special Operations Command (SOCOM) and Air Force Special Operations Command (AFSOC) are the 25 AC-130 gun ships (various models), of which 18 are relatively new. AFSOC has recently acquired some of the latest Unmanned Aerial Vehicles (UAVs) – the MQ-1 *Predator*, and the more heavily armed MQ-9 *Reaper*. The Air Force has used smaller hand-held Micro UAVs and some slightly larger UAVs.[18] Additionally, there are a potpourri of specialized aircraft in the Special Operations Squadrons (SOS), and its kin.

The aircraft requirements for special operations raise the following questions for the next administration:

- Does the United States continue to grow AFSOC's air fleet?

- Does AFSOC continue to buy 50 CV-22s, reduce the number, or add more?

- Do SOCOM and AFSOC continue the recapitalization of MC-130s with modified C-130Js or something new?

- Can JCAs substitute for some of the planned C-130Js?

- What are some new cost effective air innovations in SOCOM?

- What should SOCOM do with some of its specialized air fleet?

- Should AFSOC put more emphasis on Building Partnership Capacity (BPC)? (Historically, most of this has been done in AFSOC. If the magnitude of BPC increases significantly, it may require the BPC in other parts of the Air Force.)

Recommendations

We intend to provide viable and cost-effective solutions through our recommendations. While it is virtually impossible to get accurate cost and capability data for some of the proposed innovations because they are not available anywhere, the following recommendations are founded on an understanding of sound principles – the result of decades of experience. We believe they are worthy of serious consideration.

Spending for air refueling and airlift is at an historical high.[19] It is expected to climb higher to pay for the new tanker (the first aircraft is the KC-X)[20] as it begins production at a rate of approximately 15 tankers per year. The average spending on strategic mobility has grown significantly even without accounting for the current conflicts.[21] Since 2000, it has more than doubled. Spending on air refueling should not have to be at the magnitudes proposed, even though recapitalization is a high priority, because this is an area where we have great advantage to leverage the private sector for cost-effective solutions. There are a number of innovative options that are more plausible and attractive than other segments of the overall national defense portfolio proposed by others not contributing to this anthology.

Historically, the Office of the Secretary of Defense has generally favored strategic airlift over strategic sealift – especially in the last 20 years. Similarly, the U.S. Air Force has favored strategic airlift over tactical airlift, aerial refueling and special operations air. The strategic goal will be to continue relative dominance, but much more cost effectively while taking some allowable risk. The costs of the existing portfolios can be reduced by at least 30 percent or more with little loss of capability. In the near- to mid-term, our recommendations favor an increased emphasis on aerial refueling, strategic sealift and specialized air, with a decreased emphasis on strategic and tactical airlift, but all at significantly reduced cost compared to current plans.

Even with an increased emphasis on aerial refueling, the current plans for tankers are not realistic with respect to either cost or schedule. The yearly cost for the tanker portfolio will increase from approximately $3 billion in FY 08 to at least $7 billion in the next five or so years. Based on its plans, the U.S. Air Force will have to maintain at least that amount for 30 years ($200 billion total) according to current projections. The projected cost of just acquiring new tankers over the next 30 years is at least $100 billion.[22] Even worse, there appears to be no backup plan if the largest, oldest fleet in the Air Force is grounded or the KC-135Rs' service life is significantly reduced in the near- to mid-term. This is important as 90 percent of the strategic air refueling capacity resides in the KC-135Rs. The only options appear to be to spend more money and buy more tankers per year, or let old tankers continue to fly until they are grounded or fall apart. Unfortunately, there is an industrial capacity issue and significant resource limits on how much the nation can afford to spend per year. In order to decrease these funding requirements, we must reduce the cost of the tanker fleet, as well as the demand and/or need for tankers. This leads us to propose a force structure that permits reducing tanker numbers in the U.S. Air Force inventory by approximately 20 percent.

According to the Congressional Research Service (CRS), the Air Force strategy of tanker recapitalization, one of bureaucratic averaging, is to buy exactly 179 KC-X, 179 KC-Y and 179 KC-Z tankers.[23] To reduce the cost of the tanker fleet, the Air Force must move towards a smaller, cheaper tanker (KC-Y) as quickly as possible. That would mean stopping the KC-X buy at around 100 tankers (pending analysis of the final selection). The smaller, cheaper tanker (KC-Y) should be at least 30 percent cheaper in acquisition costs than the KC-X, and about 30 to 40 percent less expensive in operational and support (O&S) costs. It should require virtually no additional infrastructure costs – that is, to be comparable with KC-135R costs. The KC-Y tanker should be no larger than the KC-135 (in both size and weight), and the life cycle costs need to be significantly cheaper with the ability to use and transfer alternative fuels. Even though there are no commercial derivative aircraft in this class today (from either Boeing or EADS), this should help shape the aircraft industrial base on their next commercial offerings in the 2010-2020 timeframe (specifically, the Boeing/EADS follow-on aircraft). This future aircraft should be a "fly-before-you-buy" acquisition to minimize cost and capability risks. Introducing a third tanker (e.g., KC-Z) to the discussion is not cost effective for a plan going several decades into the future.

There are experts in this field who say there should not even be a thought of savings in strategic aerial refueling because this area has been woefully neglected and therefore it is time for it to get its fair share. However, neglect does not mean that we should accept OSD and U.S. Air Force plans *carte blanche*. Even with the alternatives that we recommend, there are significant additional resources for tankers. Neverthe-less, we believe there are numerous approaches to innovation that would increase effectiveness and reduce cost. Finally, we are discouraged that there are only two alternatives – either spend significantly more money or just spend less money on the same plan. Either will usher in failure.

Based on the discussion above, we make the following recommendations:

1. Reduce the total number of strategic tankers to approximately 420 total aircraft.

2. Limit the buy of KC-X to about 100, regardless if the final selection is EADS, Boeing or a combination because they are too big and too expensive.

3. Immediately begin a new competition for a smaller, cheaper commercial deriva-tive tanker – the KC-Y regardless of the outcome of the final KC-X selection.

4. Develop innovative and effective "out-of-the-box" ideas for additional capability (e.g. contract air refueling, new transfer technology, etc.).

5. Develop new concepts of operations that will permit a smaller refueling force but also one that has the needed capability. Such options would factor in the consideration that new air refuelers will be able to capitalize on each tanker being able to refuel others, as well as being able to refuel itself, and each new tanker will have boom along with hose and drogue capability.

6. The KC-X, especially, could provide a hedge in the strategic airlift because each air aircraft will be significantly better for handling and carrying cargo and passengers compared to KC-135Rs.

7. To alleviate the continued fallout with the tanker scandal, simplify and reform the acquisition system with "fly-before-buy" competition of the actual aircraft to be competed.

One of the outcomes of our recommendations will be a reduction of the cost of future strategic aerial refueling plans by approximately 30 percent.[24]

A reasonable person might ask: Why take risk in strategic airlift? The answer is that because of the U.S. Air Force's emphasis on strategic airlift since the mid-1990s, our capabilities have increased significantly in the last seven years, and our allies are starting to increase their capabilities as well (e.g., Australia (4 C-17s), United Kingdom (8 C-17s), Canada (4 C-17s), NATO (6 C-17s estimated), Japan (4 C-17s estimated), et al.).[26] Additionally, many of our allies have pledged to purchase the A-400M (which

Table 1. Strategic Air Refueling Recommendations Compared With Service/OSD Plans

	KC-X	KC-Y	KC-Z	KC-135	KC-10	Innovative Options	Totals
Service/OSD plans for aircraft in 2030	179	179	103	0	59	0	520
Recommended numbers of aircraft in 2030	100	200	0	0	59	Approx. 15% (~60 aircraft)	420
Estimated percentage cost difference	-44%	+12%	-100%	0%	-20%	Increase	-30%

Cost assumptions are based on parametric estimates from 2011-2030. Both plans assume KC-135Rs are retired by 2030. Larger, more expensive tanker aircraft are assumed to be in the "innovative options." Innovative options could also include other options such as Contract Air Refueling and other options. KC-10 savings come from OPTEMPO reductions.

is more than a tactical airlifter), as a replacement for their older models of the venerable C-130s.[27] It appears that the global aircraft industry will be producing several aircraft (e.g., Embraer C-390) as possible C-130 replacements. They would be more capable than C-130s, not as large as C-17s, but are comparable in range and payload with the A-400M, but potentially more cost effective.[28]

The U.S. Air Force will have more than just the KC-10 as a true tanker-transport. The new KC-X, manufactured by the Boeing and/or EADS winner in the tanker competition, will carry cargo and passengers similar to the KC-10. According to the Air Mobility Command, one strategy would be to fly the more efficient KC-X at a high utilization rate, so the Air Force could reduce the utilization rate of the C-17 and C-5B/M. This would save resources in the near-term, but also extend the life of those two aircraft so they do not have to be replaced as soon.[29] That would avoid or defer billions of dollars in spending over the next 20 years. Otherwise, if we keep flying C-17s at the rate we are flying them, the fleet may require replacements in the 2020s. That would require a new program in the near-term to be ready by the mid- to late 2020s.

By reducing the number of strategic airlifters by approximately 20 percent, cost benefits of more than 20 percent could be realized as the reduction avoids the need to recapitalize those assets. Furthermore, it would save operating and support costs, as well as dollars for modifications and upgrades of existing assets over the next two decades. By foregoing additional buys of C-17s (250 vs. 205), taxpayers would save at least $13 billion in acquisition costs and approximately $7 billion of operating costs for the next 20 years.[30]

Some would argue that strategic airlift is one of our largest vulnerabilities and that we cannot take risk in this area. It is clearly a critical weakness because of the way we currently fight. Heavy forces with ridiculously unrealistic strategic mobility requirements make this a strategic Achilles' heel. To fix strategic mobility primarily through airlift would require a Herculean effort in both cost and force structure. It would be better to incrementally improve strategic airlift in cost-effective and innovative ways. Hopefully, this would lead the U.S. Army to reduce its strategic air mobility requirements closer to Marine Corps standards, by enhancing mobility requirements through strategic sealift, and some additional prepositioning of material. Historically, strategic sealift ends up carrying approximately 95 percent of the total tonnage. The cost-benefit analysis is not even close.[31]

Based on the discussion above, we make the following recommendations:

1. Reduce the number of strategic airlifters from approximately 300 to 260.

2. Immediately retire 39 of the 59 C-5As.

3. Double the capacity of fast strategic sealift, then retire the remaining 20 C-5As.[32]

4. Stop the buy of C-17s at approximately 205.

5. Employ a portion of the KC-X and/or KC-10 fleets for both passenger and cargo carrying capability.

6. Increase the cargo capacity of the Civil Reserve Air Fleet (CRAF) by about 10 percent.

7. Develop innovative options (e.g. encourage more allies to focus on strategic airlift, etc.).

7. Develop new cost-effective alternatives for specialized cargo that do not require military-unique aircraft.

By implementing the recommendations above, DOD could reduce the cost of strategic airlift by approximately 35 percent from current plans.

How could we possibly reduce tactical airlift costs by approximately 20 to 30 percent and not lose capability? Current plans call for the acquisition of roughly 120-plus C-130Js, 24 C-27Js, and retaining large numbers of C-130Hs with a significant amount of dollars for C-130 modifications. Our alternative plan calls for a 15-percent reduction in total aircraft. Halting the C-130J buy at 100 would save about $3 billion in acquisition costs. Aggressively divesting C-130Hs earlier than scheduled avoids a series of unnecessary modifications and relatively high O&S costs.

Table 2. Strategic Airlift Recommendations Compared With Service/OSD Plans

	C-17s	C-5Ms	Civil Reserve Air Fleet	KC-X/ KC-10*	Sealift/ NSA†	Totals
Service/OSD Plans for Aircraft in 2030	Approx. 250	52	Status quo	0% / 0%	Status quo/NSA	302
Recommended Number of Aircraft in 2030	Approx. 205	52	10% increase	20% / 25%	2x/No NSA	257
Delta Cost percentage (est.)	-20%	0	Small cost	Small Cost	Significant Savings	-35%

*Percentage of KC-X/KC-10 fleet employed for passenger and cargo carrying capability
†NSA (Next Strategic Airlifter) is a notional replacement for the C-5/C-17.

Avoiding the Advanced Joint Air Combat System (AJACS)[33] aircraft (which will likely have a substantial R&D bill) precludes at least $5 billion to $10 billion by purchasing a modified commercial off-the-shelf New Tactical Airlifter (NTA).[34]

Based on the discussion above, we make the following recommendations:

1. Keep tactical airlifters at approximately 400 tails, with a new mix of aircraft.

2. Accelerate the retirement of C-130Es and older C-130Hs.

3. Stop the C-130J buy at approximately 100 aircraft (divert C-130J production to AFSOC aircraft).

4. Buy approximately 100 JCAs for tactical airlift, assuming aggressive acquisition-cost containment and innovation to reduce JCA total costs. If that fails, pursue other alternatives (e.g., Advanced Composite Cargo Aircraft (ACCA), et al.)

5. Aggressively pursue Building Partnership Capacity (BPC) in tactical airlift worldwide that is appropriate for partner countries.

6. Reduce the cost of modifications on C-130s significantly (e.g., scale back or cancel C-130AMP).

7. Pursue a commercial derivative New Tactical Airlifter (NTA) for the late 2010s that is more cost-effective than the C-130J and AJACS.

8. Cancel the U.S. Army's Joint Heavy Lift (JHL) and Quad Tilt-Rotor programs.[35]

By following these recommendations, we can reduce the cost of tactical airlift by approximately 20 to 30 percent.

Although we believe that Special Operations Air should have a strategic emphasis, this does not mean we cannot save significant resources and still increase capability. Our recommendations not only decrease costs, they increase capability while increasing the number of aircraft by approximately 20 percent. This number of aircraft would increase even more if we include small, manned counterinsurgency (COIN) aircraft.

We recommend that AFSOC give their CV-22s to the U.S. Marine Corps and acquire one or two helicopters variants. The CV-22 is an expensive aircraft to operate and support, and it also has a dubious history of numerous acquisition and integrity failures. With relatively high acquisition, operating and support costs, it appears that CV/MV-22s will cost much more than conventional helicopters to procure and operate.[36]

Although we recommended stopping the C-130J buy in the Tactical Airlift Section, we recommend a continued buy of C-130Js for Special Operations and converting them to MC-130s. The Service/OSD plans for MC-130s not only recapitalizes all the current MC-130s (approximately 40 aircraft), but it increases their numbers. We believe that 40 MC-130s should be recapitalized with the C-130Js. For additional capacity beyond that provided by these C-130Js, we should acquire a variant of the C-27J or something else.

The AC-130 gunship has had a successful history, but we believe it is time to move on to a smaller, cheaper variant. Once that new variant is ready for operations – Initial Operational Capability (IOC) – we recommend retiring the older AC-130s. We also

Table 3. Tactical Airlift Recommendations Compared With Service/OSD Plans

	C-130Js	C-130Hs	JCAs	AJACS	NTA	Totals
Service/OSD Plans for aircraft in 2030	127	200	24	80+	0	431
Recommended Aircraft in 2030	100	100	100	0	100	400
Delta Cost percentage Estimate	-30%	-50%	4x more	*	*	-20-30%

*The delta costs between an AJACS and the NTA is significant. There is little Research Development Test & Evaluation cost for NTA. Furthermore, the NTA flyaway and O&S costs are substantially less. Note: AJACS and NTA are notional aircraft to replace C-130s by approximately the 2020s. The AJACS would be a full RDT&E program before production while the NTA would be a modified commercial "off-the-shelf" aircraft.

envision AFSOC acquiring the New Tactical Airlifter (NTA) that we recommended in the Tactical Airlift Section that could be used in Special Operations Air for a new AC or MC variant.

Several years ago, AFSOC recommended the establishment of an Irregular Warfare Wing that would include 44 airlifters (such as the M28 Skytruck and aircraft up to C-27J class), 20 helicopters (for example, Mi-17 class), and light attack aircraft (for example, EMB314 class). These COIN aircraft would help further Building Partnership Capacity and at the same time could be used in OIF and OEF instead of very expensive fighters and UAVs. All these aircraft should cost, in flyaway dollars, about $10 million each – meaning the whole irregular warfare (IW) wing could be acquired for less than $1 billion, compared to a new F-35 wing that would be seven to ten times more costly. The IW wing would also be significantly less costly to operate each year.

Based on the discussion above, we make the following recommendations:

1. Stop the CV-22 buy immediately. Replace it with an H-X (e.g., CH-53K, H-92, CH-47, EH-101 or a combination of several).

2. Recapitalize most of the current capacity of MC-130s with C-130Js, but any additional capacity will be provided with a smaller and cheaper aircraft (e.g. C-27Js and its kin).

3. Develop lower cost alternatives to the AC-130s (e.g. AC-27J) and increase total gunship numbers.

4. Acquire the Next Tactical Airlifter (NTA) as a follow-on to the C-130J in the 2020s.

5. Instead of buying more MQ-1s or MQ-9s, buy small, manned aircraft that can do ISR, mobility and light strike (e.g. FID/COIN aircraft) to help Building Partnership Capacity.[37]

By following the above recommendations, the cost of Special Operations Air can be reduced by approximately 20 percent.

Conclusions

The current military services' and Office of the Secretary of Defense's plans for air mobility[38] should not continue. They are unfeasible and will lead to a significant loss of capability in the future. As we know from the Congressional Budget Office (CBO), the Government Accountability Office (GAO) and other reporting over the years, current plans will invariably mean significant cost growth requiring significantly

Table 4. Special Operations Air Recommendations Compared with Service/OSD Plans

	CV-22/ H-X	AC-130	MC-130J	JCAs/ AJACS†	NTA	Totals
Service/OSD Plans for aircraft in 2030	50/0	25	78	10/ unknown	0	163
Recommended Aircraft in 2030	0/60	15*	40	20-60/0	20	195
Delta Cost percentage Estimate	-30%+	-20%	-50%	2-6x	Incremental	-20%

*AC-130s are not reduced until the mini-gunships are operational.
†The proposal is to use JCAs/NTAs for a variety of specialized mission aircraft to replace and/ or supplement AC-130s/MC-130s.

higher budgets and smaller inventories than initially promised. These plans have significant program risk, too.[39] Although it is difficult to do a detailed analysis of Service/OSD force structures without discussing the details of the latest Program Objective Memorandum (POM) and Program of Record (POR) that are not publicly available, our proposals are based on years of experience, and we believe they are rational, effective and efficient.

In our recommendations, we clearly advocate a number of creative choices – a strategic focus on aerial refueling and special operations air, with less emphasis on strategic and tactical airlift. In all cases, we call for innovative solutions that run counter to conventional wisdom but allow us to lower costs without the loss of overall capability. Without these creative and innovative solutions, the Department of Defense will be forced to reduce far more force structure, leading to significantly more risk.[40]

ENDNOTES

1   It should be emphasized that most of AFSOC acquisitions of aircraft occur through Air Mobility Command (AMC).

2   William M. Leary, "Strategic Airlift: Past Present, and Future." *Air University Review*, September-October 1986, http://www.airpower.maxwell.af.mil/airchronicles/aureview/1986/sep-oct/leary. html

3   2007 CSIS Commission on Smart Power & CDI's *Honing the Sword and A Swift, Elusive Sword* (2003/2001)

4   "Building Partnership Capacity," National Defense University, May 22, 2006, http://www.ndu. edu/itea/storage/790/BPC%20Roadmap.pdf (accessed 8/23/08).

5   See Franklin C. Spinney, *Defense Facts of Life* (Westview, 1985). The bottom line is that there is a disconnect between the plan and what is reasonable or feasible from a budgetary (generally,

but not always) perspective (e.g., I want 100 of X but only enough budgeted dollars for much less than X).

6   Comptroller General of the United States, "Decision: Matter of The Boeing Company (b-311344)," June 18, 2008, http://www.kirotv.com/download/2008/0625/16708220.pdf

7   The U.S. Air Force has officially designated the KC-X as the KC-45. Due to the protest, and the uncertainty regarding which aircraft will ultimately be selected; we elected to go with KC-X in our analysis and discussions.

8   Christopher Bolkcom, "Air Force Aerial Refueling," *CRS Report for Congress*, March 20, 2007, http://www.fas.org/sgp/crs/weapons/RS20941.pdf

9   *Air Force Magazine Almanac* 2008, pp. 147-149.

10 Michael Bruno, "ARH, C-5 RERP Help Drive Up DOD Cost Growth Estimates," *Aviation Week*, November 20, 2007, http://www.aviationdaily.com/aw/generic/story_generic.jsp?channel=aerospacedaily&id=news/DOD112007.xml&headline=ARH, percent 20C-5 percent 20RERP percent 20Help percent 20Drive percent 20Up percent 20DOD percent 20Cost percent 20Growth percent 20Estimates

11 "C-5 Modernization Program Certified," *B-Net*, March 2008, http://findarticles.com/p/articles/mi_qa3731/is_200803/ai_n25419519

12 Christopher Bolkcom, "Civil Reserve Air Fleet (CRAF)," *CRS Report for Congress*, October 18, 2006, http://fas.org/sgp/crs/weapons/RL33692.pdf

13 James W Herron, "Future Airlift Requirements," *USAWC Strategy Research Project*, http://www.strategicstudiesinstitute.army.mil/pdffiles/ksil30.pdf

14 "Fact Sheet on the U.S. Air Force C-130J Transport," *Center for Defense Information*, http://www.cdi.org/pdfs/C-130JTransport.pdf; "Joint Cargo Aircraft (JCA)," *Global Security*, http://www.globalsecurity.org/military/systems/aircraft/jca.htm

15 "Taxpayers Carry the Load: The C-130J Cargo Plane Does Not," *Project on Government Oversight*, March 15, 2005, http://www.pogo.org/p/defense/do-050301-C130J.html

16 "Fact Sheet on the U.S. Air Force C-130J Transport," *Center for Defense Information*, http://www.cdi.org/pdfs/C-130JTransport.pdf; "Selected Acquisition Reports: Summary Tables," Department of Defense, http://www.acq.osd.mil/ara/am/sar/

17 "Operation Enduring Freedom," Global Security, http://www.globalsecurity.org/military/ops/enduring-freedom.htm (accessed August 17, 2008).

18 "Unmanned Aerial Vehicles Roadmap: 2002 – 2027," Office of the Secretary of Defense, December 2002, http://www.uavforum.com/library/uavroadmap_2002.pdf

19 "The Long-Term Implications of Defense Plans: Detailed Update for Fiscal Year 2008 (March)," Congressional Budget Office, 2008, http://www.cbo.gov/ftpdocs/90xx/doc9043/03-28-Current-DefensePlans.pdf

20 The U.S. Air Force acquisition strategy is to buy three different tankers – notionally the KC-X, KC-Y and KC-Z. The KC-X is the first of these three tankers.

21 Ibid.

22 The Associated Press, "Boeing: Tanker Costs Miscalculated," *Air Force Times*, June 13, 2008, http://www.airforcetimes.com/news/2008/06/ap_boeing_tanker_fight_061208/

23 Christopher Bolkcom, "Civil Reserve Air Fleet (CRAF)," *CRS Report for Congress*, October 18, 2006, http://fas.org/sgp/crs/weapons/RL33692.pdf

24 Because we do not know which Tanker OSD will actually select – it is impossible to acquire a baseline from which to compare. Nevertheless, a parametric estimate of our recommendations makes a 30-percent cost reduction reasonable. Both the Boeing and EADS offers may be too large, with O&S costs that are significantly higher than the KC-135R.

25 http://thehill.com/business--lobby/air-force-is-pressed-to-test-air-refueling--for-hire-2007-06-06.html (Last visited 8-17-08).

26 Those listed are actual contracted or delivered C-17s; the other countries listed are still in negotiation. "C-17 Globemaster III," Wikipedia.org, August 30, 2008, http://en.wikipedia.org/wiki/C-17_Globemaster_III/

27 http://www.eads.net/1024/en/eads/eads_uk/Major_Programmes/A400M.html (Last visited 8-17-08).

28 "Embraer C-390 Military Transport Aircraft under Study," Deagel.com, April 19, 2007, http://www.deagel.com/news/Embraer-C-390-Military-Transport-Aircraft-under-Study_n000001851.aspx

29 "Headquarters Air Mobility Command White Paper KC:-X: The Next Mobility Platform, The Need for a Flexible Tanker," Air Mobility Command, http://www.amc.af.mil/shared/media/document/AFD-070227-044.pdf

30 "US Strategic Airlift: The C-5 AMP/RERP Program vs. Buying C-17s," Defense Industry Daily, 2007, http://www.defenseindustrydaily.com/files/DID_EXCEL_C-5_vs_C-17_Programs.xls

31 John D. Klaus, "Strategic Mobility Innovation: Options and Oversight Issues," April 29, 2005, *CRS Report for Congress*, http://www.fas.org/sgp/crs/weapons/RL32887.pdf

32 Each LMSR (Large, Medium-Speed, Roll-On/Roll-Off Ship) has the capability of approximately 3.0 Million Ton Miles (MTM)/day per ship versus a C-17 at about 0.15 MTM/day – that is a 20-times difference in capability. See U.S. Navy's Military Sealift Command Fact Sheet, "Large Medium-Speed, Roll-on/Roll-off Ships (LMSRs)," U.S. Navy Military Sealift Command, http://www.msc.navy.mil/factsheet/lmsr.asp; Each LMSR costs about the same as a C-17. See: "Table 5: Changes in Estimated Cost at Completion of LMSR New Construction Ships," Tpub.com, http://www.tpub.com/content/cg1997/ns97150/ns971500017.htm; The operating costs per year are similar.

33 The new name for AJACS is Joint Future Tactical Lift (JFTL). JFTL includes the U.S. Army's Joint Heavy Lift (JHL) and Quad-Tilt Rotor/VTOL concepts. These later concepts are potentially even bigger budget busters than AJACS.

34 "AJACS Load: US Begins (Another) Next-Gen Tactical Transport Project," Defense Industry Daily, April 23, 2007, http://www.defenseindustrydaily.com/ajacs-load-us-begins-another-nextgen-tactical-transport-project-03230/; The AJACS is a notional follow-on tactical airlifter to replace C-130s in the 2020s. AJACS is based on a full RDT&E program, then production. The NTA is a notional modified Commercial-Off-The-Shelf (COTS) aircraft.

35 Graham Warwick, "U.S. Army Extends JHL Concept Studies," *Aviation Week*, July 1, 2008, http://www.aviationweekspacetechnology.com/aw/generic/story_generic.jsp?channel=aerospacedaily&id=news/JHL070108.xml&headline=U.S. percent 20Army percent 20Extends percent 20JHL percent 20Concept percent 20Studies

36 Lee Gaillard, "V-22 Osprey: Wonder Weapon or Widow Maker? They Warned Us. But No One is Listening," Center for Defense Information, 2006.

37 Richard Comer, "An Irregular Challenge," *Armed Forces Journal*, http://www.armedforcesjournal.com/2008/02/3608631/

38 By the way of review, this includes aerial refueling, strategic sealift, strategic and tactical airlift, and special operations air.

39 "Defense Acquisitions: A Knowledge-Based Funding Approach Could Improve Major Weapon Systems Program Outcomes," United States Government Accountability Office, July 2008, http://www.gao.gov/new.items/d08619.pdf; "The Long-Term Implications of Current Defense Plans: Detailed Update for Fiscal Year 2008," CBO.gov, March 2008, http://www.cbo.gov/ftpdocs/90xx/doc9043/03-28-CurrentDefensePlans.pdf

40 For additional discussion of the DOD phenomena of larger budgets buying smaller defense inventories and capabilities, see chapters 10 and 11.

CHAPTER 9

THE ARMY NATIONAL GUARD, THE ARMY RESERVE AND THE MARINE CORPS RESERVE

Bruce I. Gudmundsson

In the days when bronze was the material of choice for artillery pieces of the lighter sort, the practice of recasting old ordnance on new patterns allowed armies to rapidly renovate their artillery parks at relatively low cost. In the middle years of the 19th century, a time of rapid improvement in the design of artillery pieces, the benefits of this practice were enhanced by the fact that new weapons made from the old material were much more effective than the guns, howitzers and mortars they replaced. At the start of the American Civil War, for example, the typical field artillery battery consisted of four 6-pounder guns (which fired a small projectile at relatively long ranges) and two 12-pounder howitzers (which fired a larger projectile, but was severely limited in range). The melting down of these six weapons produced enough metal to make four 12-pounder Napoleons, pieces that combined the range advantage of the 6-pounder gun with the larger projectile of the 12-pounder howitzer. Thus, instead of four weapons that were useful in some situations, and two that were useful in others, each battery was provided with four weapons that could fulfill all of the tasks that it would be called upon to perform.[1]

The reforms of the Army National Guard, the Army Reserve and the Marine Corps Reserve proposed here have much in common with the recasting of bronze ordnance. The central premise is that, like the American field artillery parks of the 1850s, the institutions in question are made out of first-class material that is formed on obsolete patterns. If one accepts the axiom that America's reserve military formations are important but need significant modification to better serve the nation's needs in the 21st century, then it follows that the first step in the improvement of the Army National Guard, the Army Reserve and the Marine Corps Reserve is the creation of a set of improved patterns, the organizational equivalents of the design of the Napoleon 12-pounder field piece. The first step in this design process, in turn, is the production of a set of very basic sketches, or broad descriptions of the sort of organizations that the author would like to see created.

Like other preliminary sketches, the descriptions that follow neither condemn the present system nor defend a definitive alternative. Rather, they serve as an aid to the imagination, a means by which readers might compare the current state of affairs with a very different way of doing business. In keeping with this purpose, the descriptions are presented in the present tense to describe a hypothetically existing situation.

The Marine Corps Reserve

In times of peace, the chief task of the Marine Corps is to provide relatively small formations that can be deployed at very short notice to those parts of the world that are accessible by sea. As a rule, the operations that these formations conduct are modest in aim and limited in duration. In wartime, however, the Marine Corps conducts operations on a much larger scale, and must therefore deploy substantially larger forces for longer periods of time. The chief means of providing the additional units needed to form such forces is the Marine Corps Reserve.

Most of the units of the Marine Corps Reserve recommended here are "academic lifecycle battalions." As the word "lifecycle" implies, these units are formed, trained, maintained and disbanded according to a predetermined schedule. In particular, a lifecycle battalion exists for eight years. During the first two of these years, the unit and its members are on active duty, following a progressive program of individual and unit training. For the next four years, the unit is in first-line reserve status, subject to activation at very short notice and assembling three times for about two months of refresher training each year. At the end of its life, the battalion spends two years in a second-line reserve status. While second-line academic lifecycle battalions carry out no training whatsoever, they remain subject to recall in the event of war or dire national emergency.

An academic lifecycle battalion differs from a present-day reserve unit in a number of important ways. First, because all training periods last for two months or more, its members do not have to live within commuting distance of a particular reserve center. Second, before it goes into reserve status, the unit has been thoroughly trained. Thus, if recalled to active duty, the battalion will need little in the way of additional training before deployment. (Both the nature and the amount of additional training will, of course, depend upon such things as the intended employment of the unit and the time that has elapsed since it left active duty.) Third, the life of the unit coincides with the service obligation of most of its members. Thus, the unit will not only enjoy a high degree of unit cohesion, but will also be able to conduct truly progressive training.

The terms of service for the rank-and-file members of an academic lifecycle battalion are designed for young people who want to go to college. Once a reservist has served for two years of continuous active duty, he will be in a very good position to begin a four-year course of full-time study. His pay and benefits will be such that he will be able to pay for tuition and living expenses without going deeply into debt. His time in uniform will give him a number of habits and attitudes that will help him to succeed at university, as well as some time to ponder the particular path he wishes to take. The three annual periods of refresher training that take place during the middle years of his term of service, moreover, will provide the reservist with a well-paid summer job. Finally, the end of the most demanding period in the existence of an academic lifecycle battalion, moreover, will coincide with the completion of its members' undergraduate educations. Thus, unless there is a dire national emergency, a reservist serving in a unit in second-line reserve status will be able to focus all of his energies on his post-college career.

While on active duty, academic lifecycle battalion does a great deal to help its members prepare themselves for college. Optional off-duty classes allow future college students to fill gaps in their secondary educations, explore possible majors and tackle some of their general education requirements. The battalion guidance counselor helps Marines learn more about their particular talents, select the universities they would like to attend and complete their application forms. The officers of the battalion, many of whom are themselves alumni of earlier academic lifecycle battalions, encourage their subordinates to make the most of their educational opportunities.

The harmonization of lifecycle battalions with the rhythm of academic life encourages the recruitment of young people who might not otherwise be attracted to military service. In particular, it is designed to attract members who might otherwise feel compelled to go to full-time work and perhaps part-time community college to fulfill their better wishes and to go instead to full-time college.[2] In the past, community college students who explored the possibility of military service found themselves between two stools. Too well-educated for first-term enlistments of the ordinary kind, they lacked the academic credentials associated with officer training programs designed for full-time college students.

In addition to attracting them to service in the ranks, academic lifecycle battalions are an excellent means of interesting young people, particularly young people from traditionally underrepresented social groups, in military careers. Many officers who are serving today had not considered the possibility of devoting their lives to the profession of arms until they joined academic lifecycle battalions. There, they learned of the inherent satisfactions of military service, became aware of intellectual challenges offered by the military arts and sciences, encountered inspiring role models, and found many companions who were on the same path.

Some of the commissioned officers of academic lifecycle battalions (the commanding officer, both of the majors and a portion of the captains) are career officers. During the first two years of the unit's existence, all of these officers are present for duty with their unit. When that unit passes into first-line reserve status, some of these officers take up assignments (such as duty at schools of various sorts) that allow them to easily rejoin their battalion, whether for annual refresher training or in the case of mobilization. Other career officers will leave the battalion for assignments of different sorts, thereby creating opportunities for the promotion of those who remain.

The reserve officers of academic lifecycle battalions, who serve in billets traditionally filled by lieutenants and captains, are of three types. Many are alumni of previous academic lifecycle battalions who, having completed a college degree and basic officer training, have signed on for a second cycle of active and reserve duty. Others are prior-service noncommissioned officers who, after proving themselves as squad leaders and platoon sergeants, become warrant officer platoon commanders or commissioned officers. A few are officers who, after three or more years of service with the active-duty Marine Corps, have decided to join an academic lifecycle battalion instead of returning directly to civilian life. The common element in the civilian occupations of these reserve officers is the ability to participate in the three periods of refresher training that take place in the third, fourth and fifth year of the battalion's existence. That is to say, while a few of them work in seasonal industries other than education, the vast majority of them are school teachers, graduate students or academics.

Many of the noncommissioned officers of academic lifecycle battalions are Marines who, having already completed several years of active duty, have re-enlisted as reservists. Like those who join an academic lifecycle battalion directly from civilian life, these Marines are on a path that leads to a college degree. Other noncommissioned officers are career Marines who serve with an academic lifecycle battalion during the early years of its existence, passing on their expertise to the reserve Marines who will remain with the unit until it is disbanded. As these career Marines depart, prior-service reservists take their places. This, in turn, creates opportunities for first-term enlistees to serve in more demanding leadership positions.

In the event of mobilization, the Marine Corps can use each of its academic lifecycle battalions in one of two very different ways. If the need for additional forces is either modest or particularly immediate, a lifecycle battalion can immediately take its place in the order of battle of the operational forces. If there is a need to create new units, a mature lifecycle battalion can undergo "mitosis," providing the organizational framework for the creation of two, three or four "daughter battalions." While it would take some time to integrate new members into the daughter battalions, the cadre of such units would enjoy a high degree of internal cohesion from the very start.[3]

Most academic lifecycle battalions are either ground combat units (e.g. infantry, tank or light armor) or ground-oriented combat support units (e.g. field artillery, combat engineer or assault amphibian). In some cases, the organization and training of these units is very similar to that of comparable units of the active-duty Marine Corps. In other cases, such as those of reserve units that specialize in certain environments (e.g. cold weather) and battalions armed with weapons that are not normally employed by active component units (e.g. certain types of artillery pieces), academic lifecycle battalions will have no exact active duty counterparts. Academic lifecycle battalions of this latter sort will serve to provide the Marine Corps with capabilities that would otherwise require the maintenance of units on full-time active duty.

Not all units of the Marine Corps Reserve are academic lifecycle battalions. A number of aviation, logistics and military police units are formed, trained and employed in much the same way as the "parallel occupation" units of the U.S. Army Reserve. Thus, while all members of these units undergo the common experiences that define service in the Marine Corps, membership in these units is contingent upon the practice of particular civilian occupations. Moreover, the composition, structure and schedules of such units are custom-tailored to the peculiarities of the occupations in question.

The Army Reserve

Just as the Marine Corps Reserve serves to augment the active duty Marine Corps, the Army Reserve serves to augment the regular Army. In addition to this, the Army Reserve provides the organizational framework for the mobilization of a large national army of the sort raised for the world wars of the 20th century. While it is increasingly difficult to imagine a scenario in which such a force might be needed, it would be unwise not to make some provision for mass mobilization. Moreover, the design of the Army Reserve is such that the cost of its ability to serve as the framework for a large national army is minimal. The chief enabler of rapid expansion, the ability of the units of the Army Reserve to replicate themselves in a short period of time, is inherent in their organization.

Many of the units of the Army Reserve, including most combat and combat support units, are academic lifecycle battalions that bear such a close resemblance to their counterparts in the Marine Corps Reserve that any further description would be redundant. Indeed, the chief difference between the lifecycle battalions of the Army Reserve and those of the Marine Corps Reserve lies in the specifics of their calendars. While most lifecycle battalions of the Army Reserve follow a schedule identical to that of their Marine Corps counterparts, some (such as artillery units armed with the Multiple Launch Rocket System) spend only one year on active duty, have shorter periods of on-site refresher training and make more extensive use of online refresher training. This makes service in such units attractive to young people who are planning to pursue a technical certificate or an associate degree, rather than a traditional four-year degree.

A substantial portion of the units of the Army Reserve, particularly service and support units of various types, are "parallel occupation" units. While the civilian occupations of members of academic lifecycle battalions have little, if anything, to do with their military jobs, the members of parallel occupation units either practice or are preparing to practice civilian vocations that correspond to their military occupational specialties. That is to say, the members of overland transportation units are truck drivers and diesel mechanics, the members of military police units are police officers, and the members of construction units are carpenters, electricians and heavy equipment operators. Because of this, the training schedules of parallel occupation units can focus on those skills that are specifically military. Thus, the training schedule of a transportation unit need not devote much time teaching its members how to handle a truck or repair a diesel engine, but allows a great deal of time for such subjects as convoy operations, anti-ambush tactics and weapons training.

Most parallel occupation units have lifecycles that are similar to those of academic lifecycle battalions. That is, they are formed, trained, released from active duty, recalled for refresher training, passed to the second-line reserve and disbanded according to a pre-established schedule. The specifics of these schedules, however, vary greatly from one type of unit to another. Thus, while most parallel occupation units have relatively short periods of active duty of about one year at the start of their lifecycles, a few military police units spend three years on active duty. (These units are designed to attract young people who intend to pursue a career in law enforcement, but are too young to attend civilian police academies.) Likewise, the refresher training of parallel occupation units is timed to minimize interference with the civilian occupations of unit members. While many construction units conduct relatively long periods of refresher training each winter, military police units that spend three years on active duty have very little in the way of on-site refresher training.

A small proportion of parallel occupation units, such as mobile field hospitals, legal units and history units, lack the pre-established lifecycle that characterizes the vast majority of units of the Army Reserve. The members of these units are older than the rank-and-file of most other units, have considerable prior military service, and practice professions with long apprenticeships (whether formal or informal). Units of this sort conduct little in the way of on-site refresher training. As with members of other sorts of parallel occupation units, there are many opportunities for members of these "continuous existence" units to serve on active duty as individuals.

Most of the officers and noncommissioned officers of parallel occupation units are senior practitioners of affiliated civilian professions. In construction engineer units, for example, they are civil engineers, general contractors and foremen. Indeed, in order to obtain their rank in parallel occupation units, the reserve officers and noncommissioned officers must pass both the requisite military qualifications and be confirmed by a board that will examine their civilian qualifications. In addition to these occupation-specific leaders, each parallel occupation unit will have a small staff of military specialists, officers and noncommissioned officers whose task it is to conduct the purely military training of the unit. In other words, these military specialists will fulfill a role similar to that of the Marines who are assigned as instructors in naval construction battalions.

A small proportion of Army Reserve units are organized as "seasonal occupation" units. Recruited from among those who practice seasonal occupations (such as those related to fishing, farming and tourism), seasonal occupation battalions conduct on-site training during those months when the seasonal workers in question are most likely to be less in demand. Unlike lifecycle battalions, which front load their training during the first two years of their existence, seasonal occupation battalions divide their initial individual and unit training over several annual training periods. Many seasonal occupation units make use of the special skills of their members. Some amphibious vehicle units, for example, consist largely of fishermen. Others, such as cold-weather infantry units, exploit the fact that their training periods take place in the winter.

The benefits packages offered to members of the Army Reserve are custom tailored for each type of unit. Thus, while the default benefits package for members of academic lifecycle battalions contain generous educational benefits, the default benefits package for seasonal employment units provides things (such as comprehensive medical and dental benefits) not likely to be offered by the employers of seasonal workers. That said, many reservists have needs and goals that are different from those of their immediate comrades. Thus, each reservist is free to choose the benefits package that is best suited to his particular situation. Thus, a prior-service reservist serving in an academic lifecycle battalion who is a public school teacher by profession, and already receives educational assistance and health insurance from his civilian employer, may opt for a benefits package that offers retirement plan contributions instead of the other benefits. Similarly, a member of a parallel occupations unit who plans to go to college after completing his enlistment may opt for a benefits package that contains generous educational benefits.

The National Guard

Along with the Army, Navy, Marine Corps, Air Force, Air National Guard and Coast Guard, the National Guard is an armed service of the United States. However, while the other six services are primarily concerned with protecting the nation as a whole, the National Guard provides immediate protection to specific communities. In particular, the National Guard of the United States is an umbrella organization that encompasses and supports the National Guards of the fifty states, the District of Columbia, the Commonwealth of Puerto Rico, and the Territories of Guam and the U.S. Virgin Islands. Within each state or similar jurisdiction, the National Guard protects the people from such dangers as the collapse of local government, temporary breakdowns in public order, widespread lawlessness, terrorism, natural disasters, large-scale accidents and the aftereffects of the employment of weapons of mass destruction.

The National Guard is the direct descendent of the Army National Guard, has many Army veterans and reservists in its ranks, and often works closely with the Army on projects of mutual interest. Nonetheless, the National Guard is a completely independent service. Similarly, while the National Guard units work closely with police and fire departments of various kinds, and many of its members are police officers and firefighters, it is neither a law enforcement agency nor a public safety organization. Rather, the National Guard is a unique military organization composed largely of people who serve on a part-time basis.

In contrast to most reserve units of the Army or Marine Corps, which assemble mostly at military bases of the larger sort for relatively long periods of training, units of the National Guard are located in the communities that they protect. This arrangement facilitates preparations for local operations as well as greatly reducing the time needed to respond to local emergencies. It also makes it possible for National Guard units to conduct most of their training during relatively short periods of time – single days, weekends, single weeks and fortnights. In other words, while most Army Reserve or Marine Corps Reserve units are lifecycle units, National Guard units are "continuous existence" units.

The basic unit of the National Guard is the National Guard regiment. Just as the National Guard as a whole is a unique organization, the National Guard regiment is a unique type of unit. With capabilities in such diverse areas as local security, transportation, emergency medical care, rescue, decontamination, engineering, communications, liaison, transport and unmanned aviation, a National Guard regiment is a microcosm of the National Guard as a whole. That is, each National Guard regiment is capable of fulfilling most of the definitive functions of the National Guard with little or no reinforcement. While most National Guard units are configured as National Guard regiments, a few serve as specialized reinforcing units of various kinds. These include task force headquarters, mobile hospitals, aviation units, engineer units and logistics units.

The organization and equipment of each National Guard regiment is custom tailored to the peculiarities of the community in which it serves. For example, regiments that serve in areas plagued with forest fires are provided with a great deal of firefighting equipment, while those that are located in places that are prone to flooding are equipped with boats and amphibious vehicles. Similarly, National Guard regiments in communities where breakdowns of public order are of concern have more capabilities in the realm of "boots on the ground" local security while those that operate over large sparsely populated areas make greater use of unmanned aerial vehicles.

All members of the National Guard are either veterans of another branch of service (to include the old Army National Guard) or are members of a lifecycle reserve unit of the Army, Navy, Marine Corps or Air Force that has completed its initial period of active duty. This requirement that all members of the National Guard receive their initial training in another branch of the service relieves the National Guard of the burden of providing entry-level individual training. It also ensures that each member of the National Guard is familiar with the language, capabilities and culture of one of the other services. In addition to facilitating inter-service cooperation, the "outsourcing" of initial training also broadens the inventory of skills in each National Guard unit, thereby expanding its tactical repertoire and increasing its ability to adapt to new circumstances.

The "simultaneous membership program" encourages reservists of other branches to join the National Guard at any point after their respective units have completed their initial periods of active duty. The most obvious objection to this program, that it complicates both mobilization and training by creating the possibility that one person might be obligated to be in two different units (and thus places) at the same time, is addressed by a simple set of protocols. Reserve unit training takes precedence over National Guard training, and, while a reservist is undergoing periods of active duty for training, he is not subject to activation. In time of peace, National Guard activation takes precedence over reserve mobilization. Thus, in the (somewhat unusual) event that both a person's National Guard unit and his reserve unit are mobilized for the same crisis, that person reports to his National Guard unit. However, in the event of war, Reserve unit mobilization takes precedence over National Guard activation.

The civilian occupations of many members of the National Guard correspond to their military service. Guardsmen who are police officers, firefighters and para-medics, for example, enhance the ability of their respective National Guard units to cooperate with police departments, fire departments and rescue crews. Guardsmen who work for utility companies, departments of transportation, port authorities and other organizations involved in the maintenance of infrastructure also possess skills of great value to a unit responding to a disaster of one sort or another. Regardless of their civilian occupation, most guardsmen possess intimate knowledge of the culture, geography and peculiarities of the community in which they serve. Thus, in the event that several different military units find themselves operating in a particular part of the country, the local National Guard unit will be able to provide guides, escorts and liaison teams.

While the definitive mission of the National Guard is immediate response to short-term crises in their home communities, the peculiar capabilities of National Guard units are useful in other situations. If, for example, the collapse of public order of the sort that took place in the U.S. in the 1950s and 1960s, the organization of choice for "domestic nation building" is the National Guard. Similarly, concerted campaigns against organized crime on a large scale (of the sort that currently afflicts parts of the southwestern United States) require the intervention of civil-military task forces that usually include National Guard units. For such long-term missions, National Guard regiments form, deploy and maintain "standing companies." Com-posed of members of their parent regiments who serve on a rotating basis, standing companies are custom-tailored organizations that are capable of remaining on active duty for indefinite periods of time.

As a standing company of a National Guard regiment enjoys close links to its home community, the deployment of such a unit to a distant community in distress has the effect of forging a relationship between the two localities. This, in turn, creates the opportunity for the creation of a larger partnership, one in which civic organizations in the home community work in concert with the standing company to rebuild the social, political and physical infrastructure of the community being helped. This sort of "adoption" increases the possibility that aid is offered in an intelligent, highly specific way. At the same time, it makes the community-building process more personal, and thus inherently more humane. The same basic approach used in the deployment of standing companies within the United States is also of use in community-building efforts that take place in foreign countries. As such efforts make considerable demands upon the home communities in question, the laws governing the activation of the National Guard require that the state legislatures of the states involved give their explicit permission before standing companies can be sent overseas.

In time of war, activated National Guard units serve in two different ways. While some National Guard units provide for the immediate defense of the communities in which they serve, others are assigned to multi-service task forces of various kinds. Within these joint task forces, activated National Guard units perform services that make use of their capabilities. These services include rear-area security, the guarding of prisoners of war, the establishment of military government, and, in the case of specialized units, the provision of medical, engineering, logistics and transportation support.

Aviation Units

Most reserve aviation units belong to the Air National Guard, the Air Force Reserve, or, to a somewhat lesser degree, the Navy Reserve. Nonetheless, a proportion of the units of the National Guard, the Army Reserve and the Marine Corps Reserve are configured as aviation units of one sort or another. In particular, these units are of types that habitually work closely with forces on the ground. Thus, they are equipped with helicopters, light fixed-wing aircraft, transports and ground attack planes. (As the old cartel arrangements that precluded certain services from flying certain types of aircraft have been abolished, the order of battle of the Army Reserve includes a number of ground attack squadrons.)

As is the case with all other reserve units, the structures and schedules of reserve aviation units are custom tailored to their peculiar needs. This usually results in arrangements that resemble those of comparable units in the Air National Guard and Air Force Reserve. That is, rather than being lifecycle units of one sort or another, reserve aviation units are continuous existence units in which most members serve for relatively short periods of time. In order to provide for such things as maintenance, however, reserve aviation units are provided with much more in the way of full-time staff than other units. Some members of this full-time staff are uniformed personnel serving tours of active duty. Others are on special contracts that call for them to work as civilians at the base where the unit is stationed, but serve with the reserve unit when it assembles for training or active service.

Transition

In the middle years of the 19th century, the recasting of artillery pieces was an incremental process. At any given time, pieces cast on new patterns were arriving, the least serviceable pieces in an artillery park were being sent to the foundry, and the artillery park consisted of a mixture of old and new pieces. The reform of the old Army Reserve and Marine Corps Reserve advanced in much the same fashion. Every year, new reserve units were formed, old reserve units were disbanded, and the force as a whole consisted of a mixture of both new and old units.

In order to make full use of the services of members of the old-style, the disbandment of "one weekend a month, two weeks each summer" Army Reserve and the Marine Corps Reserve units was carried out in a slow, systematic manner. The first step was a moratorium on the recruitment of new non-prior-service reservists, those who would traditionally begin serving with the unit after six months of full-time, entry-level training. This had the effect of slowly converting units into cadre organizations composed entirely of officers and noncommissioned officers. (Had there been a general mobilization, such units would have been "filled-out" with new recruits.) After several years in a cadre status, each of the old reserve units passed its flag to the new unit and stopped drilling.

The reform of the Army National Guard was a somewhat different process. While a few new units were formed and a few old ones were disbanded, the lion's share of the change took place in the realm of equipment and training. As units of the Army Reserve took their places in the mobilization tables, National Guard units exchanged the weapons of conventional warfare for the tools of local defense. In some cases, this exchange was painfully obvious, with tanks and artillery pieces disappearing from the parking lots of drill centers. In other cases, such as those of helicopter and transportation units, the change was harder to see.

Over the years, faithful readers of the *Defense Almanac* noticed that the Army Reserve had expanded to a great degree and the Marine Corps Reserve had grown somewhat, while the National Guard, the active-duty Army, and the active-duty Marine Corps were smaller than they had been in the first decade of the 21st century. Those who gathered more detailed statistics observed that while the National Guard was getting older, the Army Reserve and Marine Corps Reserve were getting younger. At the same time, those who followed cultural trends noticed some interesting developments. Within the military, a much greater proportion of officers had served the ranks prior to pinning on their bars. In American society at large, the proportion of veterans in each group of college graduates increased with each passing year.

ENDNOTES

1   For details of the recasting of the obsolete ordnance of the field batteries of the Army of Northern Virginia, see *The War of Rebellion, United States War Department*, 1st ser., vol. 19, (I), 836-37; vol. 21, 836; and vol. 29 (II), 637-38. For background on the pieces in question, see Philip Katcher, *American Civil War Artillery, 1861-1865, Field Artillery* (Oxford: Osprey, 2001).

2   While often counted in educational statistics as if they were no different from students who are able to devote the bulk of their energies to obtaining a four-year degree in four academic years, community college students must deal with two significant handicaps. The most obvious of these is the lack of the means to pay for four continuous years of college. Less apparent, but no less powerful, is the frequent absence of the sort of intense preparation for university that goes on in some homes and many secondary schools of the more prosperous.

3   The process herein described as "mitosis" – the splitting of an experienced unit in order to provide the cadre for new units – is a time-honored technique for creating new units at a time of rapid expansion. It was used extensively by the British Army at the start of World War I and the German army in the latter years of World War II.

CHAPTER 10

LONG IN COMING
THE ACQUISITION TRAIN WRECK IS HERE

Thomas Christie

Summary

After more than four decades of supposedly well-structured defense planning and programming, combined with numerous studies aimed at reforming its multibillion-dollar
acquisition system, any informed student of our defense establishment would conclude
that the overall decision process is broken and in need of far-reaching, even radical,
remedial actions. The evidence supporting the need for drastic action abounds.

Perhaps the strongest evidence is that, despite the largest defense budgets in real
terms in more than 60 years, we have a smaller military force structure than at any
time during that period, one that is equipped to a great extent with worn-out, aging
equipment. Granted, the employment of our forces in the conflicts in Iraq and Afghanistan has contributed in a major fashion to the deterioration of our combat and
support equipment, particularly severe for our ground forces. The bill for restoring
and repairing that equipment (reported to be in the hundreds of billions) is yet to
be faced up to and will only exacerbate the already severe modernization problems
faced by all three services. Those problems have been on the horizon for some time
now and would have plagued our forces even if the Global War on Terror (GWOT)
had not evolved as it has.

The fundamental cause of the Defense Department's budget problems lies in a
long historical pattern of unrealistically high defense budget projections combined
with equally unrealistic low estimates of the costs of new programs. The net effect is
that DOD's leaders could claim that they can afford the weapons they want to buy,
and so there is no urgency to face up to the hard choices on new weapon systems,
not to mention other looming future demands on the budget, such as health care for
both active and retired personnel, and planned increases in ground forces manpower.
This confidence is, however, mistaken.

DOD's Planning and Budgeting Process

The Department of Defense's annual budget request submitted to the Congress is the
first year of a continuously updated six-year spending plan, called the Future Years
Defense Program (FYDP). Informed and effective long-range planning is necessary
because most of the programs contained in the budget entail an obligation to spend
money far into the future. For example, a decision to build a new aircraft carrier entails
a spending stream that could last as long as 50 years. In theory, the FYDP is supposed

to place such decisions in the context of their future obligations.

As pointed out so adeptly by Chuck Spinney some 10 years ago in his 1998 treatise, entitled *Defense Power Games*,[1] Pentagon planners and decision-makers have systematically downplayed these future obligations over the years by basing their decisions on three unrealistic assumptions:

- The future will be better than the past. Budgets will grow at a faster rate for the next five years than they grew over the last five years.

- The different components of the defense budget will grow at different rates. Investment (research, development, and procurement) will grow much faster than the total budget, and the spending required to operate the force (salaries, operations and maintenance) will grow more slowly than the total. New weapons will cost less to operate because they will be more reliable and easier to maintain than the older weapons they are replacing.

- Weapon system procurement costs will decrease. Weapons will cost less to buy over the next six years because increasing production rates and the effects of the learning curve will increase the efficiency of production.

These assumptions have allowed Pentagon decision-makers to front-load the first year of the FYDP (which is also the annual budget request made to Congress) with too many high-cost investment programs. The assumption of larger budgets in the later years, coupled with the biased allocation toward investment, provided a misleading picture of the total money available for developing and buying new weapons. The further assumption of sharply declining weapon unit procurement costs permitted even more weapons to be stuffed into the later years of the investment plan, a phenomenon known in the Pentagon as the "bow wave." Planners tolerated low production rates in the early years because the rising bow wave, coupled with the assumed declines in unit costs, promised higher, more efficient, rates in the later years. By the last year of the FYDP, the Defense Department would get well: more complex weapons would be produced at much higher rates; forces would be larger and more modern; training tempos would be higher because the new equipment is assumed to be more reliable and easier to maintain; and large quantities of spare parts and ammunition would be flooding into the stockpile.

Where We Are Today

The president's budget for fiscal year 2009 (FY 2009), submitted to Congress earlier this year, projected the defense top line increasing from $518 billion in FY 2009 to $549 billion in FY 2013. While this represented a slight decline in real terms over the five years when adjusted for inflation, it did not account for the administration's practice of submitting substantial supplemental requests (well over $100 billion in FY 2008) to fund the continuing operations in Iraq and Afghanistan, nor the annual Department of Energy funding of $15 billion to $20 billion for nuclear weapons research and maintenance. In any event, there is good reason to question whether these budget levels can be sustained in the future with all the other growing demands on the federal budget and the consequences of huge federal deficits yet to be addressed. Among the more disturbing aspects of these budget figures is the fact that they incorporate huge planned increases in spending on weapon systems – $104 billion in FY 2009 growing to $125 billion in FY 2013, an increase of 11 percent in real, inflation-adjusted terms. Such unrealistic planning only adds to the procurement bow-wave and puts off the tough decisions needed to prevent the coming train wreck.

It should be noted that Deputy Secretary of Defense Gordon England issued fiscal guidance in March 2008 that directed the services' FY 2010 spending blueprints, spanning FY 2010 to FY 2015, assume zero real growth compared with the FY 2009-2014 budget plan under consideration by the Congress.[2] That guidance at a minimum would allow the defense budget to increase to account for inflation and, according to a Pentagon official involved in the process, might allow for medical and fuel cost rises as well. However, it appears to preclude previously hoped-for significant increases in funding for major weapon systems or other priorities. Obviously, such budget projections should force some tough decisions with respect to major acquisition programs projected to require substantial increases in their research, development, testing and evaluation (RDT&E) and procurement funding over the next several years.

Unrealistic Budget Plans Plus Continuing Modernization Problems Mean Tough Decisions Ahead

The make-believe world of defense budgeting, however, must eventually confront the real world of weapons development and procurement, a world where hardly a week passes without some acquisition horror story emanating from the Pentagon. New systems critical to the services' modernization plans for their aging forces encounter cost overruns, serious technical challenges and schedule slips that call into question the affordability and realism of service plans for growing and/or sustaining their present force levels and structures. The following discussion provides but a few examples of the cost, schedule and performance problems associated with key service modernization programs.

The Army Banks on the Future Combat Systems (FCS) as its Key to Modernization

The Army faces daunting challenges as it looks to the future. As mentioned above, in the immediate future, the Army will require significant funding above what is included in its approved modernization budget into the out-years to repair, overhaul and replace equipment damaged, destroyed or worn-out in combat operations in Iraq and Afghanistan. On top of these immediate funding requirements, the Army is faced with the steady growth in operations and maintenance (O&M) costs that have plagued all the services over the past decades. In its annual report to Congress in early 2008, the Congressional Budget Office (CBO) reported[3] those costs grew steadily by an annual average of $2,000 per active-duty service member from 1980 to 2001 before hitting the spike resulting from the aforementioned combat operations that have been funded to a great extent by supplemental budget requests. Excluding potential unbudgeted costs for the continuing GWOT, the CBO projects a similar rate of O&M cost growth in the future. Furthermore, the Army and Marine Corps will require yet additional billions in funding in the coming years to accommodate the planned increase of 92,000 in their combined active duty end strength.

For its future modernization, the Army has built the bulk of its plan around its Future Combat Systems (FCS). Planned as a revolutionary, "leap ahead" system, it would form the centerpiece of its ground combat forces to be fielded between FY 2015 and FY 2020. Army plans describe FCS as a mobile, deployable, lethal and survivable platform, incorporating advanced technology components to enable a significant increase in combat effectiveness. The program consists of an integrated family of advanced, networked combat and sustainment systems; unmanned ground and air vehicles; and unattended sensors and munitions intended to equip the Army's new transformational modular combat brigades. Within a system-of-systems architecture, FCS now features 14 major systems (already down from its 2003 plan that called for 18 new systems) plus other enabling systems along with an overarching network intended to provide information superiority and survivability.

The FCS program was approved in May 2003 to begin its System Design and Development (SDD) phase of development. FCS plans then called for the ambitious development of the 18 individual systems that included armored ground vehicles, unmanned ground vehicles (UGVs), as well as several classes of unmanned aerial vehicles (UAVs). At that time, the Army planned to stand up an experimental FCS brigade in 2008 equipped with all the new systems.

Since that time the program has undergone numerous far-reaching restructurings. By July 2004, the Army announced that it planned early delivery or "spin out" of selected FCS systems vice the earlier plan to deliver all the systems simultaneously. This new plan called for a phased approach to "spin out" mature FCS equipment to existing forces, provided the equipment demonstrated military utility during testing, slated to begin in FY 2008. The Army, however, planned to test spinout hardware using surrogate radios because technical issues had delayed development of its family of new radios. As of the existing schedule, production-representative radios would not be available for testing until at least 2009, after the production decision for spinout items.

FCS Milestone C, with approval of initial production, was slated for 2012, leading to an Initial Operational Capability in 2014. Finally, a Full Operational Capability FCS-equipped Brigade Combat Team was planned to be available in 2016.

In August 2006, the program documented the desired functional characteristics of FCS systems and the criteria for achieving those characteristics. Although a notable accomplishment, this event should have occurred before the start of development in 2003. As a result, the program began life with more cost, schedule and performance risk than was necessary. Army officials downplayed this risk by telling the Government Accountability Office (GAO) that they could trade-off FCS capabilities to maintain schedule and cost projections.

It turned out to be a false hope. The GAO, in its March 2008 report[4], entitled *Defense Acquisitions, Assessments of Selected Weapon Programs*, shows FCS RDT&E costs, in constant FY 2008 dollars, rising from the $20.5 billion projected at program approval in May 2003 to $28.5 billion, and total acquisition (RDT&E + procurement) costs increasing from $88.3 billion to $128.5 billion.

The cost of the FCS program and its impact on the Army budget over the next decade or so is a critical issue. The following discussion is extracted directly from an excellent summary report on FCS issues by the Center for Defense Information (CDI)[5], dated May 30, 2008. This report draws data and information from various government sources, to include the GAO, the CBO and the Congressional Research Service (CRS), as well as pertinent DOD documents. The report paints a fairly bleak picture of future cost growth and raises questions about the affordability of the FCS as presently planned. Extracts from the CDI discussion of these issues follows:

"Not only has the projected cost of FCS development and acquisition increased significantly, FCS has not yet reached the critical design review (scheduled for 2011); it is *after* this point that most development cost growth occurs. The Congressional Budget Office (CBO) estimates that costs could grow 60 percent. Therefore, it is hard to have confidence in the cost estimate put forward by the Army. By the time of initial production, the Army will have spent 80 percent of its development funds, before crucial network development and demonstration. Even if all technology is developed and performs as expected, there is the danger that FCS is simply too expensive."

"Additionally, two separate entities, the Institute for Defense Analyses (IDA) and DOD's Cost Analysis Improvement Group (CAIG), have performed independent cost estimates, and their cost projections are substantially higher than the Army's. IDA examined only RDT&E (Research, Development, Test and Evaluation) costs, which it estimates to reach $38.1 billion, compared to the Army's $25.1 billion. The CAIG estimated total program costs to be between $203.3

and $233.9 billion (in then-year dollars), which is substantially higher than the Army's $160.9 billion figure. The Army has refused to reconcile the numbers offered from IDA and CAIG, arguing that their estimates for software costs were too high and that they included additional work in the later years of development."

"The Army's $160.9 billion projection is a 76-percent increase from the original $91.4 billion estimate. It is worth noting that, in 2006, 4 of the 18 systems were cut, but the $160 billion price tag stayed approximately the same; this was the second program restructuring. FY 2009 marks the first year of a planned funding shift: funds for RDT&E will start to decrease and costs for procurement will increase, respectively, $3.2 billion and $331 million.

As RDT&E concludes and procurement starts to take over, between years 2015 and 2022, the Army is projected to spend at least $10 billion a year on procurement for FCS, with CBO estimating this figure may reach $16 billion per year. The Army is projected to receive $20 billion a year for procurement for the entire service during these years. If the Army spends $10-16 billion on FCS each year, only $4-10 billion is left for all of the service's other procurement and modernization priorities.

FCS success depends on at least 50 complementary programs that are developing according to their own schedules and budgets and technological challenges outside of the FCS program itself. Three notable programs are the Joint Tactical Radio System (JTRS), Warfighter Information Network – Tactical (WIN-T) and the Air Force Transformational Satellite Communications Program (TSAT). These programs have an estimated combined cost of $80 billion, up $29 billion from their original estimates. Problems with these programs pose a significant risk to the FCS program."

The Army appears to be mesmerized by the false promises of future technological advances that are coming at the expense of its critical near-term capitalization or "reset" needs. More than five years of simultaneous wars in Iraq and Afghanistan have ground down our aging military equipment, particularly that of our ground forces. For example, Humvees travel as much as 100,000 miles per year in Iraq, five times the planned peacetime rate. Heavy armor further adds to the strain on their engines and axles.

"We must reset, reconstitute, and revitalize our ground forces," Admiral Michael Mullen, chairman of the Joint Chiefs of Staff, stated before a Senate hearing in May 2008. Army estimates of the funding needed to re-equip itself range up to $17 billion annually, for as many as three years after the wars in Iraq and Afghanistan end.[6]

With the bulk of its modernization funds tied up in the FCS program for the foreseeable future, the outlook for the Army's critical recapitalization needs is uncertain at best. Even its most optimistic projections call for the complete conversion of its forces to FCS vehicles not occurring until the 2020s, by which time a good part of its aging fleet of vehicles will be well past its shelf life. On top of the Army's huge near term capitalization bill, estimates call for annual funding of $2 billion over the next seven to eight years just for necessary upgrades and maintenance of its aging ground combat systems, some of which incorporate technologies dating back as far as the 1960s.

Add to these bills just the Army's plans for modernizing its rotary wing and theater air defense forces and one quickly concludes that, short of a huge, and unlikely, infusion of funds in future Army budgets, there is no way it can all be afforded. That appears to be true even with the unrealistic assumption that FCS encounters no further cost overruns or schedule slips.

The Shrinking Navy

The U.S. Navy keeps shrinking. At its post-Vietnam height in 1987, the Navy's battle fleet numbered 568 ships; today it is less than half that size, at 279.[7] The Navy now plans a 313-ship fleet size for the future. Sustaining that size fleet requires building at least 10 ships per year on top of an additional 30-plus ships needed to build from its present fleet size to its goal of 313 ships. At the peak of the Reagan buildup in 1986, by comparison, the Navy built 20 ships; since the early 1990s, it has never exceeded eight per year. In 2007, cost overruns and cancellations brought the number down to five. The 2009 budget requests seven.

In hearings on the Hill in early 2008, the Navy's six-year plan for building its 313-ship fleet was deemed to be impracticable. Instead of the Navy's claim of an average $15.6 billion per year needed to execute their shipbuilding plan, CBO told Congress that the Navy would actually need $21 billion per year over that period, nearly double the $12.6 billion average the Navy has been spending each year since 2003.

To make matters worse, overruns and schedule delays now threaten two new classes of ships critical to the Navy's plan to increase and sustain its combat fleet – the DDG-1000 destroyer and the smaller Littoral Combat Ship (LCS). These two classes of ships were to be the workhorse surface combatants designed to protect aircraft carriers, patrol sea-lanes and project U.S. power in areas around the world where a carrier might not be available.

The CBO has questioned the costs of the seven DDG-1000 Zumwalt-class advanced destroyers in the Navy's plan, down from the original plan to build 32. Instead of the advertised $3.3 billion costs to build each of the first two ships with subsequent hulls being cheaper, the CBO declared that $5 billion per ship is more likely, with higher figures possible. In addition, the CRS weighed in with equally alarming cost projections. In testimony before the House Seapower subcommittee in March 2008, CRS analyst Ron O'Rourke stated that the combined cost growth for the planned seven DDG-1000s would be close to $12 billion in then-year dollars, which is roughly comparable to the total amount of recent annual funding in the Shipbuilding and Conversion, Navy (SCN) appropriation account.

These cost projections, along with recent reports that the ships aren't large enough or can't be configured to incorporate missile defense radars, have completely undermined support for the program. The House of Representatives, in its FY 2009 Defense Authorization, voted for a pause in DDG-1000 construction, citing the cost of the first two ships and their dependence on yet unproven technologies. This action was followed in late July 2008 by a Pentagon decision to terminate the program following the two ships currently under construction. The Navy will ask Congress to drop the request for the third ship in the 2009 defense budget and, instead, it will build more DDG-51s, a course of action long resisted by the Navy prior to this decision, and forego plans to build the remaining four ships.

Not only was the DDG-1000 program fraught with cost and schedule problems, but the Littoral Combat Ship (LCS) also ran into serious problems. Out of the first four prototype ships, the two now in construction are well behind schedule and over cost, and the other two have been terminated outright, calling into question the Navy's planned buy of 55 LCSs. The Navy had originally estimated these first two lead ships would cost in the neighborhood of $500 million each with subsequent ships coming down in cost to $220 million. The CBO has estimated these first two LCSs could end up costing about $700 million each, including outfitting and post-delivery and various nonrecurring costs associated with the first ships of a class, but excluding mission modules. Furthermore, at the Navy's request, the FY 2008 National Defense Authorization Act lifted the cap for the fifth and sixth LCSs from $220 million to $460 million. But even that may not be enough, as the Navy has stated in a February 2008 report to the Congress on its new LCS acquisition strategy that it may be unable to stay within the new $460 million cap set for future LCS hulls.

Yet another example of "head in the sand" management on the part of the Navy is the VH-71 Presidential Helicopter program. The program, approved by the Defense Acquisition Board (DAB) in early 2005, envisioned a two-phased development and procurement strategy. Increment One would provide a "reduced capability" system in the near term with seven test articles and five production aircraft funded. Increment Two was scheduled to provide two test articles and 23 modified production aircraft equipped with the complete communications and survivability package. After encountering skyrocketing costs and significant engineering problems, many of which had been predicted by some participants in the 2005 DAB, the Pentagon put the program on hold in 2007 and undertook a series of internal reviews and discussions with White House officials about the future of the program. During that time, a Pentagon design review found that the requirements could be met for the first increment of the program, including the five production aircraft, but at a cost of $3.7 billion, an increase of more than 60 percent from the initial estimates of $2.3 billion. That review also revealed that nearly 2,000 design changes (including a new tail, transmission and rotor blades) would be needed to meet the specifications for the second increment of aircraft. Furthermore, the costs for that increment of 23 VH-71 aircraft had risen from $4.5 billion to $7.5 billion. In sum, the costs of the total 28-aircraft program had risen from the initial estimates of $6.8 billion to $11.2 billion, an increase of 65 percent in little more than two years.

There are cases, albeit rare, where the acquisition review and decision process faces up to hard realities and imposes much-needed discipline by cutting its losses on questionable programs. After more than a decade of research and over $600 million spent, the Navy announced in March 2008 that it was terminating the Extended-Range Guided Munition (ERGM), a high-tech projectile designed to be fired from Navy destroyers up to 50 miles offshore in support of ground troops. The system had repeatedly failed to perform as advertised in field tests according to the Navy with the guidance system, the rocket motor, and tail fins all flunking demonstration tests. ERGM was another classic case of a system entering Engineering and Manufacturing Development (EMD), as it did in 1996, with unproven technology. Originally scheduled for full production and deployment in 2001, the Navy finally decided that the expected costs to salvage the effort were simply too high to justify going further.

Air Force Fighter Forces – Smaller and Much Older

The Air Force faces an equally daunting task in building its six-year investment plan with sufficient funding for all its critical modernization programs. In putting together the Program Objective Memorandum (POM) for FY 2010-2015, the Air Force has struggled to accommodate a host of expensive RDT&E and procurement programs critical to its plans to modernize its existing and aging forces. Several of these high priority investment programs continue to suffer cost growth and schedule delays, creating a huge procurement bow wave and severely limiting the Air Force's ability to sustain and operate its combat and support forces. The list is indeed daunting and calls into question previous decisions that have led to this *plans/reality mismatch*, to invoke a phrase coined by Chuck Spinney in the early 1980s.

The Air Force's modernization funding (RDT&E plus procurement) request in the FY 2009 budget totals $63 billion, but does not reflect its oft-expressed desire to increase these accounts by $20 billion on average over the next 20 years in order to acquire and field a modern force that service officials call the Required Force. The Air Force indeed faces severe aging problems in its tactical air forces with the average age of its fighter/attack aircraft exceeding 20 years and growing, about twice that desired and more than twice the 10-year average age these forces enjoyed in the 1980s and early 1990s. This spike in aircraft age can be traced to the procurement "good times" of the late 1970s, when the Air Force was able to produce close to 350 to 390 fighter/attack aircraft annually for a couple years, falling to around 200-220 in the mid-1980s. It is interesting to note that DOD spent roughly $7 billion (in FY 2008 $) per year to buy those 200-plus aircraft compared to the $5 billion annual procurement bill for 20 F-22s bought each year in the 2003-2009 time frame.

This near-suspension of procurement traces its origins to the end of the Cold War in the first Bush administration. Air Force fighter procurement fell from the more than 200 a year discussed earlier to 20 or fewer aircraft per year starting in the mid-1990s during the Clinton years and continued into the first decade of the 21st century with the decision to cap the buy of F-22s at 183 aircraft, procured at an annual rate of 20 aircraft. Thus, despite parallel major reductions in Air Force fighter force levels to roughly half those of the 1980s, the "procurement holiday" of the 1990s, added to the higher-than-planned OPTEMPO of these forces in the Iraq and Afghanistan conflicts, has led to a major headache for the service's leadership. The competing demands of an aging force, becoming more and more expensive to keep operational, and the need to replenish these worn-out forces with modern aircraft is a planners' nightmare.

In order to reduce the average age of its fighter forces to its desired 10 to 15 years level in the next five to 10 years, the Air Force would need a huge spike in procurement quantities to reach that goal and then require an annual procurement rate of between 100 and 120 aircraft per year in order to sustain that average age. Unfortunately, the Air Force's aircraft procurement in its budget request totals 93 aircraft in FY 2009, of which only 28 are new fighter aircraft – the last 20 of its planned 183 F-22s and 8 F-35As – while 52 are UAVs: 38 Predators, nine Reapers and five Global Hawks.

The F-35 Will Not Solve the U.S. Air Force's Problem

The replacement of F-22 procurement with the less expensive F-35 will not solve the problem. The Air Force budget projection shows F-35A procurement rising to 48 aircraft by FY 2013 (with actual and planned procurement between FY 2007 and FY 2013 totaling 142 aircraft), still not enough to turn around the worsening force aging problem. Even this total quantity and out-year procurement rate are questionable based on the past unstable record of this program. For example, compared to the FY 2007 FYDP, the Air Force FY 2009 FYDP procures 89 less F-35As through FY 2013. Furthermore the F-35 program office has reduced the F-35A peak production rate from the previously planned 110 aircraft per year to 80 aircraft per year in FY 2015 and beyond. These relatively small quantities appeared even more questionable in light of reported reductions in out-year funding in the fiscal guidance for the prepara-tion of the FY 2010 budget combined with yet more cost growth as discussed in the following paragraphs. In any event, even these planned procurement quantities are not sufficient to attain the Air Force's average age goal, much less maintain it into the next decade. The obvious result will be either a further reduction in its fighter forces or their ever-increasing age or a combination of the two.

It should be noted here that subsequent to issuing its fiscal guidance to the services for their FY 2010-2015 budget, the DOD added $5 billion to the Air Force's procurement accounts that would allow it to accelerate purchases of its planned 1,753 F-35As. Given these added funds become and remain a reality, the Air Force reportedly plans to use them to buy 100 or more per year by FY 2015, back up from the 80 planned for FY 2015 and beyond.

On the other hand, rumors of significant cost overruns in the overall F-35 program continue to surface, affecting not only the Air Force's F-35A, but the Marine Corps F-35B and Navy F-35C as well. Depending on which "independent" cost estimate one believes, the program could be underfunded by as much as $30 billion to $40 billion, and the schedule likely to slip up to two more years. Such impending cost increases will obviously only make matters worse, most likely resulting in further schedule slips and reduced procurement quantities in the coming years.

Table 1, extracted from the GAO March 2008 report on the Joint Strike Fighter[8], summarizes the result of three independent cost growth and schedule slip estimates for the F-35 program.

The F-22 Experience Made a Bad Problem Worse

This serious situation borders on a fiasco for all three services involved in the F-35 program, but it is certainly a potential disaster for the Air Force. This is the inevitable consequence of the Air Force having first put all its eggs in the super-expensive F-22 program during the 1990s, and all but eliminating further F-15 and F-16 production in order to protect its new fighter development. Approved for Demonstration/Validation (Dem/Val) in 1986 and Full-Scale Engineering Development (FSED) in 1992, the Air Force originally planned a buy of over 700 F-22s. By 2000 that number had been reduced to 346 aircraft with a total acquisition costs projected to be $61.9 billion. F-22 procurement started in FY 2001 and, after encountering and addressing numer-

Table I. Independent Estimates of F-35 Cost and Schedule Growth
(GAO JSF Report: Recent Decisions by DOD Add to Program Risk, March 2008)

Assessing Organization	Projected Cost Growth	Projected Schedule Slip
OSD Cost Analysis Improvement Group (CAIG)	$5.1 billion for RDT&E $33 billion for procurement	12 months
Naval Air Systems Command	$8-$13 billion for RDT&E/tradeoffs that add to procurement costs	19-27 months
Defense Contract Management Agency	$4.9 billion to Complete Lockheed Development Contract	12 months

ous technical problems, the F-22 finally completed its Initial Operational Test and Evaluation (IOT&E) in 2004, several years later than planned, and obtained approval for full-rate production in early 2005. Nearly 20 years and close to $40 billion after its beginning, the F-22 achieved an Initial Operational Capability (IOC) in December 2005. By that time, cost and schedule problems had led to the Pentagon's decision to limit the production run to some 180 aircraft and close the line following procurement of the last F-22s in FY 2009. The total acquisition costs for this drastically reduced buy is now projected at $64.5 billion, slightly more than projected nine years ago for nearly twice the number of F-22s.

But the F-22 Wasn't the Only Culprit
To exacerbate the Air Force's dire predicament even further are other large modernization programs that will demand an increasing share of its potentially lower investment accounts in the coming years. Among the big programs are: the Next Generation Tanker Aircraft; the Space-Based Infra-Red System-High (SBIRS-H), the National Polar-orbiting Operational Environmental Satellite System (NPOESS), the GPS-III, the Air Borne Laser, the Joint Air-to-Surface Standoff Missile (JASSM), and the Global Hawk High Altitude Endurance (HAE) unmanned aerial vehicle (UAV). Several of these programs are plagued with significant cost growth, performance problems and schedule delays that will put increasing pressure on Air Force modernization plans into the next decade.

The previously referenced GAO report, entitled "Defense Acquisitions, Assessments of Selected Weapons Programs," and dated March 2008, provides a wealth of information on the status of these programs among a total of some 95 DOD acquisition programs evaluated in the report. It is the primary source of the following discussion of cost and schedule problems facing Air Force acquisition officials as they cope with the dilemma of funding these programs in the coming years at the same time that they strive to modernize their tactical air forces.

The SBIRS-H satellite system is being developed to replace the aging Defense Support Program (DSP) in meeting requirements for missile launch warning, technical intelligence and battlespace awareness missions, critical to the success of planned missile defense systems. SBIRS-H plans call for a constellation of four satellites in geosynchronous Earth orbit (GEO), two sensors on host satellites in highly elliptical orbit (HEO), and fixed as well as mobile ground stations. Projected SBIRS-H RDT&E costs have more than doubled, from $4.4 billion to $8.5 billion, while total program cost grew by 140 percent to $10.5 billion in constant FY 2008 dollars in the decade since development started in FY 1997.

The Air Force has restructured the program more than once since its outset due to technical, cost and schedule problems that resulted in Nunn-McCurdy breaches. The Nunn-McCurdy amendment to the Defense Authorization Act for Fiscal Year 1982 was an attempt to limit cost growth in defense programs. It called for the termination of weapons programs whose total costs had grown by more than 25 percent above original estimates, unless they were certified as critical systems by the secretary of defense or if the cost growth was attributable to certain specified changes in the program. After delays of nearly two years, two HEO sensors have been delivered and, according to program officials, the first sensor's on-orbit performance is "exceeding expectations." The first GEO satellite launch has been delayed to at least late 2009/ early 2010, a schedule slip of a year. Design problems have recently emerged making further schedule slippage of the GEO launches likely. For example, testing has uncovered deficiencies in the flight software that controls the health and status of the space vehicle. Both hardware and software changes may be necessary to correct the problem and could cause a further delay of at least a year and up to a billion dollars in additional funding.

In a similar vein, several other Air Force space programs are troubled with growing costs and schedule delays. For example, in the five years following a production decision in August 2002, NPOESS RDT&E costs increased from $5 billion to almost $8 billion, total program funding requirements grew to $10.7 billion from $6.3 billion, and the schedule slipped almost a year and a half. These cost problems resulted in a Nunn-McCurdy breach and subsequent Air Force restructure of the program finalized in June 2007.

The Global Hawk program is yet another system beset with significant cost, schedule and performance problems. Global Hawk is a high altitude, long-endurance unmanned aircraft with integrated sensors and ground stations providing intelligence, surveillance and reconnaissance capabilities. It entered development and limited production in March 2001. Soon after its start, the Air Force restructured the program from a low-risk, incremental approach to a high-risk, highly concurrent strategy. Specifically, the restructuring aimed to develop and acquire the larger RQ-4B aircraft with more advanced but immature technologies on an accelerated production schedule. Significant cost increases between 2002 and 2005 culminated in a Nunn-McCurdy unit-cost breach, which led to certification to Congress. The program has been re-baselined three times, and aircraft unit costs have more than doubled from $81 million to $178 million in FY 2008 dollars since program start. After several restructures and re-baselinings, the current program plan procures seven aircraft similar to the original demonstrators (the RQ-4A) and 47 of a larger and more capable model (the RQ-4B).

However, the program continues to encounter cost, performance and schedule problems. The RQ-4B aircraft had its first flight in March 2007, more than a year behind schedule. The first flight had been delayed, in part, due to problems identified during testing. Differences between the two models turned out to be much more extensive and complex than anticipated, resulting in extended development times, frequent engineering changes and significant cost increases. The schedules for integrating, testing and fielding the new advanced sensors continue to suffer delays, raising questions as to whether these new capabilities will satisfy the warfighter's requirements. An operational assessment, completed over two years late in March 2007 on the RQ-4A, identified performance problems in communications, imagery processing, and engines. Any independent observer would have to assess Global Hawk as a high-risk program, as the most advanced aircraft variant will not be fully tested until mid-FY 2010, by which point, the Air Force plans to have purchased over 60 percent of the total aircraft quantity.

Broken Defense Planning and Acquisition Processes and Structures

The examples cited above provide ample evidence for concluding that DOD has systemic problems in how it develops and buys major weapon systems and, furthermore, that these problems extend back several decades. Clearly, any astute observer would question the effectiveness, if not the competence, of decision processes that result, in case after case, of plans and reality mismatches. Astute observers have indeed reached that conclusion, and the past 40 years have seen several high-level efforts aimed at reforming both the planning and budgeting and the defense acquisition processes. In some cases, these efforts were established in response to the egregious examples of mismanagement or acquisition horror stories that plague defense today. While DOD's acquisition policies and directives have adopted many of the more substantive findings and recommendations of these reviews, too often, unfortunately, the people managing this process lacked the will to carry through and implement them in program decisions.

Recurring Management Reform Efforts

Instead, what has happened is that, every three or four years, yet another high-level study is commissioned to review DOD management in general and the acquisition process in particular. The 1970 Fitzhugh, or Blue Ribbon Commission, was followed by the 1977 Steadman Review, the 1981 Carlucci Acquisition Initiatives, the 1986 Packard Commission and Goldwater/Nichols Act, the 1989 Defense Management Review, the 1990 Defense Science Board (DSB) Streamlining Study, yet another DSB Acquisition Streamlining Task Force in 1993-1994, the Total System Performance Responsibility (TSPR) initiative of the late 1990s, the early 2000s focus on Spiral Development and Capabilities-Based Acquisition, and so on.

The common goal for many of these reform efforts was streamlining the acquisition process itself in order to reduce the burgeoning costs of new weapons. In doing so, these commissions and task forces hoped to drastically cut system development and production times (and thereby costs) by reducing management layers, eliminating certain reporting requirements, using commercial-off-the-shelf (COTS) systems and subsystems, reducing oversight from within as well as from outside DOD and eliminating perceived duplication of testing, among other initiatives.

After 40 Years, Cost and Schedule Problems Persist

What went wrong? After all these years of repeated reform efforts, major defense programs are taking 20 to 30 years to deliver less capability than planned, very often at two to three times the cost and schedules planned. These continuing problems are obviously worsening the severe force modernization shortfalls that face the military services now and into the future, made even more critical by the loss and heavy use of equipment in the Iraq and Afghanistan theaters of operation. The following table, extracted from the March 2008 GAO Assessments of Selected Weapon Programs, not only depicts the cost and schedule problems plaguing defense acquisition programs since the outset of this decade, it shows that the situation continues to deteriorate, despite all the rhetoric about transformation and reform.

Recognizing that the situation has only worsened in the past few years, John Young, who assumed the position of defense acquisition executive in 2006, has issued several policy directives aimed at restoring discipline and good business practices to DOD's acquisition process. Among these practices are competitive prototyping, budgeting to independent cost estimates, emphasis on reliability/availability/maintainability (RAM) during the system design phase and early development testing and development of well-grounded business cases for new system developments, among others.

While applauding these attempts to address the process's most persistent problems, it should be noted that there is nothing new in these new "initiatives" – they have all been on the books, so to speak, at one time or another. However, experience over the years has convinced many astute observers that the fundamental shortcoming in the process has been, and continues to be, the failure of the acquisition community – from

Table 2. Cost and Schedule Growth for DOD Acquisition Programs
(GAO Report-08-467SP, Assessment of Selected Weapon Programs, March 2008)

Year When Evaluations Were Performed by GAO	FY 2000	FY 2005	FY 2007
Number of Programs Evaluated	75	91	95
Total Planned Costs (FY 2008 $ Billion)	$790	$1, 500	$1,600
Costs Yet to Go (FY 2008 $ B)	$380	$887	$858
Δ RDT&E Costs from 1st Estimate	27%	33%	40%
Δ Program Acquisition Costs from 1st Estimate	6%	18%	26%
Estimated Total Program Cost Growth (FY 2008 $ B)	$42	$202	$295
Share of Programs Exceeding 25% Program Acquisition Unit Cost Growth	37%	44%	44%
Average Months Delay in Delivering Initial Capabilities	16	17	21

program managers to senior decision-makers and their advisors – to implement and carry out the letter, much less the intent, of DOD's existing acquisition policy directives and guidelines. These guidelines have evolved over the years, and include many of the critical findings and recommendations emanating from the aforementioned reform efforts of the past 40 years.

Key Findings from Previous Studies

Some of these findings and recommendations are worth noting here in light of these latest initiatives. One key misconception should be put to bed right up front – a finding borne out in spades during the 1990 DSB review: *While oversight by government agencies and their reporting requirements can indeed be burdensome, they clearly are not the causes of the continuing miserable record of program stretch-outs and cost growth.* This is true, independent of whether those agencies and their reporting requirements are internal to DOD, such as the Defense Contract Management Agency (DCMA), Independent Cost Analysis groups, Operational Test and Evaluation organizations; or those external, such as the congressional committees and their staffs and the GAO.

Instead, that 1990 review, covering some 100 major defense acquisition programs, concluded that failure to identify and admit to technical issues and solutions, as well as real costs, before entry into what was known as Full-Scale Engineering Development (FSED) – now referred to as System Design and Development (SDD) – was the overwhelming cause for subsequent schedule delays, often in terms of years, and the resulting cost growths. To the extent oversight played any role in these delays, it was the discovery and reporting of test failures during FSED/SDD that often necessitated additional time and dollars for system redesign, testing and retesting of fixes, as well as costly retrofits of those fixes.

Despite the overwhelming evidence that oversight per se was not the cause of continuing cost and schedule growth, Pentagon leadership in the mid-1990s implemented the strategy known as Total System Performance Responsibility (TSPR) for several key acquisition programs. This strategy, in essence, relieved development contractors of many reporting requirements, including costs and technical progress. In essence, it built a firewall around the contractor, preventing government sponsors from properly overseeing the expenditure of the taxpayers' dollars.

Several major acquisition programs contracted for their development and engineering activities under the ballyhooed TSPR strategy. Needless to say, many of these programs soon hit the headlines with huge technical and cost problems. For example, the Army's Theater Area Air Defense (THAAD) experienced several high-profile missile failures in development testing.

A high-level independent technical review of the program, undertaken in the late 1990s, found that the contractor, trying to maintain cost and schedule, had skipped or postponed some basic ground testing of the missile and its subsystems before proceeding with the doomed full-up missile shots. When questioned by the independent review panel as to how this had come to pass, the THAAD program manager stated that he had no contractual means to pressure the prime contractor, Lockheed-Martin, to carry out the planned ground tests. It was this review of THAAD which coined a most appropriate phrase, "rush to failure," to describe the sequence of events leading to the test fiascos.

Underestimating Technical Problems is a Major Cause of Program Problems

One need only examine the history of three of DOD's largest and most controversial programs undertaken in the past 20-plus years to further substantiate that launching into major developments without understanding key technical issues is the root cause of major cost and schedule problems. The Army's Comanche armed reconnaissance helicopter program began in 1981 as the LHX, planned at the time to replace the Army's fleet of UH-1 utility and AH-1 Cobra attack helicopters. After spending billions of dollars over two decades and undertaking several restructures of the program, the latter brought about by continuing technical problems and cost growth, the Army's leadership canceled the program in 2003.

The Department of Navy's MV-22 program had a similar checkered history. Initiation of the joint Army/Marine Corps JVX program was approved in the fall of 1981, followed by approval to enter the Demonstration/Validation phase in 1982. Later, a Milestone II review in 1986 approved the program's entry into FSED/SDD. Designed as a much-needed replacement for the Marine Corps aging CH-46 medium-lift helicopter fleet, the MV-22 finally completed its second Operational Evaluation (OPEVAL) in 2005, a prerequisite for the full-rate production decision that followed later that year. In the meantime, the Marine Corps had procured over 50 MV-22s in Low-Rate Initial Production (LRIP) over the previous six or more years, running the risk of needing additional funding for these aircraft to incorporate fixes to problems uncovered in testing after their procurement. In any event, close to 25 years and about $15 billion later, the Marine Corps finally reached the point of replacing its 1960s vintage CH-46s.

In a similar vein, the early 1980s witnessed a debate about the scope and requirements for the Air Force's Advanced Tactical Fighter (ATF) program which eventually became the F-22. As discussed earlier, with respect to Air Force fighter/attack aircraft modernization, the F-22 encountered unforeseen technical problems during its FSED/SDD. Operational testing was delayed several years while unexpected problems with complex software and avionics reliability were discovered during development testing and time-consuming fixes were designed and implemented. In the end, these problems along with large cost increases resulted in a procurement program of about one quarter the number of aircraft originally planned.

The Front-End of the Process Sows the Seeds of Future Problems

These programs also epitomize what astute observers have found to be a fundamental deficiency in the overall defense acquisition process – the front-end of the process. They have pinpointed the development and setting of requirements, both technical and operational, as sowing the seeds for these future problems. Among the proposed remedies in this area has been the repeated call for attainable, affordable and testable requirements based on realistic budget toplines and threat projections and performance/cost tradeoffs that, in turn, rely on the projection of realistic system lifecycle costs and force levels.

Unfortunately, the process has whetted, if not heartily reinforced, the appetite of the users for quantum leaps in capability that are reflected in high-risk, sometimes unattainable, technical and operational requirements. Many of these "reach for the moon" system performance goals have resulted from the salesmanship of the DOD research and development communities, combined with industry lobbying, in successfully convincing the user that advanced capabilities could be delivered rapidly and cheaply. Over the years, this process has been warped by the ever-optimistic projections of available funding both in the near-term as well as into the out-years, in essence relieving the decision-maker of any need to make the hard choices.

Part and parcel of this effort to sell a new program – to get the camel's nose under the tent, so to speak – is the so-called "buy-in" syndrome, whereby costs, schedule and technical risks are often grossly understated at the outset. These low-ball estimates mesh right in with the optimistic overall budget top line projections into the out-years, especially the procurement accounts. As illustrated earlier in this chapter, in case after case, Pentagon decision-makers have acquiesced to programs entering FSED/SDD and even low-rate initial production before technical problems are identified, much less solved; before credible independent cost assessments are accomplished and included in program budget projections; and even before the more risky requirements are demonstrated in testing. The overwhelming abundance of such data clearly points to a problem with the DOD acquisition system itself that cannot be written off to poor management of individual programs, although this does occur sometimes as well.

This root of the problem is well known: The aforementioned process reviews have repeatedly found that we should "fly and know if it works and how much it will cost before buying." Building and testing competitive prototype systems and subsystems before proceeding with FSED/SDD has been a recommendation of several of these studies and, as discussed earlier, directed by Young. In that same vein, these reviews have called for up-front funding of robust efforts to demonstrate technology maturity as a prerequisite for program approval. DOD's acquisition policy and directives have incorporated these recommendations. Unfortunately, the rising operating and support (O&S) costs of the existing forces, and the fact that there are more acquisition programs being pursued than DOD can possibly afford in the long term, have combined to intensify the competition between programs for dollars. This, in turn, has led to decision-makers sanctioning low-balled program costs and overly optimistic schedules at the outset of major programs, most often at the expense of building and testing prototypes and critical technology risk reduction efforts.

Having obtained approval to enter FSED/SDD with unrealistic costs and schedules based on rosy, if not surreal, technical risk assessments, programs inevitably encounter problems early-on. These problems, in turn, set off the spiral of schedule stretches and ballooning costs that have come to plague the vast majority of DOD acquisition programs. Unfortunately, too often, program managers attempt to limit the damage by trying to maintain the schedule at the expense of critical test events and design fixes for obvious deficiencies. The net result is a schedule-based strategy, rather than the event-based program strategy that the myriad of DOD acquisition directives stress.

With our emphasis on the GWOT for the next decade or so, it would seem that there is far less need to cut corners and field these technologically advanced systems without thorough testing as we have been wont to do over the past few decades. It isn't as if the Taliban will be fielding stealth fighters or some semblance of the FCS anytime soon. Furthermore so-called "peer competitors," Russia and China face daunting technical and manufacturing challenges in their attempts to mimic us and field F-22/F-35 generation aircraft. The DOD should take the necessary time to build and test competitive prototypes for major future systems and make sure it has mature technology in hand before proceeding, or at least understand and plan for the technical hurdles before it. In essence, it is worth repeating, "fly and know if it works and how much it will cost before we buy."

Schedule-Driven Versus Event-Driven Strategies

The past several years, particularly after U.S. forces entered combat in Afghanistan and Iraq, the pressure has intensified to keep programs on schedule, even to accelerate the process, in order to get equipment in the hands of troops sooner than later. As a result, some systems with serious reliability and maintenance problems found in development and operational testing have been waived through the decision process into production and deployment.

It appears that often the programs fail to carry out adequate testing; and in those cases where they do, they often fail to take the necessary corrective actions based on that testing before proceeding with full production and deployment. A Defense Science Board Task Force on Development Test and Evaluation[9] reported that, in the 10-year period, 1997 through 2006, roughly 70 percent of Army systems had failed to meet their specific reliability requirements in operational testing. See the Figure below extracted from the Task Force Report, dated May 2008. Nevertheless, many of these programs proceeded into production and deployment to the operating forces. The Task Force found that similar problems existed with the programs of the other

Figure 1. Army Systems Failing Reliability during Operational Testing (1997-2006)

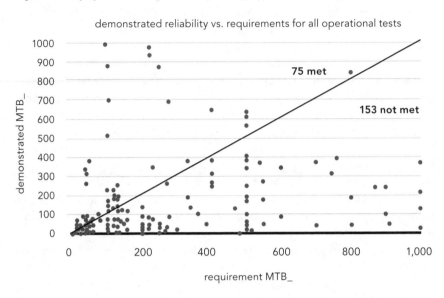

services. These problems with attaining realistic reliability, availability and maintainability goals result in increased logistics burdens on our operating forces and a *de facto* reduction in force effectiveness attributable to low equipment availability.

More recent experience shows that, with all the streamlining of the acquisition process, the number of systems failing to meet reliability requirements continues to be a major problem. For example, of the 28 systems for which the Pentagon's Director of Operational Test and Evaluation (DOT&E) submitted Beyond Low-Rate Initial Production (BLRIP) reports to the Congress between 2001 and 2006, over half were found not operationally suitable or assessed to have major suitability deficiencies. The trend in suitability results is disturbing, as more systems are going to the field despite being unsuitable as tested.

What is Needed is Discipline

In keeping with the overall thrust of this discussion, any recommendations for fixes to the much-maligned defense PPB and acquisition processes would feature enforcement of the existing directives and instructions that supposedly govern the process. They are the product of numerous high level, often insightful, reviews of that process stretching over some 40 years. There isn't much new under the sun, so to speak, that knowledgeable observers of, and participants in, this process haven't already identified as problems and proposed solutions for. Pointing the finger at oversight agencies in the executive and legislative branches for the lengthy times from program starts to deliveries to the troops in the field doesn't get at the root causes for those schedule slips. Neither does the cyclical invention of acquisition strategies with catchy buzz-word titles, such as TSPR and Simulation-Based Acquisition (SBA), for example, come to grips with those root causes.

The bottom line is that the basic policies and directives DOD has on the books, particularly for its acquisition process, are fundamentally sound. They incorporate more than four decades of experience and findings of numerous reviews. Unfortunately, many of the major acquisition decisions over those years have not reflected adherence to those policies and directives. Too often, Pentagon acquisition officials have approved low-balled estimates of the costs and time required to deliver new capabilities, even when other independent assessments are obviously more realistic. Time and again, early-on funding for building and testing prototypes to better understand technical and operational issues has gone by the wayside in the competition for dollars, and program managers have approved programs proceeding into FSED/SDD before these issues are addressed.

In most cases, by the time the technical and cost issues come to the fore in spades, few, if any, of those involved in the process can bring themselves to admit they were wrong, to cut their losses before inevitable further cost growth and schedule slips, or to demonstrate much-needed discipline by making an example of program officials and their contractors who have sold the department and the taxpayers a bill of goods. By the time these problems are acknowledged, the political penalties incurred in enforcing any major restructuring of a program, much less its cancellation, are too painful to bear. Unless someone is willing to stand up and point out that the emperor has no clothes, the U.S. military will continue to hemorrhage taxpayer dollars and critical years while acquiring equipment that falls short of meeting the needs of the troops in the field.

Laying the Ground Work for a Disciplined Process

Certainly, it is clear that more discipline is sorely needed on the part of DOD decision-makers and it is easy to criticize its apparent absence over the past decades. However, until incentives are in place that encourage hard-nosed decisions, whether it be in the programming and budgeting or in the acquisition process, the department will continue down the same paths that have gotten it into the dire straits it faces today. As long as decision-makers are presented with inflated threat assessments; grossly optimistic budget projections, particularly with respect to available funding for ac-quisition programs; as well as the patently unrealistic estimates of costs, schedules, technology maturity levels and performance projections; there are little or no incen-tives to face up to reality and take the heat for making hard choices. To proceed with major force structure and acquisition decisions unconstrained by realistic funding considerations simply continues the road we are on now-shrinking and ever aging forces at ever increasing costs,

Coming to grips with these issues will not be easy. While these impediments to rational defense program planning have been well known for decades, there have been few lasting initiatives that address them coherently. In both his previously referenced work, "Defense Power Games," and his June 4, 2002 testimony[10] before the House Subcommittee on National Security, Veterans Affairs and International Relations, defense analyst Chuck Spinney spelled out a set of step-by-step procedures to address these long standing impediments. While many defense observers and certainly insiders may consider his recipe for success to be a series of drastic, even bureaucratic, steps, the defense plans/reality mismatch that we have on our hands today cries out for similar drastic action.

At a minimum, the department, in concert with the Congress, should take the first of these steps by undertaking Spinney's recommended crash effort to "clean up the books." In the next chapter in this series, Winslow Wheeler takes a major page from Spinney's work with his discussion of specific initiatives aimed at dealing with defense's overall budget and financial management mess. Such efforts would start with the commitment on the part of the White House and the Congress to fund the continuing war on terror on a "pay as you go" basis. In essence there would be no further supplemental budget requests to cover the operations in Iraq, Afghanistan and other theaters around the world. At the same time, DOD and Congress would agree on a year's pause or freeze in the department's core programs while a concerted effort on the part of the various government audit agencies, to include the GAO, and aided by private accounting firms as needed, is undertaken. This effort would strive to complete a thorough audit of all components of the defense establishment, to include combat and combat support forces, their equipment levels and readiness, their operating and support costs, as well as all the programs underway in various stages of development and acquisition.

While this intense "scrubbing of the books" is underway, an independent panel or commission of professional experts, agreed upon by both the executive and legislative branches of the government and adequately staffed with impartial, yet knowledgeable, personnel, would undertake the tasks spelled out in Wheeler's chapter under the heading, "Sorting Out the Mess." This panel or commission would combine its evaluation of the potential threats facing the nation over time with its assessments of the forces and programs needed to meet those threats, to evolve a realistic defense funding top line over the next decade and beyond, as well as the relevant forces and programs that meet those threats and fit within the financial constraints imposed by that top line.

Wheeler's chapter provides more details concerning this crucial effort to rectify the Pentagon's financial books and its future budget projections with practicality and to independently evaluate and scrub its acquisition programs in particular. While those details need not be repeated here, two aspects of these far-reaching initiatives are worth a few points of discussion here.

One big concern, also treated by Wheeler, is that finding the "right" individuals to agree to take part in such an independent panel, either as members or supporting staff, will not be easy. Over the past 20 or so years the DOD and its components have deliberately and systematically decimated their in-house technical capabilities to the point where there is little, if any, competence or initiative left in the various organizations tasked with planning and executing its budget and acquisition programs. The results of those years of congressionally and DOD-directed reductions in personnel involved in its complex acquisition programs and processes, to include the related oversight functions, are evident in the rampant cost, schedule and performance horror stories that persist to this day. The situation clearly calls for a hard-hitting, tell-it-like-it-is panel or commission, perhaps along the lines of the National Commission on Terrorist Attacks Upon the United States, the so-called 9-11 Commission, that issued its independent report in 2004.

The other aspect is the recommendation espoused by Wheeler and one that merits serious consideration is institutionalizing this panel as a continuing entity overseeing and guiding the planning and execution of the defense program. The panel would continue to operate at least until the new administration and the Congress are satisfied that the DOD has reached a point of competence and backbone that it would no longer need the external review and oversight of its decisions and processes.

Specific Acquisition Process Discipline Measures

Hard-nosed discipline on the part of decision-makers at the front-end of the acquisition process should curb the appetite of the requirements community and preclude launching into a major system development that rests on immature technologies and optimistic projections of both system costs and the overall availability of resources in the future. Realistic independent cost estimates and technical risk assessments, developed outside the chain of command for major programs, should inform the defense acquisition executive as to the viability of a new program's cost, schedule and performance projections.

The decision authority should impose event-based (vice schedule-based) strategies on programs to include meaningful and realistic exit criteria for each stage of development and production. Only if these criteria are successfully demonstrated and satisfied, should a program be allowed to proceed to its next stage – e.g., (Dem/Val) to FSED/SDD or from FSED/SDD into production. Of critical importance is demonstrating the technical maturity of the technologies embedded in a new system development prior to proceeding into FSED/SDD. Sufficient upfront funding and time for robust system and subsystem prototype demonstration and testing should be programmed and fenced to enable an informed decision as to the technical risk entailed in proceeding. When a program enters FSED/SDD and subsequently encounters technical, schedule or cost problems, the decision authority should not permit the program to enter LRIP until the program has demonstrated that the problems have been solved satisfactorily. Otherwise, we will continue to deliver large numbers of systems over several years of LRIP prior to the completion of the statutorily required Initial Operational Test and Evaluation (IOT&E), as was the case with the MV-22 and F-22 aircraft programs. Similarly, programs that have failed to meet either their effectiveness or suitability requirements in IOT&E should not be accorded a green flag to enter full production.

In summary, more informed management attention and discipline at the front-end of the process and due consideration of independent assessments of cost schedule and performance throughout the development and testing of new systems should go a long way to solving many of the problems plaguing defense acquisition. There's nothing new here – time and again major defense management reviews have come to the same conclusions. It's high time decision-makers took these findings seriously, most of which are embedded in existing directives and instructions that govern the overall budget development and acquisition processes, and made them an integral part of their program review and decision process.

ENDNOTES

1   "Defense Power Games," *Defense and the National Interest*, November 27, 2007, http://www.d-n-i. net/dni/military-in-society/defense-power-games

2   Inside the Pentagon, *DOD Tells Military to assume Zero Real Growth in FY-10 Budget*, March 20, 2008.

3   Congressional Budget Office, *The Long-Term Implications of Current Defense Plans: Detailed Update for Fiscal Year 2008*.

4   Government Accountability Office Report, GAO-08-467SP, *Defense Acquisitions, Assessments of Selected Weapon Programs*, March 2008.

5   Valerie Reed and Jessica Guiney, "*Future Combat System: Is It Worth It?*" Center for Defense Information, May 30, 2008, http://www.cdi.org/pdfs/FCS.pdf

6   "Military May Face $100B In Repairs," *USA Today*, June 26, 2008.

7   Sydney J. Freedberg, Jr., "The Bills Come Due," *National Journal*, March 15, 2008.

8   Government Accountability Office Report GAO-08-388, *Joint Strike Fighter, Recent Decisions by DOD Add to Program Risks*, March 2008.

9   Defense Science Board Report on Developmental Test and Evaluation, May 2008.

10 Statement by Franklin C. Spinney before the House Subcommittee on National Security, Veterans Affairs and International Relations.

CHAPTER 11

UNDERSTAND, THEN CONTAIN AMERICA'S OUT-OF-CONTROL DEFENSE BUDGET

Winslow T. Wheeler

The foregoing chapters have described how America's armed forces are manned and equipped to fight, at best, enemies that do not now exist and may never again in the foreseeable future. I say "at best" because there is much evidence, cited here and elsewhere, that the hugely expensive and extraordinarily complex programs that the Pentagon and Congress describe as vital for national defense are not even good ideas to fight the Second Generation Warfare which U.S. armed forces would seem best suited to conduct. Indeed, for Third Generation Warfare, which many in our armed forces seem very interested to talk about but which their leadership mostly does not seem to comprehend, such systems are little, if any, help. And, in Fourth Generation Warfare, such programs and policies – and the thinking that goes with them – lend a clear advantage to the enemy and almost guarantee our own defeat.

Almost as disturbing is the condition of the defense budget. Our problems are redoubled: it is not that the defense budget adequately supports our irrelevant, even counterproductive forces. For that to be the case would be a significant improvement. Instead, to promote armed forces that fight the wrong type of war in the wrong places – liberals, moderates and conservatives in the Pentagon, Congress, think tanks and the White House have over time constructed an edifice that makes our forces smaller, older and less ready to fight, all at dramatically increasing cost. And, we have done so with a system that, quite literally, does not know – or apparently care – what it is doing.

Do You Know What Your Defense Budget Is?

Each year, when the new defense budget is released, the media discusses it with great precision – always careful to cite it to at least the first decimal. The vast majority of those ostensibly precise newspaper articles have the numbers quite wrong – not just to the right of the decimal point; they are often off by tens of billions of dollars, and by some measures, they are off by hundreds of billions. Their reportage on George W. Bush's defense budget request for fiscal year 2009 (FY 09) was no exception.

On Feb. 4, 2008, the Department of Defense (DOD) briefed the press on the new 2009 defense budget, citing its total, $515.4 billion. President Bush's Office of Management and Budget (OMB) released the same budget on the same day, citing it to be $518.3 billion. That's a $2.9 billion difference. OMB was accurate; the Pentagon "forgot" to include some permanent appropriations (also called "entitlements" or "mandatory" spending) for retirement and some other non-hardware spending. Nonetheless, the vast majority of the press used the Pentagon's number. Going to DOD's budget "roll out" press briefing is an annual ritual for defense journalists, as is regurgitating the numbers in the Pentagon press release with little, if any, meaningful review.

All the numbers cited above were quite wrong. They did not include $70 billion that was also requested to pay for the wars in Iraq and Afghanistan. While some journalists did include that number in their articles, $70 billion was also inaccurate. It did not include enough money to fight the wars for more than a few months in 2009. Doubling that number, if not more, is necessary. As this anthology is released, no one knows the right number; neither the White House nor Congress have bothered to put together a properly documented estimate of what amount will likely be needed. It is something responsible politicians would do, especially in Congress which is the definitive constitutional authority on such matters. Previous presidents and congresses did; today's politicians have not.

To do so, however, would only be part of what will ultimately be appropriated to fund American security for FY 09. The Pentagon's budget, plus the full amount needed to conduct operations in Iraq and Afghanistan, does not include:

- Department of Energy (DOE) funding for nuclear weapons research, storage and related activities. Bush requested $17.1 billion for 2009.

- An additional $5.7 billion for miscellaneous defense activities in other agencies, such as the General Services Administration's National Defense Stockpile, the Selective Service and the FBI's international activities, all of which OMB includes in its so-called "National Defense" budget category.

If you add these estimates, you get a total of $611.1 billion for 2009. It is a number most journalists ignore; most likely for the simple reason that it's not in the Pentagon's press release.

However, there is more.

Any inclusive definition of U.S. security spending should also include the budget for the Department of Homeland Security (DHS): add $40.1 billion for 2009.

There are also important security costs in the budget of the State Department for diplomacy, arms aid to allies, U.N. peacekeeping, reconstruction aid for Iraq and Afghanistan, and foreign aid for other countries. These and other international activities are clearly intended to contribute to U.S. national security: add $38.4 billion.

U.S. security expenses might also include the human costs of past and current wars: add another $91.3 billion for the Department of Veterans Affairs.

We could add the share of the 2009 payment for the national debt that can be attributed to national defense spending. While few agree on what that share is; one reasonable calculation argues that the "National Defense" budget category constitutes 21 percent of federal spending, and that percent of the 2009 payment on the debt should be calculated. That would be $54.5 billion.

There's more; add the costs to the U.S. Department of the Treasury for military retirement that are not counted in the DOD budget; that's $12.1 billion. Some would also add the interest earned in the Treasury's military retirement fund, another $16.2 billion.

Altogether, the total security bill for America for 2009 comes to $863.7 billion. (Actually, it will be more – once Congress and the White House adopt a spending figure for Iraq and Afghanistan that approximates reality.)

Table 1 recounts these numbers.

Some will argue that the $863.7 billion figure inflates what we spend for national defense. It is, of course, significantly more than what we are asked to pay for the Department of Defense ($588.3 billion), but it can be argued that the figure that is $275.4 billion higher (not including the full cost of the wars) better characterizes what we pay for national security.

Table 1.
Total National Security Costs as Requested in President George W. Bush's Fiscal Year 2009 Budget

Category	2009 Request
DOD	518.3
War Funding	70.0
"Atomic Energy Defense Activities" (DOE)	17.1
"Defense Related Activities" (GSA, etc.)	5.7
Homeland Security (DHS)	40.1
Veterans Affairs (DVA)	91.3
International Affairs	38.4
Non-DOD Military Retirement	28.3
21% of Interest on the Debt	54.5
Grand Total	**863.7**

Source: Office of Management and Budget

A Comparison to History and Other Nations

Even if you count just Pentagon spending for 2009, it is a historic amount. It is more than we have spent for the Department of Defense at any time since the end of World War II.

Figure 1 on the next page shows post-World War II Pentagon spending; the dollars are adjusted for inflation.

Notice in Figure 1 how far above average Cold War spending we are today. With no superpower opponent challenging the United States, this is remarkable. A less powerful threat means a larger budget.

It is also notable that what the U.S. government spends for national defense is an amount that approximates what the rest of the world spends. Depending on which

Figure 1. Post-World War II DOD Spending, Constant 2008 Dollars

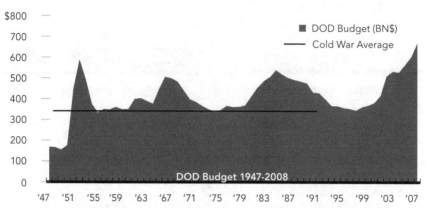

Source: National Defense Budget Estimates for the 2008 Budget ("Greenbook"), Department of Defense.

estimate one uses, the United States spends slightly less than, or significantly more than, the rest of the world combined. See Figure 2 below.

The figures above show not just America's enemies or potential enemies, but the entire rest of the world. In the 19th century, Great Britain adopted a standard to assure security for its navy – a navy that dominated all others: to possess as many capital ships as the next two most powerful navies combined, whether friend or foe. America has gone well beyond this measure; we have adopted not a "Two Power" standard, instead we have adopted a standard that approaches all 191 other members of the United Nations.

Spending amounts that approximate the combined budgets of just so-called threat nations would mean virtual evisceration of the Department of Defense budget. The defense budgets of the remaining "Rogue States" (Iran and North Korea) are tiny in comparison. Adding Cuba to the mix, adds virtually nothing. Even if we were to consider significant defense spenders like Russia and China to be enemy-, or potential-enemy states, the grand total comes to less than one-third of the current DOD budget.

As Col. Chester Richards pointed out in Chapter Two – and others elsewhere – the United States and China are major trading partners, and the U.S. and Russia, while competitive on various international issues, have a relationship nothing like the Cold War posture we had with the Soviet Union. In addition, 65 years of post-World War II history have shown that nuclear powers – like the United States, Russia and China – go to great lengths to avoid direct military confrontations. It would require leadership of incomprehensible incompetence or virtual clinical lunacy to permit war among nuclear powers. Many use the possible threat of Russia and China to justify adding programs

Figure 2. United States Defense Spending Compared to Worldwide Military Expenditures

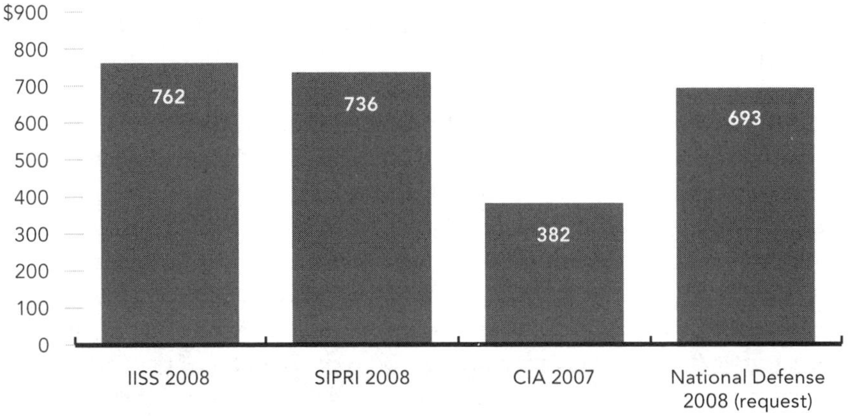

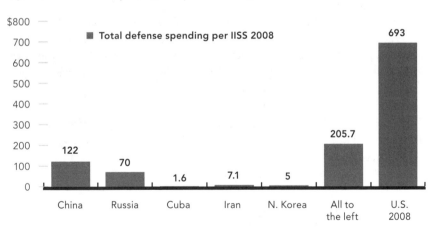

Sources: International Institute for Strategic Studies, The Military Balance for 2008; Stockholm International Peace and Research Institute, Yearbook for 2008; Central Intelligence Agency, The World Factbook, 2007.

Figure 3. U.S. Defense Spending Compared to "Rogue" & Other Non-Allied States

Source: International Institute for Strategic Studies, "The Military Balance, 2008."

to the defense budget, but it is ludicrous to think these two nations, and any other possible foes, such as Iran and North Korea, justify a defense budget more than three times the size of what all these countries spend on defense collectively.

Figure 3 above shows the U.S. defense budget in relation to these others.

224 • Understand, Then Contain America's Out-of-Control Defense Budget

It is apparent that no measure from threat countries, or from any other external source, is used to size the Pentagon budget. The only limit would appear to be how much money the politicians in the Pentagon, Congress and the White House are willing to throw at it.

Non-Threat Based Justification for Larger Defense Budgets

A significant number of important people in government and think-tank punditry have adopted a measuring system to size the U.S. defense budget independent of the external world. It is a system that – conveniently – can justify an even larger, indeed ever growing, defense budget. At the head of this highly politicized parade is the Chairman of the Joint Chiefs of Staff, Adm. Michael Mullen. He has been advocating a defense budget based on the size of the U.S. economy. The Pentagon's "base" budget should,[1] he says, increase from 3.3 percent of America's Gross Domestic Product to 4.0 percent.

His is an advocacy of stupendous brilliance and stupidity at the same time.

The amount sounds modest, just 0.7 percent more. Why should that be any problem, especially if, as he and others say, we spent much more during the Cold War, such as the 8.9 percent we spent in 1968 during the Lyndon Johnson administration?

Data from the Treasury Department shows the Gross Domestic Product, the approximate size of the U.S. economy, to be $13.4 trillion. If we increase the Pentagon's "share" of it from 3.3 to 4.0 percent, that 0.7 percent increase comes to $94 billion. On top of the $518 billion Mullen is also asking for, it is no small amount.

It is a lot more than a large increase masquerading as a puny percentage; it seeks to base the top-line amount of the U.S. defense budget on something that poses no threat to the United States. He wants to size the defense budget based on an internal attribute of the country, the national economy, that makes us stronger, not weaker. It is only because the U.S. economy has been growing more than the defense budget over time, that it makes the defense budget appear to have become smaller when it has, in fact, grown larger. Moreover, using this measure, it can be argued that we have somehow become laggards with our current all-time high defense budget. (Recall Figure 1.)

The admiral's argument also implies the extra dollars to expand defense spending are easy to find. Now spending "only" 3.3 percent compared to percentages twice that, and more, in the past gives one the sense that the money now "missing" from the defense budget can be found lying around, performing no useful function. In truth, you have only three places to find the "extra" money: 1) through increased taxes, 2) in other federal spending, or 3) from growing the federal deficit. Admiral Mullen and the other advocates of this measure of the defense budget forget to tell us which they prefer.

The specious nature of this measure is apparent when you consider what Mullen would also link defense spending to. As the economy has grown, so too have the number of McDonald's hamburger franchises in the country. It would be just as "rational" to base Pentagon spending on the number of golden arches in American towns and cities.

What Our Expanding Defense Budget Has Bought

While many appreciate that Pentagon spending is now higher than it has ever been since the end of World War II, it should also be conventional wisdom, yet isn't, that our military forces are smaller than they have ever been since 1946. Major categories of equipment are also, on average, older than they ever have been before; and key elements of our most important fighting forces are not ready for combat.

The wars in Iraq and Afghanistan are not the cause. The negative trends have been around for decades.[2] The wars have not siphoned off money from the non-war parts of the Pentagon budget. While the Pentagon has received more than $800 billion for the wars in Iraq and Afghanistan, since 2001 it has also received $770 billion more than was anticipated for it for the years 2001 to 2009. One would hope this huge "plus-up" for the "peacetime" (or "base," non-war) budget would have addressed some of the decades-old problems. It did not, and today they are worse.

The "base" DOD budget has increased, in inflation-adjusted dollars, from $370.8 billion in 2001 to $518.3 billion in 2009, a 40-percent increase.[3] Comparing the actual annual Pentagon base budgets to the base budgets planned at the start of the first George W. Bush administration (for the years from 2001 to 2009[4]) computes to an added $770 billion. These data are shown in Table 2.

Assessing the plus-ups each of the military services has received will demonstrate how more money has made our problems worse.

Table 2. Additional Funding in the "Base" DOD Budget[5]

	2001	2002	2003	2004	2005	2006	2007	2008	2009	Total
2001 "Plan" (Extrapolated for 2006-2009	291.1	294.8	301	308.3	316.4	325	335	346	358	2875.6
"Base" Budgets	295	327.8	378.6	379.6	402.6	421.1	441	483.2	518.3	3647.2
DOD "Plus-Up"	3.9	33.0	77.6	71.3	86.2	96.1	106	137.2	160.3	771.6

The Army

In early 2001, the Army anticipated an approximate budget of $719 billion for the period 2001 to 2009. Not counting the $387 billion subsequently appropriated for Army participation in the wars in Iraq and Afghanistan, the Army's "base" budget was increased by $191 billion to $911 billion. The data used for these calculations are displayed in Table 3 on the next page.

And yet, the $191 billion plus up the Army received in its base budget for 2001 to 2009 resulted in no increase in the Army's size. In fact, the historic trend is for more

Table 3. U.S. Army Funding: 2001-2009[6]

	2001	2002	2003	2004	2005	2006	2007	2008	2009	Total
2001 "Plan" (Extrapolated for 2005-2009	70.6	74.4	76.1	78.0	79.9	81.9	84.0	86.2	88.4	719.5
Base Budget Requests	73.0	80.1	90.8	93.8	97.0	98.5	110.3	128.4	139.0	910.9
Base Army Budget above 2001 Plan	2.4	5.7	14.7	15.8	17.1	16.6	26.3	42.2	50.6	191.4
Total Appropriations (including War Funding)	77.0	85.9	121.1	153.1	152.8	174.9	218.5	175.4	139.0	1297.7
Calculated War Funding	4.0	5.8	30.3	59.3	55.8	76.4	108.2	47.0	-	386.8

Figure 4. Army Division Equivalents and Budget (with Trendlines) (Billions, FY 2009 Dollars)[11]

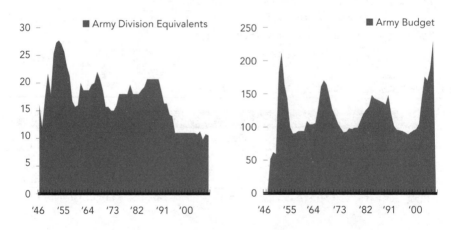

money to result in a smaller Army. The publicly available budget and force structure data for the Army for the post-World War II period are shown in Figure 4 above.

As shown, the Army's "division equivalents"[7] have declined over time to a post-World War II low at about 11 divisions. Army budgets have shown highs and lows, but the overall trend is one of growth, and the Army budget is now at an all-time high.

A key equipment inventory – ground fighting vehicles – continues to age while it also shrinks. The Congressional Budget Office measures that this inventory will continue to shrink even as the number of combat units has stabilized in the early 21st century. It is a trend that Army plans will accelerate in future years.[8]

Evidence on readiness is also discouraging. Army budget materials for 2009 state the Army achieved 459 tank training miles (per tank per year) in 2008. During the Clinton administration, the Army set a goal of about 800 tank miles per year but did little better than 650. During the previous George H.W. Bush administration, the Army had a goal of 1,000 miles, and 800 were sometimes achieved. In other words, in 2008, tank crews are training at a level less than half of what was considered optimal in the early 1990s.

The Army asserts today that all units sent to the theaters in Iraq and Afghanistan are "fully ready." This assertion is suspect. Training time in the continental United States for unconventional war has been reduced thanks to the high operating tempo and the recurrent deployments of the same units back to combat after just 12 months back home. Only a portion of the non-deployed time is spent retraining for redeployment. More importantly, during that limited training time, units do not always have available to them the proper equipment with which to train, and the people in those units get truncated time to train together – whether or not they possess the right equipment – with new personnel. This makes it very difficult, if not impossible, to achieve the kind of intra- and inter-unit cohesion that the Army has come to understand is needed to give soldiers the best chance to survive and prevail in combat. Few, if any, units inside the United States are rated as fully combat ready, and yet when they go into Iraq or Afghanistan they are rated as such. While the units deploying to Iraq and Afghanistan may be officially designated as "ready," those ratings are based on the subjective assessment of unit commanders in a command atmosphere that appears not to welcome "bad news."[9]

The Army is not alone in facing these problems.

The Navy

In early 2001, the Navy anticipated an approximate budget of $900 billion for itself and the Marine Corps for the period 2001 to 2009.[10] Not counting $95 billion subsequently received for the wars in Iraq and Afghanistan, the Navy/Marine Corps "base" (non-war) budget was increased by $174 billion to $1.07 trillion. The data used for these calculations are displayed in Table 4 on the next page.

As with the Army, a significant budget plus-up resulted in a stagnant force structure. Over time, the trend is – again – worse: more money means smaller forces. The publicly available budget[15] and force structure data for the U.S. Navy for the post-World War II period are shown in Figure 5 on the next page.

As shown, the fleet today is as small as at any point in the post-World War II period. From a 1953 high of 835 combat ships, it persistently hovers in the 21st century at about 300.

The budget shows ups and downs, but the overall trend is for it to increase in "real" dollars.[16] In recent years, the Navy's budget has increased sharply, mostly for

Table 4. U.S. Navy & Marine Corps Budget[12]

	2001	2002	2003	2004	2005	2006	2007	2008	2009	Total
2001 "Plan" (Extrapolated for 2005-2009)	91.7	90.8	94.1	96.4	98.7	101.6	105.8	108.7	111.9	899.7
Base Budget Requests	92.6	98.7	108.2	114.5	119.2	125.4	127.1	139.5	149.0	1074.2
Base Navy Budget above 2001 Plan	0.9	7.0	14.1	20.1	20.5	23.8	21.3	30.8	37.1	174.5
Total Appropriations (including War Funding)	95.5	102.4	124.1	124.3	131.7	143.8	150.3	147.7	149.0	1168.8
Calculated War Spending	2.9	3.7	15.9	9.8	12..5	18.4	23.2	8.2	N.A.	94.6

Figure 5.
Navy Active Duty Combat Ships and Budget (with Trendlines) (Billions FY 2009 Dollars)[13]

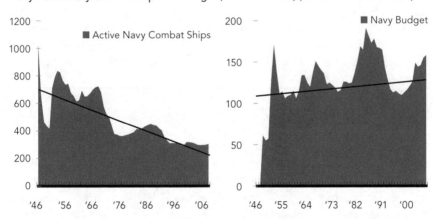

expenses not related to the wars in Iraq and Afghanistan, and yet the force structure remains flat.

In the Air Force, things are the same.

The Air Force

Since early 2001, the Air Force has received more than $200 billion above what was then planned for its "base" budget.[17] The data used for this calculation are displayed in Table 5 on the next page.

Table 5. U.S. Air Force Budget[15]

	2001	2002	2003	2004	2005	2006	2007	2008	2009	Total
2001 "Plan" (Extrapolated for 2006-2009)	85.3	88.3	89.3	90.9	93.3	96.3	100.3	104.3	108.3	856.3
"Base" Budget	85.4	95.3	106.9	113.7	120.4	127.4	130.3	136.4	143.7	1059.5
"Base" Budget above 2001 "Plan"	+0.1	7.0	17.6	22.8	27.1	31.1	30.0	32.1	35.4	203.2
Total Appropriations (including War Funding)	89.5	100.2	125.2	125.6	127.9	141.7	148.9	139.2	143.7	1141.9
Calculated War Spending	4.1	4.9	18.3	11.9	7.5	14.3	18.6	2.8	N.A.	82.4

Figure 6. Air Force Active Fighter & Attack Wings (Equivalents)[21] and Budget (with Trendlines) (Billions, FY 2009 Dollars)[22]

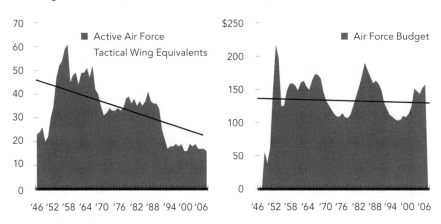

Source: National Defense Budget Estimates for FY 2009, Office of the Under Secretary of Defense (Comptroller) March 2008 and Air Force Historical Research Agency (Maxwell AFB) analysis, "Force Structure, United States Army Air Forces and United States Air Force."

The budget and force structure data for the Air Force for the post-World War II period are shown in Figure 6 above.

The tactical inventory of the Air Force is as small today as at any point in the post-World War II period. From a 1957 high of 61 "wing equivalents," it persistently hovers in the 21st century at 16 to 18.[18]

There have also been budget ups and downs, but the overall trend is for the budget to remain constant in inflation adjusted dollars, and today the amount of spending for the Air Force is above the overall trendline. Thus, at a level of spending today higher than the historic norm, we have an Air Force tactical inventory that is as small as it has ever been.

While shrinking, the overall Air Force inventory has aged further. Each year, *Air Force Magazine* publishes an almanac that presents data on the age of the "Active-Duty Fleet." The 2001 U.S. Air Force Almanac shows the average age of the total Air Force "active-duty fleet," all types of aircraft, to be 21.2 years, a then historic high. The 2007 almanac shows the current "active-duty fleet" to have further aged to 23.0 years, a new historic "high."[19]

Perhaps the most important measure of readiness to fight effectively in the air is pilot skill. One way to measure that is the number of hours each month pilots practice air combat in the air, known as "flying hours." In 2006, Air Force representatives informed the author that F-22 pilots receive just 10 to 12 hours of air combat training in the air per month. Air Force budget justification data assert that F-16 pilots receive 16 to 18 hours per month. In the late 1990s, Air Force fighter pilots were receiving 18 to 20 hours per month. During the Vietnam War, about 25 hours per month was considered just adequate. In the 1960s, when they were at the height of their proficiency, fighter pilots in the Israeli Air Force were getting 40 to 50 hours per month. Anywhere from 10 to 18 hours each month is completely inadequate. In wartime, one would hope and expect air combat training hours to rise.[20]

Given the failure of the $200-plus billion the Air Force received from 2001 to 2009 to stem the shrinking, aging, less ready nature of the Air Force, there is no reason to think that throwing still more money at the Air Force will do anything but perpetuate the problems.

Where Did the Money Go?

Considering the $191 billion plus-up for the Army, the $174 billion added for the Navy, and $203 billion for the Air Force, it is reasonable to ask: "Where did the money, $568 billion, go?"[23]

Pork

Congress added approximately $60 billion in pork to post-Sept. 11 defense bills. The impact on national defense is a matter of apparent indifference to Congress. Pork projects are added without an objective estimate of their cost, without an independent evaluation of their need or efficacy, and certainly without the politically risky idea of competing the contract. Competition for pork contracts is especially unpopular on Capitol Hill. It might permit non-preferred contractors, universities or other trough feeders to receive money that a member of Congress intends for someone else.

It is not unreasonable to consider every penny of the $60 billion to have been squandered.

Hardware cost growth

If one inspects the Defense Department's Selected Acquisition Reports (SARs)[24] for just before and at the end of the George W. Bush administration, one finds two types of pathologies: programs that increased in cost, and programs that increased in cost to buy fewer weapons. For example:

- In 2000, DOD planned to buy 458 V-22s for the Marines for $38.1 billion (unit cost: $83.2 million per V-22). In 2007, the same 458 V-22s were rescheduled to cost $54.2 billion (unit cost: $118.3 million).

- In 2000, 30 SSN-774 Virginia-class submarines were going to cost $65.7 billion; today, the same 30 will cost $92 billion. Unit cost increased from $2.2 billion to $3.1 billion.

These would appear to be the better-managed programs. In other cases, we don't get the same quantity for more money. We get fewer systems for more money.

- In 2000, the Air Force promised 341 F-22 fighters would cost $61.9 billion ($181.5 million each). Today, the estimate is $64.5 billion for 184 aircraft ($350.5 million each). Program cost went up 4 percent. Unit cost increased by 185 percent. The inventory to be bought shrank by 46 percent.

- In 2000, the Navy projected 12 LPD-17 amphibious warfare ships for $10.7 billion ($891.7 million each), while today we are to expect 9 LPD-17s for $14.2 billion ($1.6 billion each). Program cost went up 33 percent; unit cost increased by 179 percent. Inventory decreased by 25 percent.

Taken together, the Government Accountability Office (GAO) found that major system costs from 2000 to 2007 escalated by $295 billion.[25]

Some of these systems never have and never will appear in the wars in Iraq and Afghanistan. Given their irrelevance to war as we currently know it, one must also consider whether not just the cost growth should be considered waste but rather the entire cost of the program.

Understanding how these ultra-high-cost programs were started and are sustained is essential to recognizing the nature of the problem, as well as the character of the solution.

Getting the camel's nose under the tent

Some advocates of high-cost weapon systems will claim that the reduced size of the military force structure is offset by "tremendous" advances in capability. These advocates are quick to skip over the aging nature of these "high-tech" inventories and the serious readiness problems.

Advocates of high-cost and -complexity weapons also ignore two other key attributes. First, the equipment is far more expensive than they allow. They describe costs in terms of "flyaway" unit cost that ignores development and testing expenses, and they routinely understate the cost relationship with equipment being replaced. Systems end up costing far more than what is promised at the "buy-in" stage, and they often cost multiples of what they are replacing, even more when maintenance costs are considered. Second, the advocates grossly overstate how well complex systems perform, both initially in theoretical discussions and in combat after they are deployed.[26] For some systems, real improvements do occur, but they are far less than what is advertised, as well as virtually never being commensurate with the cost increase. Other times the new, more expensive system brings no meaningful improvement, and by virtue of the smaller, less ready force size, real-world capability is significantly reduced.

Understanding this "buy-in" process in detail is important. There is no better explanation of the intricacies and implications of it than in some remarkable congressional testimony offered by Franklin C. Spinney to the House of Representatives in June 2002.[27]

"Chuck" Spinney had come to the end of a long career in the Defense Department. I must disclose that he is a personal friend, and a professional colleague on numerous efforts over the years. He is also well-known among countless defense journalists and analysts in the Pentagon, Capitol Hill and Washington, D.C. think tanks. Time and time again he produced thoroughly documented forensics on fundamental Pentagon pathologies, including the budget and warfighting consequences of the ever increasing complexity of U.S. weapon systems ("Defense Facts of Life"), the un-realism of future spending plans ("The Plans/Reality Mismatch"),[28] the politicization of weapons acquisition in the Pentagon, industry, and Congress ("Defense Power Games"),[29] the wars in Kosovo, Iraq and Afghanistan, and much more.[30] Relentlessly following the data to wherever it led, Spinney had the habit – most unwelcome in Washington – of presenting data and analysis that made it all too apparent that much of the conventional wisdom in Washington that surrounded weapons, budgets and policies were not just poorly informed, but driven by selfish agendas.

The process that builds the defense budget and the system that measures it, the financial management system in the Pentagon, are both broken. As Spinney describes it – an observation endorsed in the previous chapter by Thomas Christie and his four decades of intimate observation of the system – when various entities put together the Pentagon's spending plans, they bias their cost estimates downward, their performance estimates upward and they resist any effort to correct the inaccuracies. A fundamental characteristic of this system is not just its refusal to measure its past, present and future, but also its inability to do so accurately, were it ever to try.

Imagine the implications: when managers in the Pentagon make a program decision, they cannot accurately identify the effects of what they are doing. For some, this is a matter of choice as they do not want to scare off support (due to "sticker shock") for the system being advocated. For others, it is a question of being unwilling to challenge the generally accepted wisdom that advocates in the military services, industry, think tanks and Congress promote as well-informed, "pro-defense" thinking.

Spinney starts his analysis with the Pentagon's Future Year Defense Plan (FYDP). It is the Pentagon's programmatic and budget road map for five or six years into the future. It is approved by the secretary of defense and the president; it is the definitive statement of what the Pentagon says will happen to programs and budgets "over the long term if Congress appropriate[s] the funds to pay for the first year of that plan."[31]

It is not just that this long-range plan is consistently wrong; it is consistently biased in a certain direction. The same biases consistently re-occur every year. Spinney came to this conclusion based on his analysis of 26 separate FYDPs. He examined how accurately the cost, quantity and budget predictions of earlier FYDPs matched up with what actually happened. His testimony cited the example of the Navy's F-18 fighter-bomber.

The first major bias is that the FYDP predicts significantly larger annual production runs than the ones that actually occur. This has major implications. For the F-18, peak production rates of 150 to 200 were predicted; the actual rate never exceeded 84 per year. The optimistic predictions persisted until late in the program, "Long after it should have been clear that the production plan was a pipe dream."[32]

It is important to note that the reason for the production cutbacks was not a lack of money. In the case of the F-18, more money was appropriated than predicted in the first six years of the program, and for the rest of the program, despite a few outlier FYDPs that envisioned bigger budget growth, the amounts spent stayed roughly on track. With production rates being less at predicted or higher levels of spending, it was the unit cost of the F-18 that showed the impact, and the error was not small. Actual production costs, per unit, were commonly twice as much than what was initially predicted.

This mismatch between plans and reality in the F-18 was no exception; Spinney found it in program after program.[33] The results are always the same, regardless of military service, manufacturer, or whether the program is originally based on a domestic or foreign design. He came to the inescapable conclusion that there was a deliberately "low-balled" estimate of future costs early in the program. This bias had the important effect of helping to ensure the program's approval inside the Pentagon and shortly thereafter in Congress.

This "front-end loading" was just the first step in a two-step process. Next came the "political engineering" to lock the program in. An essential partner to the buy-in price was the effort by the advocates to parcel out production of F-18 components and subcomponents to as many congressional districts as possible. It is a practice I observed many times on Capitol Hill. Early in the program, before the real costs or other potential downsides of a program are made apparent in actual budgets, the manufacturer ensures that each senator and representative is made fully aware of the production, and jobs, that will occur in their political district. With the member of Congress now "locked in" with the prospect of jobs and spending ("pork") in his state, and with the public being made fully aware of the negative economic consequences if the program fails or is terminated, political support from the vast majority of states and congressional districts is guaranteed. With these commitments being secured before reality in the form of higher costs (and lower performance) set in, the stage is set to continue to support the program – no matter what. When the actual, higher costs do emerge, decision-makers in the Pentagon and on Capitol Hill take the easy way out by cutting back production rates to keep total costs at an "affordable" level. In the face of adversity, the politicians on both sides of the Potomac make a decision based not on the data and its long-term implications but on the risks presented to their own livelihood and bureaucratic careers.

With many "front-loaded" programs receiving the same buy in, the FYDP becomes overstuffed with unrealistically priced programs. The inevitable result is ever-rising pressure to grow the entire defense budget to accommodate the massive unit cost expansion.

There are important effects at this stage. With the political engineering scaring decision-makers away from permitting program terminations, the resulting lower production rates naturally decrease the inventory being purchased to a rate lower than the aging rate of the existing inventory. Weapons become older and thus more expensive to operate. These higher operating costs face severe resistance due to the drive to find additional money to support the inadequate production rate of the newer, politically engineered weapons. As a result, raids on the operating budget mean less maintenance and repair for both the old and new weapons, and less money available for training as well.

There, you have it: the shrinking, aging, less-ready military force we spoke of earlier. Spinney explained the essential dynamics.

Not keeping track

The Pentagon's broken financial management apparatus is an essential part of this busted system. It is dysfunctional beyond dispute. More than twenty years of reports from GAO and the Pentagon's own auditor, the Inspector General (the DOD IG), make that abundantly clear.

What is less clear – at least to many in Washington – is what that means. Spinney explains it; there is no reliable data link from the past to the present, nor from the present to the future. Because the Pentagon cannot link financial inputs (appropriations) to results, managers cannot consistently and reliably identify what their weapons, forces, and policies are now costing, will cost in the future, or even what they really cost in the past.[34] Simple questions such as, the actual cost of a component for a weapon system, the amount paid to the contractor and whether the contractor was overpaid, under paid, or did not paid at all, are, in today's system, answered only by the contractor. Incredibly, we rely on the contractor to keep our records for us. DOD's Comptroller (the department's CFO) has estimates, but they are exactly that: estimates.

It is not just a question of satisfying the arcane requirements of green eye-shade accountants. It is a question of having a process to know accurately and understand past, present and future costs, and use that knowledge to inform contemporary decisions. As Spinney puts it, "Today's budget should reflect a sound appreciation of and account for the intended consequences of past decisions as well as the future consequences of current decisions."[35]

The most likely consequence of a decision to fund a weapon program suggested by a military sponsoring service is not identified. Decisions are made not just in an information vacuum, but in a forest of misinformation – all biased in one direction.

The Pentagon's response is to refuse to solve the accounting problem. As noted above, there are decades of GAO and DOD IG reports detailing the intricacies and depths of the problem, and there are recurring promises from secretaries of defense and DOD comptrollers to solve the problem. Not once have they met their own self-imposed, and relaxed, deadlines. In the late 1980s, Congress, tired of the empty promises from DOD and many other federal agencies, imposed the Chief Financial Officers Act of 1990. It demanded, at long last, that DOD and all the rest clean up their books and prepare themselves to pass an audit. Most did, but not DOD. After a few more years, and more failures, DOD requested, and Congress granted, what amounted to a wholesale exemption from the CFO Act for DOD exclusively. It is today the only major federal agency that not only cannot pass an audit, but that still cannot be audited. The difference is significant. One fails an audit when the accountants track the money and find it misspent. In DOD, the accountants cannot track how the money was spent.

The Pentagon's solution

Instead of accountability, the Pentagon has a solution it strongly prefers: send it more money.

Advocates in the Pentagon and on Capitol Hill complain that the defense budget is being "starved" while it is at historically high levels. For example, today, as it has each year since the mid-1990s, the U.S. Army is seeking to supplement its own budget with extracurricular money, mostly in the form of a "wish list" that it sends to Congress each year after an eagerly anticipated congressional request for it. Citing the many problems it currently faces, the Army seeks a $3.9 billion supplement. Taking into account the amount by which the 2009 Army budget has already been increased over and above the extrapolated 2001 plan for 2009, $50.6 billion (see above), it is apparent that the Army is actually seeking a $54.5 billion "wish list plus-up."

The Navy is doing the same. Citing the shrunken size of the fleet, the Navy seeks $7 billion more than it requested in its official 2009 budget request, $149 billion, which is an amount well above the Navy's post-World War II average. Taking into account the amount by which the 2009 Navy budget has already been increased over and above the extrapolated 2001 plan for 2009, $37.1 billion, the Navy is actually seeking a $44.1 billion plus-up.

Even though it is the service least involved in the wars in Iraq and Afghanistan, the Air Force is seeking the largest "wish list," $18.7 billion. Taking into account the additional money already built into the Air Force budget above the 2000-2009 "plan," $35.4 billion, the Air Force is actually seeking a $54.1 billion plus-up.

Having failed to reform a system that requires an increasing amount of money to shrink, age and blunt the armed forces, each of the military services can only suggest one solution: more of the same. The military services have put themselves and the nation on a treadmill of squandered resources with no positive result. They operate in an environment, both in the Pentagon and Congress, where no one fundamentally questions their self-scripted vision of the past, present and future.

Time is way overdue to break the self-destructive chain of declining forces at increasing cost.

Recommendations
Real reforms do not need to be complicated or elaborate, but simplicity does not mean the implementation will be easy. The business–as-usual crowd in Congress, industry, and the Republican-Democratic national security think-tank apparatus will aggressively oppose them.

De-grease the pork
Ending the addition of billions of dollars of dubious pork projects to defense bills each year requires a process to sort out the junk from the worthy projects, if any exist.[36] Members of Congress who argue that their earmarks are good ideas should have no problem with competent, independent evaluation of their proposals and a good-government process for implementing them. Any earmark proposed to any defense (or any other) bill should have:

1. An estimate from the Congressional Budget Office for all costs, past, present and future.

2. An evaluation from an independent entity (one with no material interest in the project, which eliminates the Pentagon) to determine if the project is needed and, if needed, whether the proposed solution can be effective. In most cases, GAO can and should provide such evaluations.

3. A requirement that any earmark that successfully emerges from the CBO and GAO evaluations must be submitted to a competitive bidding process, both for initial and for any follow-on work.

This proposal will be vehemently opposed by the vast majority of today's Congress. Members will insist on controlling the evaluation of any earmarks and where the contracts for them are awarded. After all, the whole idea is to send the money to a pre-designated client. To affect real reform, Congress needs – and currently lacks – an uncompromising and uncompromised reformer to make the existing system too painful and politically costly to continue further.

Rectify the books[37]

No weapon acquisition or policy decision can properly be made in the absence of accurate data about the past and the present, and an objectively obtained view of the likely future. Up to now, the system has been operating in the absence of such data. That must be changed. The first, indeed mandatory, place to start is DOD's program and accounting books. I refer not just to the well-defined, but very important, regime of financial management, but more broadly to accurate information and reliable analysis.

The place to start achieving a rectification of various forms of data in DOD is with financial management. The reform must spread thereafter to the broader realm of the analysis and evaluation of programs and policies.

The new president and the secretary of defense should announce together – to obviate dissension – a "budget pause" at the level of spending Congress has set for the previous fiscal year, 2008. That level would constitute a ceiling, not a floor, for ongoing spending. The purpose is to buy time, without making new financial commitments, to scrub the books. With war funding fully provided at the all-time high 2008 level, Pentagon decision-makers should avoid any new, non-war-related contract or other spending obligations. For example, all weapons program milestone decisions would be frozen, with existing programs sustained only at the level authorized by previously signed contacts. No programs would start or advance to a new milestone, with the possible exception of truly extraordinary, not conjured, circumstances.

The Defense Department's audit agencies, with the help of GAO and private accounting firms as needed, would undertake a maximum effort to complete a comprehensive audit of all DOD components, programs and systems. Simultaneously, war-related managers would perform a comprehensive readiness audit of the military services and their readiness-related functions, such as training, exercises, spare parts inventories, weapons maintenance and manning.

The point is to find the weaknesses, both in substance and in the quality of information. Problematic programs and policies (and the managers associated with them) would be identified and put on a watch list for ongoing, continuous oversight until the program in question is cancelled or all discovered problems and data uncertainties are resolved.

The purpose of this vital step is to understand current programs and the financial consequences of past decisions. It provides the essential information baseline for going forward. Programs and entities that are so incompetently managed that they cannot comply are obvious candidates for termination, both for the program and its management.

The failure to fix the Pentagon on this essential measure will mean that no other reforms will be meaningful. How can you control an acquisition process that you cannot accurately measure in terms of cost, schedule and performance? We cannot begin to clear out the dubious programs, and, more importantly, end the biased "front-end loading" and the "political engineering" to buy unrealistically assessed new programs without these steps.

Sorting Out the Mess[38]

During this period and its immediate aftermath, a new series of decisions would be called for by a special panel that would address the relevance, efficacy and affordability of the existing and proposed programs and policies of all DOD components. A new panel of uniquely professional and objective individuals should be convened for two core purposes:

The first purpose is to combine the data made available from the above described process on cost, schedule and performance with an all-source analysis of the overall world situation. Information on the relevance of programs and policies to current threats and realistic future U.S. needs would be combined with more realistic assessments of the programs' and policies' cost, schedule and performance.

The second purpose is to take into account the arguments of all program advocates, from inside the military services, Congress, industry and any other entity interested to make a pleading for – or against – specific programs and policies.

The panel would then make recommendations to the secretary of defense and the president. In some cases the executive branch might be able to cancel contracts for programs that fail to measure up – either for cause or for the "convenience of the government." However, in many cases the president will likely have to forward legislative recommendations to Congress, perhaps with a recommendation for urgent action.

The panel's recommendations to the secretary of defense, president, and Congress will have to acknowledge real-world budget constraints in several respects. In the past, more money has made our problems worse (as explained above). The implications of the recommendations for force structure and how and when to use those forces as outlined in this volume, and the calls on the U.S. federal budget for other purposes – such as healthcare and social security reform – are issues that a responsible president will need to seek for Congress to address.

Purists will argue that this will mean that crass budget considerations will be allowed to drive program and security decisions. Correct; it means exactly that. The availability of resources is a necessary and proper consideration in determining strategy and the implements to carry it out. While many in Washington will be horrified that strategy and weapons should be affected by acknowledging whether money is available, the simple truth is that affordability has been in other times and, in fact, should continue to be as a matter of course. To select a strategy and its implementation unconstrained by budget considerations simply facilitates the situation we are now in: a shrinking, aging, less ready national security apparatus at ever-increasing cost.

As a matter of historical record, consideration of strategy, implementation and budget have been, and should be in the future, interactive and nonlinear. To consider the former two in the absence of the latter is to dwell in a cloud-cuckoo-land most typically found in end-of-war bunkers and politically driven prognostications from advocates of an agenda.

With only a very few exceptions, such "blue-ribbon" panels have a poor record of past performance.[39] Learning from the failures and the successes of the past, certain characteristics are essential.

While the views of the defense corporations, the military services and other interested parties should be heard, their membership on such a review panel must be barred for it to have any credibility. Similarly, retired military officers who have any pecuniary relationship with defense corporations must also be barred. Finally, any person accepting membership on the panel, as well as staff, should be barred from accepting any future position with any entity that can gain, or lose, from the panel's decisions.

Business-as-usual apologists will complain that such rules for membership on a program review panel would call into question their integrity. They will be correct; it does.

They will also ask where the appropriate expertise will be found if the usual legions of interested parties are barred from participating. There are many retired military officers, previous civilian Pentagon officials and former members of Congress who have declined association with the many vested interests that gain from weapons procurement decisions. That they are not prominent among those who typically opine publicly about hardware decisions says more about how America conducts its defense business than it does about the fitness of such people to make these decisions.

If the panel can perform as hoped for by using the data to identify an array of defense programs and policies that should be retained, terminated and significantly modified, the president should institutionalize the panel as a continuing body in DOD. Indeed, the implementation of the associated recommendations may take several years, and each year there will likely be new, necessary reviews and decisions as the process whittles down to a national security apparatus outlined in this book, or at least one approaching its less bloated dimensions. The continuing work will require its own advocate and basis of authority.

It would help immensely for this process to occur in an atmosphere of "adult supervision," especially in Congress. Major reforms will be needed there as well if Congress is to re-learn how to perform serious oversight and to legislate in a manner consistent with its own findings.[40] In an atmosphere of foreknowledge that someone will be looking over their shoulder, asking informed questions and holding them responsible for their promises and their actions, decision-makers and advocates in the Pentagon might become infected with an appreciation for reliable, accurate predictions of the future, along with valid descriptions of past and current events.

The question naturally occurs why the military services and Pentagon officials should be deprived of controlling the acquisition process and whether that "deprivation" should be permanent. Acquisition decisions have been made in the Pentagon by military and civilian bureaucrats for decades, and they have the expertise and resources to make an effective system work properly. A "blue-ribbon panel" would not possess the infrastructure to do everything.

The problem we are trying to address is that the military services have not exercised their control of the system with a positive result. Indeed, their influence in, if not control of, the process in the Pentagon up to now has been such a disaster that clearly a completely new approach must be tried. However, as the independent panel described above – perhaps to be called the "Defense Evaluation Board" – performs its duties, it will require the cooperation of the military services and of civilian bureaucracies in the Pentagon. The military services are sure to be generally hostile to the idea of people beyond their control deciding the fate of their budgets, programs, and policies – a loss of control earned by decades of mismanagement. As the work of the Defense Evaluation Board unfolds, many in the military services and the civilian parts of the Pentagon bureaucracy are sure to be frustrated and uncooperative. Some will attempt to undermine the changes.

As the Defense Evaluation Board's work progresses, however, a new operating and managerial ethic may become apparent. Some in the military services, or the services themselves as a corporate entity, may learn to "get with the program." The positive effects, namely more effective fighting forces with adequate support operating in an ethical environment that strives to understand events and to prepare for a complex and difficult future without selfish agendas, will hopefully be manifest. Such an atmosphere is likely to attract strong support from military service members and professional civilian bureaucrats. At some point, the military services – or perhaps components within those services – may demonstrate their willingness and competence to resume control of their programmatic and budgetary fate.

All services and the components within them will not progress at the same rate. That those that progress rapidly to understand and cooperate with the new environment are duly rewarded will serve as incentive for those that find it more difficult to discard old, ineffective and force-eviscerating management techniques. In the final analysis, it will be important for the military services to "buy in" to the new set of moral, mental and written rules of a reformed Pentagon acquisition system. Failure to do so will imply the need for a wholesale reorganization of the Pentagon, perhaps in a rewriting of the 1947 National Security Act, where completely new approaches to acquisition with less control by the military services may be needed.

Before that bridge is crossed, however, it needs to be established that the decision to allow the re-entry of the military services and other Pentagon bureaucracies to control their budgetary and programmatic fate would be up to the Defense Evaluation Board – in consultation with the secretary of defense and other officials deemed appropriate. Whether even more radical ideas than the Defense Evaluation Board need to be explored should be a matter that is ultimately laid before the military services and the Pentagon bureaucracy to contemplate.

One Final Word

In a system that measures merit by the amount of money spent and maintaining that flow, these changes will meet huge resistance. The changes described here call for a presidential leader with an iron will who will require real, not cosmetic, reforms of a system determined to and skilled at countering any real change. It will also require a president who will stick with the process for years, continuously making decisions that will ultimately reverse the present disastrous course U.S. national security is now on.

The journey will be a difficult one, and many opportunistic politicians – in Congress, the Pentagon and the military services – will attack and attempt to undermine the fundamental changes that need to be made. The one thing that is sure to be more problematic for all than the comprehensive reforms set forth in this volume is the failure to start them and to persist to the end.

ENDNOTES

1 The so-called "base" Pentagon budget is that part that does not include special, "emergency" appropriations to fund the wars in Iraq and Afghanistan.

2 These trends are addressed in detail in an analysis by Franklin C. Spinney, "Defense Death Spiral," put together in the late 1990s. It is available at http://www.d-n-i.net/fcs/defense_death_spiral/ contents.htm. However, Spinney's briefing does not include the additional funding that has

been put into the Pentagon's budget since 2000, both for the wars in Iraq and Afghanistan and additional money not related to the wars.

3   Also, substantial amounts of non-war spending have been added to appropriations for the wars. Such spending includes additional money for C-17, V-22, F-16, and other aircraft, which are highly unlikely to see service in Iraq or Afghanistan, and money for a reorganization of the Army, initiated well before the wars started. The $770 billion "plus-up" in base Pentagon spending is a likely understatement.

4   The budget plan specified in early 2001 extended to 2005. For the years 2006 to 2009, an extrapolation was made, citing the largest increases consistent with the 2001-2005 plan.

5   Source: National Defense Budget Estimates, volumes for 2001-2009, Office of the Under Secretary of Defense (Comptroller).

6   Source: National Defense Budget Estimates, volumes for 2001-2009, Office of the Under Secretary of Defense (Comptroller).

7   This analysis includes both divisions and separate combat regiments, brigades, and modern brigade combat teams. Earlier independent brigades and regiments are counted at the rate of three per division equivalent. Given the reduction of full size maneuver battalions in modern brigade combat teams, those are counted at the rate of four per division equivalent.

8   See Figure 3-5 of "The Long Term Implications of Current Defense Plans: Detailed Update for Fiscal Year 2008 (March 2008)," Congressional Budget Office, at http://www.cbo.gov/ftpdocs/90xx/doc9043/03-28-CurrentDefensePlans.pdf.

9   The assertions by the author are based on messages from and conversations with direct observers of the character of units deploying to Iraq.

10 The budget plan specified in early 2001 for the Navy & Marine Corps extended to 2005. For the years 2006 to 2009, an extrapolation was made, citing the largest increases consistent with the 2001-2005 plan.

11 Sources: National Defense Budget Estimates for FY 2009, Office of the Under Secretary of Defense (Comptroller) March 2008; Center of Military History, Historical Perspective on Force Structure Reductions 1946-1988, (Washington, D.C.: 1989); Department of Defense Annual Reports, and Department of Defense Appropriations Bill Reports from the House Committee on Appropriations.

12 Source: National Defense Budget Estimates, volumes for 2001-2009, Office of the Under Secretary of Defense (Comptroller).

13 Sources: National Defense Budget Estimate for FY 2009, Office of the Under Secretary of Defense (Comptroller) March 2008, and Navy fleet data from annual Department of the Navy Budget Estimates, the Congressional Research Service, and Department of Defense Annual Reports.

14 Source: National Defense Budget Estimates, volumes for 2001-2009, Office of the Under Secretary of Defense (Comptroller).

15 Budget data for this period of time that separate the Navy from the Marine Corps, or naval shipbuilding from the Navy's other expenses are not readily available.

16 FY 2009 "Constant" dollars.

17 The budget plan specified in 2001 for the Air Force extended just to 2005. For the years 2006 to 2009, an extrapolation was made, citing the largest increases consistent with the 2001-2005 plan.

18 The 16 to 18 "wing equivalents" cited by the AFRHA for the 21st century may be an over-count; Air Force budget justification materials cite just 10 "Air Expeditionary Wings" available during this period. It is not clear to what extent these AEWs may be larger than historically typical wings, thereby justifying the AFRHA count of 16 to 18 "wing equivalents."

19 Find *Air Force Magazine's* Almanac editions for these and other years at http://www.afa.org/magazine/almanacs.asp.

20 The standard Air Force position on these issues is that the technology it pursues may cost more, but it brings extraordinary results on the battlefield. The F-22 is a typical example. As a fighter, it depends on the efficacy of a technological road that has not proven itself in real war. The "beyond visual range" radar-based air war the F-22 is highly specialized to fight is yet to be proven workable, let alone effective, in real-war aerial engagements involving more than a very few aircraft. Moreover, some serious experts, including the designers of highly successful combat aircraft such as the F-15, F-16, and A-10, argue that the F-22 is a huge disappointment in the actual performance characteristics that count in real-world aerial warfare. Also, the costs to acquire these "highly capable" systems are far more than what the advocates will tell you. The dollar's value has inflated by a factor of twelve since the end of World War II. But the cost of the F-22 has inflated by a factor of 273 the cost of 1946-47 fighter aircraft. Surely, the F-22 performs at a level barely imagined in 1946 by the designers of the Air Force's first jet fighter, the P-80. But, just as surely, the F-22 does not bring an increase in effectiveness against its likely enemies, even remotely like its cost increase.

21 Consistent data on the size of the Air Force in terms of aircraft are not readily available. In lieu of a year-by-year count of actual tactical aircraft for the 1946 - 2008 period, the Air Force Historical Research Agency (AFHRA) at Maxwell Air Force Base has published an analysis of "wing equivalents" of the Air Force's force structure since the late 1930s. Find this analysis at http://www.afhra.af.mil/timelines/. Although this analysis does not track the shrinkage and growth of the Air Force combat aircraft inventory with the best measure (actual aircraft) and may over-count the forces available in more recent times compared to the past, it is used here as the only Air Force data available to the public from 1947 to the present day.

22 Sources: National Defense Budget Estimate for FY 2009, Office of the Under Secretary of Defense (Comptroller) March 2008 and Air Force Historical Research Agency [Maxwell AFB] analysis, "Force Structure, United States Army Air Forces and United States Air Force."

23 All Pentagon components received a non-war "plus-up" of $772 billion. The balance left from the $568 billion absorbed by the Army, Navy, and Air Force ($204 billion) went into defense-wide spending for DOD components such as missile defense, special forces, and OSD operations.

24 Available at http://www.acq.osd.mil/ara/am/sar.

25 See GAO testimony at http://www.gao.gov/new.items/d08674t.pdf.

26 For example, for an analysis of actual high tech system performance in Operation Desert Storm against Iraq in 1991, see "Operational Desert Storm: Evaluation of the Air Campaign," General Accounting Office, June 1997, GAO/NSIAD, 97-134.

27 See Statement by Franklin C. Spinney before the Subcommittee on National Security, Veterans Affairs and International Relations of the Committee on Government Reform, House of Representatives, June 4, 2002. Also available at http://www.d-n-i.net/fcs/spinney_testimony_060402.htm.

28 See "Defense Facts of Life: The Plans/Reality Mismatch," Franklin C. Spinney, (Westview Press, 1985).

29 See "Defense Power Games," Franklyn C. Spinney, Fund for Constitutional Government, 1990; available at http://www.d-n-i.net/fcs/def_power_games_98.htm.

30 These "blasters" and other comments and analyses by Spinney can be found at http://www.d-n-i.net/dni/about/spinneys-comments/.

31 See Spinney Testimony, p. 7.

32 See Spinney Testimony, p. 9.

33 See "the Plans/Reality Mismatch" in "Defense Facts of Life, Franklin C. Spinney, Westview Press, 1985.

34 This is not just Spinney's conclusion, it is that of virtually any auditor who has reviewed the

Pentagon. Beyond GAO and DOD IG reports, see also "Transforming Department of Defense Financial Management: A Strategy for Change," April 13, 2001, a special report commissioned by the Secretary of Defense to review the situation.

35 See Spinney testimony, p. 1.

36 See "Congress, the Defense Budget, and Pork: A Snout to Tail Description of Congress' Foremost Concern in National Security Legislation," Winslow T. Wheeler, Independent Institute Policy Report. Copies are available from the author at winslowwheeler@msn.com.

37 Important elements of this section are borrowed from Chuck Spinney's thinking in his statement to Congress in 2002. See statement by Franklin C. Spinney before the Subcommittee on National Security, Veterans Affairs and International Relations of the Committee on Government Reform, House of Representatives, June 4, 2002. Also available at http://www.d-n-i.net/fcs/spinney_testimony_060402.htm.

38 Important elements of this section are also borrowed from Chuck Spinney's work. See statement by Franklin C. Spinney before the Subcommittee on National Security, Veterans Affairs and International Relations of the Committee on Government Reform, House of Representatives, June 4, 2002. Also available at http://www.d-n-i.net/fcs/spinney_testimony_060402.htm. Also see, "Defense Power Games," Franklyn C. Spinney, Fund for Constitutional Government, 1990; available at http://www.d-n-i.net/fcs/def_power_games_98.htm.

39 For a discussion of the negative record of many such panels, see Chapter 1 of "Military Reform: A Reference Handbook," Winslow T. Wheeler and Lawrence J. Korb, Praeger Security International, 2007.

40 For a discussion of this author's proposed reforms for restoring oversight on Capitol Hill, see "The Wastrels of Defense," U.S. Naval Institute Press, 2004.